It is so refreshing to read what Bishop David Zac Niringiye, long-term friend and brother, has to say about the church. On the one hand I am personally warned of how easy it is for us, lost in the exuberance of our inventions and redefinition of the church, to lose our bearing with regards to God's purpose for the church. On the other, I am reminded of why the church today should be a continuing story, journey and witness of the people of God to his kingdom.

In a contemporary age in which the identity of the church has been re-created in our image – be it ethnic, social, economic or whatever else, with all their attendant paraphernalia, Bishop Zac's clear word is a call for sober reflection regardless of our church tradition. Rather than just a lamentation of how church easily slides from being "all about God" to "all about us" or even just "me", this is a prophetic call to rediscover and return to God's original purpose for the church in relation to his kingdom.

I commend this book to all who long for the church to be the church as communities of God's people "announcing and demonstrating the Kingdom of God by the grace and power of the Holy Spirit."

Femi B. Adeleye, PhD
Director of Church Partnerships
Global Centre Christian Commitments, World Vision International

David Zac Niringye is for me a modern hero of the faith. He has been so helpful to our community of hundreds of students and all nations and ages at the heart of Oxford. When he gave up his role of Bishop to work for the cause of justice in Uganda and beyond some feared he might forget the Church. But this brilliant book shows the opposite is true. He writes movingly about the people of God on the journey of God and invites us winsomely to join in the advancing kingdom of God. Get this book to get in touch with your destiny.

Charlie Cleverly
Rector of St Aldates Church,
a house of prayer for all nations at the heart of Oxford, UK

Congratulations to David Zac!

This is a brilliant piece of work. The subject is timely, coming at a time when the church is expanding rapidly, yet declining and disintegrating with equal speed. David Zac has captured both the rise and fall of God's community in a technical yet easily readable manner. It is theologically sound, historically accurate, but more importantly, culturally relevant for the church's new centre of gravity – Africa. What comes out clearly is that the church is, as David Zac puts it, *a community in the Spirit, a dwelling of God in God!* No gates of hell can prevail against.

If you are interested in the development journey of the church, this is a great read. If you care little about the church, here is a must read.

Rev David Oginde, PhD
Presiding Bishop, Christ is the Answer Ministries (CITAM)
Nairobi, Kenya.

Every journey I have taken with Bishop Zac has been both challenging and life-giving. This book is no exception. Like a knowledgeable *safari* guide, Bishop Zac points out the highs and lows as he takes us on an extraordinary biblical journey through what it means to be the community of God's people – from Creation to New Creation. Godly discontent over the mismatch he has seen between much contemporary church and the biblical vision of a community of faith, hope and love, drives Bishop Zac to ask us to take stock of our part of the community of God. To be read carefully, prayerfully and humbly by all who profess Christ's name wherever they are in the world – so that the community of God may reveal Christ to the world, not hide Christ from the world.

Rt Rev David Williams
Bishop of Basingstoke, UK

As an evangelist among people of other faiths, I have struggled with the huge chasm between our understanding and teaching of who we are as God's people in the world and our practise of church. Reading this book will help us to define the essence of our existence as a people of God in the world. Bishop David Zac makes a bold clarification of a rather hazy view of the church as God's pilgrim people that has been clouded with our propensity to settle for mediocrity.

Canon Francis Omondi
All Saints Cathedral Nairobi, Anglican Church of Kenya
Chairman of CMS Africa, Director of the Sheepfold Ministries

I can think of few people from whom I would rather hear about the church than from David Zac Niringiye from Uganda. He is biblically focused, intellectually careful, diagnostically truthful, courageously honest, emotionally bold, relationally sincere, and publicly fearless. Hearing his voice and seeing his life as a brother and mentor has changed my life. This book will hopefully open that experience to many others as well. If the body of Christ is to be God's light and salt in the real world, we need Bishop Zac to confront and inspire us to new and vigorous life.

Mark Labberton, PhD
President, Fuller Theological Seminary
Pasadena, USA

Global Christian Library Series

The Church

GLOBAL LIBRARY

The Church

God's Pilgrim People

David Zac Niringiye

© 2014 by David Zac Niringiye

Published 2014 by Langham Global Library
an imprint of Langham Creative Projects

Langham Partnership
PO Box 296, Carlisle, Cumbria CA3 9WZ, UK
www.langham.org

ISBNs:
978-1-78368-972-9 Print
978-1-78368-970-5 Mobi
978-1-78368-971-2 ePub
978-1-78368-887-6 PDF

British Library Cataloguing in Publication Data
Niringiye, David Zac author.
  The Church : God's pilgrim people.
  1. Church. 2. Communities--Religious aspects--
  Christianity. 3. Christian life.
  I. Title
  262-dc23

  ISBN-13: 9781783689729

Cover & Book Design: projectluz.com

Contents

To Theodora, my dear wife and our children
– Joshua, Grace, Kirabo, and Abigail –
for being God's ambassadors in my life.

Acknowledgements

I started working on this book in 2000 at a major turning point in my life and work. It would take another book to acknowledge all those who have contributed to this work in its entirety. Therefore, I mention here only those that have made a direct input towards this book.

My deceased parents, Cyprian Edward and Erina Joy Ruzasigande, whose godly parenting grounded me in the faith, rooted my identity in the wider family of Christ, and modeled for me (and all my siblings) real faith anchored in community.

Theodora, my dear wife, and our children (all those that call us Daddy and Mummy – biological and non biological), not only believed I would finish the book but did all they could to nudge me on. Aryantungyisa took it a level higher. She offered her editorial skills and read through the entire first draft. I must mention in particular Joshua, Grace and Abigail, our biological children. They are God's ambassadors in my life. Although they endured long periods of my absence, I cannot recall them ever complaining, except for the continued question: "When will you finish the book?" Our dear children, I hope you find this book a satisfactory answer to your question.

My deceased mentor and dear friend, Dr John Stott, tops the list of my international friends and family. Without Uncle John's encouragement and faith, I would never have started the project. I regret that he answered the heavenly call before I finished work on the manuscript. Our deep fellowship and friendship with John and Celia Wyatt, Vinoth and Karin Ramachandra, Mark and Jeannette Labberton, Steve and Dot Beck, Meritt and Steve Sawyer, Roger and Gail Wells, Roger and Gill Northcott, Tim and Pippa Peppiatt, Charlie and Anita Cleverly, Barry and Paula Davis, Francis and Anne Omondi, Kamal Fahmi, Femi and Affy Adeleye, Paul Robinson, Ceasar Molebatsi, Diane Stinton, and Ruth Padilla DeBorst enabled me not to lose faith in the church as authentic global community. Meritt Sawyer, then serving with Langham Partnership International, was always keen to be sure that I was not deterred by lack of space and time-out to think and write. My dear brethren, Nick-Wayne Jones, Roger and Gail Wells, Jürg Pfister and David Williams, also provided resources and space for quiet study and writing.

I have visited several libraries in the course of research and study. I gratefully acknowledge the help and support by libraries and librarians at All Nations Christian College; International Christian College, Glasgow; Fuller Theological Seminary, Bishop Tucker Theological College, Mukono; and Makerere University. The Church Mission Society, where I served as director for its work in Africa for close to five years, provided me priceless exposure to the churches in Africa. I have also received inspiration from many churches among whom I have exercised a teaching and preaching and (in some) a pastoral ministry, notably: Nairobi Chapel; Christ Church, Beckenham; St Paul's Church, Howell Hill; First Presbyterian Church, Berkeley; Christ Church (Anglican), Overland Park; Christ Church Winchester; and St Aldate's Church, Oxford. Kampala Diocese in the Church of Uganda holds a special place in my life, as it is where I ventured to live and work out what I understood "church" to be, while serving as a bishop for close to eight years. I am grateful to my brother, Bishop Michael Ssenyimba, for his mentorship and my fellow ministers in churches in Kampala for letting me be one among them. My brethren in the Revival Fellowship in Kampala taught me authentic Christian community.

I must also acknowledge many whose comments and input added much value. Dr David Smith was the first to see my outline and first drafts of what was then the introduction and chapter 1. His critique was pivotal in shaping the overall project and study. Aggrey Mugisha, Mark Labberton, Meritt Sawyer, Aryantungyisa Kaakaabaale and Francis Omondi made valuable input at various stages of the work. I am grateful to my friends and other sources for many of the anecdotes in the book. Vivian Doub of Langham Partnership was very instrumental in encouraging me to the finish line; Suzanne Mitchell, editor, painstakingly worked through the entire work and provided the much-needed editorial support.

To God be the glory!

David Zac Niringiye

Kampala, August 2014

Introduction

The People of God: The Church?

Watch out for false prophets. They come to you in sheep's clothing, but inwardly they are ferocious wolves. By their fruit you will recognize them. Do people pick grapes from thorn bushes, or figs from thistles? Likewise, every good tree bears good fruit, but a bad tree bears bad fruit. A good tree cannot bear bad fruit, and a bad tree cannot bear good fruit. Every tree that does not bear good fruit is cut down and thrown into the fire. Thus, by their fruit you will recognize them.

Not everyone who says to me, "Lord, Lord," will enter the kingdom of heaven, but only he who does the will of my Father who is in heaven. Many will say to me on that day, "Lord, Lord, did we not prophesy in your name and in your name drive out demons and perform many miracles?" Then I will tell them plainly, "I never knew you. Away from me, you evildoers!" (Matt 7:15–23)

Churches: A Bewildering Story

Within a radius of two miles from All Saints Cathedral on Nakasero Hill in Kampala, where my work as a bishop in the Church of Uganda was based from 2005 until 2012, there are no fewer than fifteen gatherings of churches on a Sunday morning. One block from All Saints Cathedral is a temple of the Universal Church of the Kingdom of God; three blocks away is the recently rebranded Watoto Church, formerly Kampala Pentecostal Church; then there is a breakaway group from the Church of Uganda, called the Charismatic Church of Uganda, that meets in the YMCA building a block away from the Watoto Church; and across the valley is the Deliverance Church, which is down the road from Holy Trinity Kivulu, an Anglican Church. Down the hill is the Eden Revival Church, which meets in a building that was once a motor mechanic's workshop; and in the city centre, less than a mile away, is Christ the King, a Roman Catholic Church. There is also the World Trumpet Centre, Calvary Chapel, the Redeemed Society of the Lord, and several others.

All these gatherings and groups, with their apostles, prophets, evangelists, bishops, reverends and pastors, claim to be churches – meeting and working in the name of Christ. Although they may categorize themselves differently they would all claim to base their work on the same Holy Scriptures, the Bible. On a Sunday morning in Kampala, one has the sense of being in a religious supermarket of churches; and as with choosing a supermarket, the choice of church is yours. All of them are competing for your attention, in God's name. What is puzzling and even disconcerting is that there is no evidence that any of these churches collaborate in mission projects in the city, except for the occasional evangelistic crusade when an international evangelist is in town.

Churches! They are so different. Kampala is not unique. One could cite the proliferation of shapes, sizes, styles of architecture, aspects of doctrine (or lack of them), paraphernalia and regalia. Visit any city in Africa south of the Sahara and you will be greeted by a plethora of worship centres and styles: in cathedrals, tabernacles and temples; in schools and cinema halls; on mountain tops and under trees; in brick buildings and papyrus-mat or cardboard shacks. The variety and creativity of the names is also startling. I am not speaking here of the traditional imported ones – Anglican, Lutheran, Methodist, Presbyterian, Reformed and so on – but the home-grown varieties in Africa, such as Miracle, Prayer Palace, Victory, Deliverance, Deeper Life, Winners, Bethany, Bethel, and Repentance and Faith. Some of them are named after their founding leaders. The forms of expressions of church are as diverse as their names and their meeting centres. Is it any wonder that many who do not associate with a particular church cannot easily make out where the coherence lies in the diversity of meanings attached to "church", meanings that often don't appear to have much in common? Those of us who call ourselves Christian and call our communities "churches" do not attach the same meaning to those words and are often in conflict and competition with one another.

Senzani's story shows how confusing this phenomenon of churches and Christian organizations can be. I met Senzani on a flight to Nairobi from Malawi early in 2002. We introduced ourselves and just got talking as two strangers would, asking about our destinations and work, and talking about the sights and sounds around us. She was from Zimbabwe and a professional in marketing. The discussion became friendly enough for me to ask her whether she attended a church regularly; her answer was in the affirmative. I asked which church, to which she confidently answered, "The Jehovah's Witnesses Church." I had been taught as a believer in my youth that the Jehovah's Witnesses were a cult and that I should not associate with any of them. But now Senzani was proudly calling them a church. I asked her to tell me more about her church pilgrimage.

Senzani's parents were Anglican and she was a baptized and confirmed member of the Anglican Church. She attended Roman Catholic Church-founded primary and secondary schools, where it was required that she attend Mass at the local Catholic church. While at university in Harare she would go to any of the worship services on the university campus or in the city – including Baptist, Pentecostal, Anglican, Methodist, Roman Catholic and Congregational. This remained her habit after she graduated from college. However, one day on a business trip she met a Jehovah's Witness who, according to her, explained the way of salvation extremely clearly, something that she had yearned for but had not been offered by the other churches. Now she was very grateful to God that she had found a "truer" church, one in whose disciplines she longed to grow and nurture her family. Given my Evangelical Anglican background and my understanding of the Jehovah's Witnesses as a heretical cult, I did not want to believe what she told me: that she had found Christ – or rather Christ had found her – in the Jehovah's Witnesses Church.

Some people are quick to rejoice at the proliferation of churches as evidence of the progress of God's work and the gospel of Jesus Christ. But consider the events in the central African country of Rwanda in 1994. What are we to make of the tragedy that befell that land – a genocide in which an estimated eight hundred thousand Rwandans died at the hands of fellow Rwandans in a country that was reckoned to have well over 95 per cent of its eight million-strong population claiming some church affiliation? In fact, Rwanda was reputed to be the first Catholic nation in Africa. It is fair to conclude that the 1994 genocide in Rwanda was a case of church members killing fellow church members. It is not just the fact of genocide that is perplexing, but that so-called Christians took machetes and hacked to death their Christian neighbours – people who possibly went to the same church building on Sunday morning. How could churchyards and buildings be turned into killing fields?

Or consider countries such as Kenya, Uganda and Nigeria, countries that pride themselves on the fact that the majority of their citizens belong to some form of church. Kenya boasts of over 70 per cent of its population being Christian; Uganda, over 85 per cent; and Nigeria, over 50 per cent. Yet it is these same countries which, according to Transparency International (TI) corruption indices, continue to compete for a slot among the ten most corrupt nations of the world since the 1990s. Demographics of HIV/AIDS prevalence in Africa in the late 1990s showed that countries that claim to have the largest Christian populations had the highest rates.

The events following the disputed presidential elections in Kenya in December 2007 are another sad commentary on the influence of the churches. The elections were the second multiparty elections following the long rule of President Daniel Arap Moi, a professing Christian who had ruled the country for over twenty years in a one-party regime. The three main presidential contestants in the elections were the incumbent, President Mwai Kibaki, ethnically a Kikuyu from Central Region; Raila Oginga Odinga, ethnically Luo, from Western Kenya; and Kalonzo Musyoka, ethnically Kamba from the South-East. The short version of a very complex story with a long history is that in these elections the fault lines were along ethnic and regional divisions. In what was clearly a rigged voter-counting process, Mwai Kibaki was announced the winner. Mayhem and violence broke out in all the major cities of Kenya between the different ethnic groups. Homes and villages were burned, thousands were killed and hundreds of thousands displaced. The issue here is not just the violence, but rather that such a "godly country" could descend to such violent levels; it is not that the violence was inter-ethnic, but that it was the same story in many of the churches. There were reports that members of one ethnic group took refuge in a church, and when fellow church members of the rival ethnic group learned of it, they set fire to the church, killing all who had taken refuge there.

But there is another story line. It is not about the numbers, institutional power, social services, denominations, factions or money. It is the quiet influence of bands of believers, Jesus' people, desiring to be all that Christ has called them to be. Often the secret is the leadership. I think of a church in one of the worst slums in Kampala, which is home to sex workers, drug users and addicts, and thieves; an area of the city that floods whenever it rains, with casualties: drowning, epidemics of water-borne diseases and more. Frederick, the pastor, moved there from his decent home in one of the other areas of Uganda. Members of the local youth club, which targets the restoration of thieves and drug users, call him their patron. His wife, an educationalist, took over the management of a school that had been run down by the previous leadership; enrolments grew by 100 per cent in three years. Their youngest daughter attends the school. The church is now home to an HIV/AIDS post-test club, an African Medical and Research Foundation (AMREF) health and skills centre for sex-workers, established to wean them away from that very dangerous and dehumanizing business, and a vibrant youth ministry. Not only is the attendance on Sunday growing; people are turning their lives over to Jesus. It is exciting. It is challenging. It is also depressing to see the conditions in which the people live. But Frederick and his family live there too.

And there are many more such stories, everywhere. There are amazing stories from North Africa, the Middle East and South Asia of Muslim communities of "followers of Jesus". They meet together regularly to read the *Ingil* (Gospels), not on Sunday mornings but rather on Fridays, and not in a church building but in a mosque. They have neither "churches" nor "vicars", "pastors" nor "bishops", "apostles" nor "priests"; but their devotion is to Jesus, *Issa Messiah*, as Saviour and Lord. Kamal Fahmi, a dear friend and long-time missionary serving with Operation Mobilisation in North Africa and the Middle East since the 1980s, shared with me in email correspondence the story of one house church in Sudan and one of the members, Al Faki, as reported by the house-church leader.

> Every Friday, during the Muslim holy day, a special group of Christians meets in a house. "Friday is the day for meeting people and gathering to talk or share entertainment," said the group's leader, "so our group does not attract attention." The reason for the group preferring not to attract attention is that it consists of Muslims who have become Christians. The group is one of a few in Khartoum and neighbouring Omdurman that caters especially for people from other religious faiths. "It is hard for a Muslim to become a Christian here," said the group leader. "He or she will not be able to continue in their environment without their family noticing. That is when the trouble starts. They believe that someone born into Islam

has no right to choose for themselves. Leaving Islam is like betraying your family and God, and that is blasphemy. All blasphemy in Islam is punishable by death," he explained. Al Faki is one of many examples.

Al-Faki was a teacher in a government school in Sudan. He had spent five years in further education in the Gulf and taught in the Gulf for a while. It was on his return that he became interested in Christianity. "When Al-Faki became a Christian, he tried to witness to his family, but then he suffered terribly," said the church elder. "He spent a year and a half in prison, where he was tortured by the security police. During this time in prison he suffered a stroke and his right side was partially paralysed. Fortunately, we were able to get him out of the country. He is just one of several who have been persecuted and tortured for becoming Christians."

These stories of persecuted Christians in Sudan are just some of many examples around the world, and through the history of the Christian faith, of faithful Christian communities in hostile contexts.

Who Is the Church? My Journey

Who, then, is the church? What distinguishes and authenticates a particular community as "the people of God"? Many Christians dismiss this question. Do we not all know who the people of God are? Do we not see them, especially on Sunday mornings, with their different traditions and forms? Do we not know their leaders: apostles, prophets, evangelists, bishops, priests, pastors, reverends, fathers, mothers, brothers and sisters?

The question becomes critical when one considers on what basis people consider themselves to be "church". Is it because of the day on which they gather? Is it because of the building in which they meet? Is it down to the structures of their leadership and organization; the Scriptures they read; the songs they sing; or the rituals they practise? Does any claim to some devotion to the Bible legitimize a group as church? Is it enough that people call themselves Christians and invoke the name of Jesus?

The question "Who is the church?" is deeply personal. I was born and grew up in it; married in it; my wife and I brought up our children in it; and I have given most of my life to its service, knowing and trusting that I was serving the Lord. What I write in this book emerges out of my story, and in many ways is part of my story.

I grew up in a Christian family. My father and mother were deeply committed to Christ and the church, something they had learned through the East African Revival movement,[1] of which they were first-generation adherents. My father served as an itinerant evangelist, catechist and lay reader in the then Native Anglican Church (currently known as the Church of Uganda). At that time, a lay reader, in addition to being in charge of a church covering a village area, had oversight of other churches within a sub-parish area. I recall that at one stage he was overseeing ten churches. The administrative tradition in the Native Anglican Church was to transfer priests and other pastoral church workers from one parish to another, each spending on average between two and ten years in one area. As a family we were moved around a lot in several sub-parish areas in my native area in the south-west of Uganda, as my father evangelized villages and nurtured young congregations. So I grew up as a child of the church, drinking her milk and eating her readily available bread, of which my father was a chief dispenser. Baptized as an infant, I was nurtured in the faith by my parents. I learnt how to read and write, not in a nursery school, but alongside the catechism classes that my father conducted in a "church school". My father tells me how as early as age six I used to sing with joyful faith and sure certainty the song "When the trumpet of the Lord shall sound, and time shall be no more ... I will be there".[2] My parents' faith was truly mine.

All my primary-school education was in church-owned schools, with "school prayers" every morning and compulsory attendance of church services on Sundays. When I completed primary school and went to boarding secondary school I looked forward to freedom, not only from the watchful eyes of my parents, but also from church. To my joy, chapel was not compulsory at this school. So I not only strayed away from church; I also strayed away from the faith of my childhood, into all manner of youthful pursuits.

I guess I had, as a young child, taken church for granted. It was in my third year of high school that I heeded the call of Christ and recommitted

---

1. The Revival, a movement reckoned by some analysts to be the most important development in the church's life in Uganda in the twentieth century, was one of protest, renewal and reform. It originated among the indigenous lay people of the church in Uganda, Rwanda and Burundi, and missionaries, members of the Ruanda Mission, a small mission formed out of the Church Missionary Society (CMS) in the late 1920s. The movement spread to the East Africa countries of Kenya, Tanzania and Southern Sudan.

2. James M. Black, 1893.

myself to him. At the time, another revival had broken out in the schools and colleges in East Africa. Thus, although I reconnected with church, it was not church as I had known it while I was growing up. I got very involved with a Scripture Union group, through which we would meet with other Christians for fellowship and outreach. I learned to read the Bible for myself and with others. This was life: exciting, challenging and worth fully signing up to! I had questions about the church I grew up in. The nominalism and lack of vitality that I saw in my mother church created unease within me about the Church of Uganda. I was particularly perturbed by priests and other pastoral workers who seemed to live double lives; they did not practise what they professed. Some even spoke derogatorily about the work of the Holy Spirit – in particular, about speaking in tongues, an experience I had grown to cherish. I therefore preferred to be connected henceforth with the new charismatic and youthful Deliverance Church. I even got rebaptized by immersion, renouncing my infant baptism as ineffectual and invalid since it had been done for me and was by sprinkling, a form that I had now been persuaded was unbiblical. At university I did not really care much about which church I attended on Sundays. It did not seem to matter, provided it was not Roman Catholic or Seventh-Day Adventist, or part of those other cults that we had been warned about in the Christian Union!

It was in the middle of my graduate studies in 1980, while pursuing a master's degree in physics on a career path to teach at university, that the quest deepened. It became clear to me then that my life-long vocation and service was not to be in the teaching of physics at university. The moment of reckoning for me came when I was confronted with Paul's testimony of the vision of his life, as he enunciated it to the elders from the church in Ephesus in Acts 20, in particular verse 20: "However, I consider my life worth nothing to me, if only I may finish the race and complete the task the Lord Jesus has given to me – the task of testifying to the gospel of God's grace."

Thereafter, at the invitation of the national evangelical student movement in Uganda, the Fellowship of Christian Unions (FOCUS), I quit graduate school and took on a vocation of an evangelist, Bible teacher, trainer and coordinator for Christian ministry among students. I was involved in it for just over twenty years, both at national and international level, with FOCUS and the International Fellowship of Evangelical Students (IFES), respectively. My first encounter with IFES was as a young staff member at an international students' conference in Austria in 1980, an experience that expanded my horizons to appreciate diversity in the community of the kingdom of God.

FOCUS was a member movement of IFES as well as one of many "para-church organizations". We prided ourselves on serving the church among students, without being committed to any particular denomination (non-denominational). Without saying it out loud we really believed we were the real church – more "church" than the denominational churches. Moreover, those of us who served as leaders in the para-church movement considered ourselves to be Christian leaders.

I could not avoid the question of committing to a local church for too long, however. When my wife Theodora and I got married in 1983, she demanded we commit to a particular local church, a church where we would feel at peace providing a context for the nurture of the faith of our children. I knew what she meant: the Church of Uganda. I was uncertain, because at the time I really had issues with some of the practices in the Church. I cannot remember that I prayed much over this decision. It was more a matter of retracing my footsteps back to the church of my childhood. My brothers and sisters in the Deliverance Church dubbed me their missionary in the Church of Uganda!

It was the idea that I was a Christian leader that caused me to consider ordination. How could I be a lay Christian leader without that sense of belonging and being accountable to a particular local church? I had an uneasy feeling of being a Christian leader without accountability to a leadership in a local-church structure. By this time I had completed a course in theology at Wheaton Graduate School in the USA, so I was also referred to as a lay theologian. In 1995, therefore, I was ordained in the Church of Uganda and continued my service in the student movement. I was amazed at how my being an ordained minister caused some of my colleagues in the student movement to treat me with suspicion. In 2001 I joined the Church Mission Society – the missionary society that had sent pioneering missionaries to Uganda – as director for its work in Africa. For four and a half years I lived on two continents: Europe and Africa. I was licensed as a minister in a church in a suburb of London and I spent a lot of time travelling across Africa, meeting with church leaders – in particular archbishops and bishops – talking about evangelism and mission. I also spent many hours in mission conferences in the UK and in Africa. I was stretched in my faith and understanding of the church.

I was deeply troubled to discover a depressed church in the UK, the home of the missionaries who had evangelized many peoples in Africa. I will never forget my visit to a church in a village in the UK. There must have been about fifty people in the congregation. The singing was more like a dirge. I gained a clearer picture of the congregation when the service came to an end. As each person walked out, half the congregation needed the physical support of the other half. I reckoned that those who were supporting others would themselves need that support in the not-too-distant future. The average age of the congregation must have been well over seventy-five years. At the end of the service I asked the priest, a middle-aged man, where the "others" were (by which I meant young families, the middle-aged, teenagers and so on). With a tinge of weariness in his voice he said, "They do not come to church."

I was also distressed as I travelled in various African countries. The much-talked-about vibrant church across Africa troubled me, as I came across countless situations where the churches were evidently part of the problem and not always the solution. Granted, there were great numbers on Sunday morning flocking to the church centres and buildings for worship services, but where was their impact on Monday to Friday in the market place?

As mentioned in connection with Senzani's story earlier in this introduction, when I travel I often take the opportunity to speak to strangers that I meet on flights or at the various airports as I wait. I often ask about religious or church affiliation as a conversation starter. I recall asking a man, while we sat together in a lounge at Nairobi airport, whether he went to church. "I used to go many years ago," he answered. "I stopped because going to church was like going to a party. When it is all over, people just walk away without even talking to you. I got nothing out of it." He said it in a matter-of-fact way. There are many like him who have rejected church, not because they have rejected God or faith in Jesus, but because of its trappings and traditions, conflicts and wars that are part of the history of the church: a history that posits Christianity as religion. The perception of "church" as another religion is repulsive to them. "Church" for them is one of the factors for the fracturing of society; it alienates them; it does not help them to deepen their relationship with God, but rather seems to be disconnected from and out of touch with the world as it is in their daily lives and routines. For them, "church" is a negative experience and something to shun.

I was once on a short holiday at a resort hotel on the shores of the Indian Ocean in Kenya. I got chatting with Julie and her teenage daughter Emma, who hailed from Essex in England. As is usually the case, after I had introduced myself as a bishop the conversation turned religious. We talked about church. I confessed how reluctant I often am to introduce myself to strangers as a bishop because of the stereotypes of church ministers. Julie, however, wanted me to feel at ease. She quickly explained to me, "Religion is the job you do." I quickly interjected that it was important to distinguish religion from faith. I admitted, "Yes, religion may be seen as the job I do; but faith is the life I live. I do what I do because of faith." Emma then said, "Not everyone has to be religious, but everyone has to have a faith." Julie explained that the church they knew was the Church of England. "My mother used to say to me when I was young that you did not have to go to church to be a good Christian," she explained. Emma chipped in: "She was right. I hate going to church. It's boring." She hoped that my church was different! You can imagine my embarrassment, given that my church is part of the same tradition. It was clear to me that neither of them wanted any association with church as they had come to know it.

I was ordained as a bishop in the Church of Uganda and served in the heart of Kampala as the Assistant Diocesan Bishop. There my restlessness with the contemporary church grew even deeper. It was the same story: large numbers but little impact on society. I have been amazed at how much people love the trappings of religion. The official way I was addressed was "My Lord Bishop". I tried, with not much success, to stop people calling me this, knowing that this "lordship" was not only irrelevant in Uganda, but in fact a title loaded with a history in Europe that we should be ashamed of. Moreover, it was a title that carried with it notions of episcopacy and episcopal power that were contrary to its essence. Some leaders and many Christians in the Church of Uganda consider me cantankerous for refusing the title. What is more, bishops are also called "religious leaders" and treated as such. They are the chief doers of religion. I am numbered among them, but I am restless. There is something about it all that does not feel right.

What has given me most joy is not all the religious "stuff" that comes with the office of a bishop. It was not even my visits to the largest of the congregations, whose contributions to the diocesan quota was large. It was the time I spent with young people in residential camps where denominational affiliation did not matter; with children in children's churches with their vulnerability and abandon visible in their singing; with the thriving and yet financially struggling congregations in the slums of the city, where I seemed to find vitality and religion-less desire for God and authentic, transforming faith. There are two congregations where my faith was rekindled and a hunger for more of God was awakened: in the death-row section of the national Maximum Security Prison in Luzira, and the chapel at the Mental Health Referral Hospital, Butabika. I often wonder what it is about these two Christian congregations that gave me that deep sense of the presence of God and his people and made me long for more. The worship services were electric, with an air of expectation that God was present to give hope and courage to face an uncertain future.

Five years into the work as a bishop in Kampala, I began to feel restless, wondering whether the Lord was calling me to follow him into the trenches of advocating and championing the cause of justice and dignity for all people, irrespective of creed. Reading in the Gospels about Jesus' passion for justice, as well as in the prophets – particularly Isaiah, Jeremiah, Amos, Hosea and Micah – and seeing the context of injustice, deprivation, greed, idolatry and oppression in Uganda, combined with the deafening silence from ecclesiastical officialdom, I became even more restless. It became clear to me in June 2011 that the call on my life at this season was to move on. I therefore decided that I would take an early retirement from my position as a bishop to dedicate my life to the cause of social justice from the platform of civic organizations rather than the church. Isaiah's prophecy concerning the call of the servant of the Lord in 42:1–4, quoted in Matthew 12:18–21, is poignant: "A bruised reed he will not break, and a smouldering wick he will not snuff out, till he has brought justice through to victory"! I submitted my request for early retirement to the Archbishop of the Church of Uganda. The House of Bishops accepted my request in January 2012 and I retired from my work as Assistant Diocesan Bishop of Kampala at the end of June 2012.

The Presence of God among the People of God

The presence of God: not a passive "God-is-everywhere" type presence, but a presence that stirs and gives life, joy, wonder and praise; a presence whose evidence is in the character of the community, both in its internal life and in relation to those outside. The people of God: identifiable because they display something of God's nature and character. In the words quoted at the start of this introduction Jesus warned that we should not be in haste to conclude that anybody with religious titles or forms and who speaks the right language of "Lord, Lord …" belongs to him. He challenged us to look more deeply, at the fruit of their lives.

We may need to be more sympathetic to those who have lost interest in the church or have rejected it outright. The fruit they have seen in the lives of Christians and indeed the life of the churches they know is not attractive or tasty. For many, both inside and outside the church, the words "church" and "Christian" have become a hindrance to their search for God, conjuring images of manipulation, corruption, sectarianism, "tribalism", irrelevance, domination and even sometimes abuse among those who have had damaging experiences of church. But Jesus was very clear on how his own would be identified: by the fruit of their lives. There are communities and groups that may carry the label "church" when in fact they are not or have ceased being his people. They are something other than church: simply clubs, some unashamedly so, judging by their names. I was amazed while visiting the USA to find a church called Country Club Christian Church!

We need to heed the words of Jesus today. We need to hear him warn us to watch out for false churches, dressed in "sheep's clothing ... and yet inwardly they are ferocious wolves". Let us not be deceived by our forms, structures or numbers. It is the fruit that counts; fruit that is a sign of the kingdom of God at work; fruit that glorifies God. It is those who do "the will of my Father in heaven".

1

Becoming and Being Church, the People of God

Jesus replied, "Blessed are you, Simon son of Jonah, for this was not revealed to you by man, but by my Father in heaven. And I tell you that you are Peter, and on this rock I will build my church, and the gates of Hades will not overcome it. I will give you the keys of the kingdom of heaven; whatever you bind on earth will be bound in heaven, and whatever you loose on earth will be loosed in heaven." (Matt 16:17–19)

Again, truly I tell you that if two of you on earth agree about anything they ask for, it will be done for them by my Father in heaven. For where two or three gather in my name, there am I with them. (Matt 18:19–20)

It is interesting that every time I have asked people how their church came into being, they have referred to their denominational roots or their founding fathers and mothers: the former, to the European or North American missionaries who pioneered the work of those churches; and the latter, to their charismatic founding leaders. Most quickly refer me to the name of their church and the denomination they are associated or affiliated with: Catholic, Baptist, Pentecostal Assemblies of God, Miracle, Deliverance, Word of Life, Christ is the Answer, Reformed, Anglican, Methodist, Presbyterian,

Christ Apostolic, Mennonite, Lutheran … The catalogue of names and denominations is endless.

It is even more instructive to inquire what constitutes their being church. Many will quickly make reference to what happens on Sundays when they gather or during the week days, "at church"; others may point to their leaders or leadership structures and doctrinal emphases and biases. When one inquires deeper into the basis and foundation of these structures and practices, they have little to say. Being church for them is being part of a denomination; and becoming church is primarily about going to a place for some Christian activities.

However, there is increasing disenchantment among many, especially young people, with "church" simply as a denomination or religious institution. I have been involved in work among Christian young people in Uganda for three decades and I have noted that in Kampala, for example, where there is a myriad of churches, young people no longer ask, "What church do you belong to?" or "Which church do you go to?" but rather "Who do you fellowship with?" Church for them is space where they connect with each other. This may also be reflected in the words they use to describe their worship services.

I was intrigued when I first visited St Paul's Church Howell Hill, an Anglican church in one of the suburbs at the south-west edge of London. I discovered that the name of the youth ministry and their worship service on Sunday evening is Reality. I inquired what kind of young people came to Reality. I discovered that over 30 per cent may be characterized as "unchurched" – that is, with no church background. They came because their friends invited them. Although there was a structure to the service, it could not be described as Anglican. There were no visible priests with priestly regalia, no altar or pulpit and no chairs. They began their meeting at 6:30 p.m. with a social time comprising drinks, toast and games. Then they moved from the "clubroom" into the worship area, where they spent time singing, led by a band. They had a leader who ensured some kind of flow to the service. After the songs (they do not call them hymns) of worship, there was a time of sharing personal stories; then one of them stood to give a "talk" (not a "sermon"). This was followed by a time of praying for one another in small circles of six to ten. Such is "church" that gives young people the opportunity to connect together as they connect with God, share their stories and express their youthfulness. I guess that is why it is called Reality.

This ministry Reality is part of what today is called the Emerging Church Movement – new expressions of church in the postmodern era.

But even these Emerging Churches could become the next-generation denominations with new religious bureaucracies. Today's denominations were a church phenomenon born with the modern era in Europe and which were later exported by European and North American missionaries. Every culture and generation emerges with forms and expressions of church. So it is important that we start our journey of exploring how the church came into being with the story of the one to whom the founding of the church is credited: Jesus of Nazareth.

Jesus and the Church

The leading question is: Was or is the church Jesus' idea? Did Jesus have in mind the birth of a community that would be identified as church? And was that "church" what would constitute the new people of God, in continuity with ancient Israel? Then come the follow-on questions: What does "church" that is true to Jesus' idea of church look like? And is the church in its diverse forms today what Jesus conceived?

There are only two passages in all the four Gospels – Matthew, Mark, Luke and John – in which Jesus made explicit reference to the church. The first is Matthew 16:17–19.

> Jesus replied, "Blessed are you, Simon son of Jonah, for this was not revealed to you by man, but by my Father in heaven. And I tell you that you are Peter, and on this rock *I will build my church*, and the gates of Hades will not overcome it. I will give you the keys of the kingdom of heaven; whatever you bind on earth will be bound in heaven, and whatever you loose on earth will be loosed in heaven [italics mine].

The second, also from Matthew, 18:15–20:

> If your brother or sister sins against you, go and point out their fault, just between the two of you. If they listen to you, you have won them over. But if they will not listen, take one or two others along, so that "every matter may be established by the testimony of two or three witnesses." If they still refuse to listen, tell it to the *church*; and if they refuse to listen even to the *church*, treat them as you would a pagan or a tax collector.

Truly I tell you, whatever you bind on earth will be bound in heaven, and whatever you loose on earth will be loosed in heaven.

Again, truly I tell you that if two of you on earth agree about anything they ask for, it will be done for them by my Father in heaven. For where two or three gather in my name, there am I with them [italics mine].

Experts in the languages in which the Gospels were originally written tell us that it is difficult to determine exactly what words Jesus used that are translated "church" in these passages. The English word "church" is the translation of *ekklesia* in the common Greek language that was spoken in first-century Palestine; it meant a citizens' assembly in a city to decide the matters that affected their welfare – a political gathering or simply a gathering. It was therefore also frequently used instead of the term *sunagoge* – translated "synagogue", the local gathering of Jews for preserving and nurturing the Jewish faith during the post-exile period. The term *ekklesia*, however, does not have an inherently religious (or later on, cultic) meaning. It is uncertain whether Jesus used a Hebrew or Aramaic word that translates *ekklesia* for temple. He may have used the Hebrew words *edah* or *qaha*, or the Aramaic equivalent, *edta*, which simply means the community of Israel. Yet another possibility is the Aramaic word *kenista*, which could be used of either a local Jewish community or just the Jewish people.[1]

Whichever of these words Jesus may have used, they all communicate the idea of a community identifiable by their gathering as well as by what happens when they gather, as was the case with the Israelites. In the affirmation "I will build my church", Jesus makes clear whose initiative and responsibility it was to bring the community into being and to whom the community would belong. Like the citizens' gathering and Israel, they would have a shared consciousness of the group's identity. However, their identity was grounded not simply in their belonging together, but rather in the one to whom they belonged. The community was to derive its character not from its membership but from the one who called it into being. Jesus was to be the author and reason for gathering. Furthermore, he pledged to be personally present in the gathering. It was Jesus' gathering in every sense: his people, and by extension, God's people.

---

1. Kevin Giles, *What on Earth Is the Church?* (London: SPCK, 1995), 37.

Unfortunately, the contemporary church scene speaks more of the presence of a denominational character than that of Jesus. I fear that in a lot of instances it is not Jesus gathering his own but rather us gathering those who are like us. Is it not true that the churches as we know them today – such as the ones described in the Introduction – are associations rather than assemblies of Jesus? Don't the rivalry, competition and conflict, and our inability to work together reflect the fact that our primary rootedness and calling as communities is in our worldly credentials – ethnic, social, regional, structural, stylistic and formal – and not in Jesus? I have been amazed when visiting congregations in my work as bishop in Kampala to find that some of them have felt more like tribal meetings because, in spite of the cosmopolitan nature of Kampala, the members of these congregations came from one ethnic or regional groups. The history of the churches in Kenya is such that particular denominations are associated with particular ethnic groups: Presbyterian for Kikuyu; Methodist for Meru; African Inland Church for Kalenjin; and so on.

It is unfortunate that the significance of Matthew 16:17–19 in defining the purpose of an authentic Jesus community has been lost in theological and ecclesiastical debates over what Jesus meant by "on this rock" and "the keys of the kingdom". Too much energy has been devoted to determining whether Peter was that rock and who his successors are! By focussing on this we miss the major subject of Jesus' words, which concerns the nature and purpose of community. Jesus' statement "I will build my church" is a clear expression of his intention to bring into being a visible community. Church was not accidental or incidental to his mission.

But the community was not to exist for its own sake. A closer look at the life, mission, message and ministry of Jesus as recorded in the Gospels shows that it was not the community that was Jesus' preoccupation but rather the kingdom of God. It is noteworthy that while there are only two references to the church in all the Gospels, there are 76 independent sayings on the kingdom of God, or 103 if the parables are included.[2] It was Jesus' messiahship that would be the foundation of the kingdom; the keys to Peter symbolized the work of "unlocking" through his apostolic leadership and declaration of the finished work of Jesus as Messiah. The kingdom of God was the reason Jesus was revealed. The purpose of the community is the kingdom of God.

The church was not the good news that Jesus preached; that good news was the kingdom of God. It is the kingdom of God that defines the

---

2. Giles, *What on Earth Is the Church?*, 27.

church, not vice versa. The church does not possess God's reign; it is to be possessed by it. Jesus' presence in the world would continue "*where* two or three are gathered" in his name. This would especially be the case after his physical departure from them, for he would be present for ever among them by his Spirit, whom the Father would send in his name (John 14:16–21). The community was to be a bearer of the kingdom of God in the world, by the presence and power of the Holy Spirit. This should act as a corrective to many erroneous notions of the church "building the kingdom of God". As Craig Van Gelder has observed:

> It is not uncommon to hear such concepts as "the church is responsible to build the kingdom of God", or "the church is to extend God's kingdom in the world", or "the church must promote the work of the kingdom of God", or "the church is to help establish God's kingdom in the world". These images of build, extend, promote and establish stand in sharp contrast to the biblical language used to define the relationship of the church to the kingdom of God.[3]

The kingdom of God is a greater and more encompassing reality; its vision much more liberating and inclusive; and its scope, spanning time and eternity. The kingdom of God is the reason for the church.

K. E. Skydsgaard has expressed it thus:

> The Kingdom of God is the conception placed above that of the church; the church is not the Kingdom, but the church owes her existence to the Kingdom. She exists for the Kingdom; she represents the Kingdom of God on earth in the present age till through the coming of Christ in power God will grant full and final victory. In the Kingdom of God the Church has her ultimate frontiers; from the kingdom she receives all her substance, her power, and hope.[4]

The missionary vocation of the church is to receive, enter, seek and inherit the kingdom of God. As pointed out by Lesslie Newbigin, the British

---

3. Craig Van Gelder, *The Essence of the Church: A Community Created by the Spirit* (Grand Rapids, Mich.: Baker, 2000), 87.

4. K. E. Skydsgaard, "Kingdom of God and the Church", in *Scottish Journal of Theology*, 4 (1951), 386.

missionary to India who later became bishop in the Church of South India, in his essay "On Being the Church in the World", there are at least three ways in which the church is to reflect the kingdom: as a sign pointing to a reality beyond what is visible now; as an instrument through which God's will for justice, peace and freedom is carried out in the world; and as a foretaste of the presence of the kingdom.[5]

Jesus' instructions on the ordering of the community's internal relationships in Matthew 18:15–20 give us a glimpse of his idea of what the community of the kingdom of God looks like. Firstly, there is a tacit assumption in his words that as part of its community life, they *should* gather together. The visibility of the community is in its gathering. But it is important to keep reminding ourselves that the distinguishing feature of the community is not just in its gathering, but rather in the cause for its gathering – Jesus' name. Jesus' name is the grounds on which members of the community gather. We get the full power of the significance of what Jesus said to his disciples when we remember that the people he was addressing regularly gathered in the synagogues and on occasions in the temple at Jerusalem. The community Jesus was bringing into being was not an add-on to the synagogue Jewish communities, but a radically new community whose life and health depended wholly on him.

Secondly, restoration and reconciliation are to characterize the common life of the community. The purpose for bringing the unrepentant brother or sister to the congregation (Matt 18) is so that they may be led to repentance, leading to reconciliation with those they have offended. For, "where two or three are gathered in my [Jesus'] name", Jesus – the one who loves, forgives and reconciles – is present. It is important to note that the one who sins is part of the community. But the one sinned against is also part of the community. In other words, the community that Jesus brings into being is not perfect. Members of the community sin and that creates conflict. But it is not permissible to live in conflict and division. Those Jesus gathers he also reconciles. Those who refuse to acknowledge their sin and folly are to be treated as foreigners to the community – pagans. Jesus counselled his disciples that should the sinner not repent of their wrongdoing and "refuse to listen even to the church, treat them as you would a pagan or a tax collector", meaning that they will have revealed where they belong: not to the kingdom

---

5. J. E. Lesslie Newbigin, "On Being the Church in the World", in *The Parish Church? Exploration in the Relationship of the Church and the World* (ed. G. Ecclestone; Oxford: Mowbray, 1988), 25–42.

community where Jesus rules, but rather to the community of the rebellious. The church that Jesus is building is the community of love, of forgiven and forgiving sinners; the place where the good news of the kingdom – love, forgiveness and reconciliation – is experienced. The church is a people shaped by the redemptive reign of God.

The act of forgiveness and reconciliation points to a third dimension of the life of the community: hope. The community has not yet reached perfection but rather is on a path towards complete victory, because the gates of hell will not overcome it. The redemptive reign of God is yet to be fully consummated. While on the journey there is a struggle with sin on the one hand and "the gates of hell" on the other, but neither will overcome the community. The community brought into being by Jesus is to keep its sights on his triumph as it lives out its missionary calling as the agency of the kingdom of God.

This is the community Jesus had in mind as constituting his church – the new people of God – when he said, "… I will build my church, and the gates of Hades will not overcome it": imperfect but on a path to victory. During the three and a half years of his ministry Jesus was forming the nucleus of that community through which he would continue his mission. Jesus' prayer was that the new community would be a sign of the kingdom in the world; a community that lives beneath the kingly rule of God, acknowledges it and proclaims it; daily praying to the Father, "May your kingdom come on earth as it is in heaven" and looking forward to its final manifestation. He came to the world that we may have "life … to the full" (John 10:10), life in its fullness in time and eternity. So, Jesus' people, while in the world, must be a sign of that life that he gives.

Thus, although Jesus did not make many direct references to the church, the creation of a new community was central to his life, teaching and ministry. Clearly, he envisaged a community that would continue after his death, resurrection and ascension, embodying and continuing to declare the kingdom of God.

Every church I know – indeed every one of the churches referred to in the Introduction – would argue that their claim to "being church" is their connection to Jesus. They invoke the name of Jesus as the reason for their gatherings. They would argue that their sense of community, group identity or self-consciousness has something to do with Jesus. What we must ask is whether their community life in their contexts and cultures is consistent and in continuity with Jesus' life and mission. We must ask whether they are in

Kampala, for example, as a sign, instrument and foretaste of the kingdom of God. If they are not, they may be invoking the name of Jesus in vain.

The Bible and the Church

All churches, in addition to invoking the name of Jesus, claim authenticity on the grounds that their common life is governed by the Bible; that their use of the Bible qualifies them to be church. If we were to go by this rule, all groups and communities that use the Bible in one form or another would rightly claim to be true to the vision of Jesus for the church. But we know that that is not the case, for even witchdoctors and diviners use the Bible. A friend of mine told me of a diviner in a village in a part of Uganda where the Church of Uganda (Anglican) has been strong. Among the tools of her trade are the Bible and the Book of Common Prayer, both in the language of the people she serves. There is a rebel group in Uganda called the Lord's Resistance Army that has waged a senseless and vicious war in Northern Uganda since 1986. They loot, rape and kill. One of the ways for recruiting in their ranks is abducting children – both boys and girls. They maim and kill those who resist them. They claim that their inspiration is the Ten Commandments. Clearly, the use of the Bible cannot be grounds enough for a community or group to claim to be an authentic church.

Some may object to the examples I have given above, arguing that they demonstrate misuse rather than use of the Bible. But that is the point. We have been drawn into the debate on use and misuse of the Bible and labelling churches according to which side of "use" and "misuse" they are – fundamentalist, evangelical, liberal; and neo-fundamentalist, neo-evangelical and neo-liberal. Is it not true that rather than the Bible being a uniting factor, it is a battleground for much of the infighting and rivalry among churches? It is often the reason for the proliferation of churches. Churches split because of disagreements over use and misuse. The Bible has become a problem for churches today!

I suggest that one of the reasons why the Bible is often misread and misused is that it is considered and handled primarily as a book. Granted, it is in "book form" that we encounter it: so, like any other book, it is for us to read or not read; to use and misuse; and dispense with if we do not like it. It is a tool in our hands. This is precisely what was rejected by Jomo Kenyatta, the freedom fighter and leader of the Kenya African Union (later renamed the Kenya African National Union) agitating for Kenya's independence from Britain in the 1950s. In his book *Facing Mount Kenya*, a study of the culture and customs as well as of the economy of the Gikuyu people prior to independence, Kenyatta argued that, since the Bible had been used as one of the tools to colonize Africans, in order for the Kenyan people to be freed from the shackles of their British colonial masters they needed to reject Christianity as "the white man's religion" and the Bible as their tool of suppression. He lamented that when the missionaries came from Europe to Africa they had the Bible and the Africans had the land. He said that the missionaries had used the Bible and taken advantage of the hospitality and generosity of the Africans to dispossess them of their land and sovereignty.[6]

Unfortunately, Kenyatta had a point. The same thing happened during the apartheid era of South Africa. The Dutch Reformed Church justified the doctrine of racial segregation on the basis of the Bible. No wonder the communist ideology had a very strong appeal to the anti-apartheid movement. I contend that it was not a rejection of God as such, but rather the God of the Bible that had been used as a tool of oppression.

But the Bible is not primarily a book. In fact, it is not a book, but an anthology of books, with one story. The organizing principle of the biblical text – how different texts and sources were put together into the books, when and how they were collected and arranged into the Bible as a whole – is the story of Jesus the Christ and of the community whose life was fashioned along that story.[7] Jesus is the link between the Old Testament and the New. The Old Testament story points to and is completed in him. God, who in the beginning created the heavens and the earth (Gen 1:1), is the one whom John identifies in his Gospel as revealed in Jesus, the Word, who "was with God, and … was God" (John 1:1). The first five books (from Genesis to Deuteronomy), commonly called the Books of Moses, recount the story of how the Creator God formed for himself a people through whom all creation would be blessed. Their promise, and indeed the promise for all peoples of the world, was the Messiah, whom God would send and who would come from among them. The prophets' work was to keep this hope alive, reminding the people that God would be true to his promise.

All the Gospel records link the story of Jesus to the account in the Old Testament. Matthew made it clear that the Jesus story did not begin with his birth in Bethlehem of Judah, because Jesus was "the son of David, the

---

6. Jomo Kenyatta, *Facing Mount Kenya* (Tel Aviv: Am Hassefer, 1963), 305.

7. Neil R. Lightfoot, *How We Got the Bible* (2nd ed.; Grand Rapids, Mich.: Baker, 1988).

son of Abraham" (Matt 1:1). He therefore began the account of Jesus' life with the patriarchs: Abraham, Isaac and Jacob. Then follows the ancestral line of David, including Tamar, Rahab and Ruth, who were of Gentile descent; and then the ancestral line of Joseph, during the monarchy, exile and the restoration. Luke records an incident after the crucifixion when two of Jesus' disciples were mourning his death, not realizing that he had risen from the dead "according to the Scriptures" (1 Cor 15:4). Then, "beginning with Moses and all the prophets, [Jesus] explained to them what was said in the Scriptures concerning himself" (Luke 24:27). Jesus is the key to understanding the story of Israel.

The Acts of the Apostles is an account of what Jesus continued to do through his apostles by his Spirit – bringing his own together into gatherings in Jerusalem, Judea, Samaria and beyond, throughout the Roman Empire. Thus Peter, in explaining the outpouring of the Spirit to the Jewish Pentecost gathering in Acts 2, referred to Joel's prophecy of many centuries before, predicting that God would pour out his Spirit. He pointed to Jesus as the one through whom that promise had been fulfilled. The rest of the New Testament is the continuing account of Jesus' work among his followers, looking towards its consummation in eternity, the vision laid out in the book of Revelation. Jesus is thus the centre of the entire biblical narrative. It is the story of Jesus Christ that is the one thread that joins the whole biblical account together.

The purpose of the record of the story of Jesus is for his community to live by that story. The immediate audience of the four Gospels was the second- and third-generation followers of Jesus. John the evangelist summed up the purpose of the Gospel accounts: "Jesus did many other miraculous signs in the presence of his disciples, which are not recorded in this book. But these are written that you may believe that Jesus is the Christ, the Son of God, and that by believing you may have life in his name" (John 20:30–31).

The epistles were written to the various emerging communities who had come to faith in Jesus as a result of the witness of the first apostles and disciples of Jesus. Paul encouraged the early followers of Jesus to devote themselves to the Scriptures of the Old Testament because it was through them that their faith would be nourished. The New Testament communities understood themselves to be in continuity with the Old Testament community. Hence Paul, writing to first-century believers in Corinth, appealed to the record of the pilgrimage of the Hebrew people from Egypt to the land of Canaan as a warning to the believers in Christ:

Now these things occurred as examples to keep us from setting our hearts on evil things as they did. Do not be idolaters, as some of them were; as it is written: "The people sat down to eat and drink and got up to indulge in pagan revelry." We should not commit sexual immorality, as some of them did – and in one day twenty-three thousand of them died. We should not test the Lord, as some of them did – and were killed by snakes. And do not grumble, as some of them did – and were killed by the destroying angel.

These things happened to them as examples and were written down as warnings for us, on whom the fulfilment of the ages has come. (1 Cor 10:6–11)

The faith experience of those who had gone before the Corinthian believers was to serve as a challenge and an encouragement for their faith in Christ.

As succeeding generations of believing communities and people ploughed through the different texts there was a resonance between their story and faith, and the story and faith they encountered in those texts and narratives. So in the process the canon of Scripture was established, based on a faith-consensus: a consensual decision as to what "is God-breathed and is useful for teaching, rebuking, correcting and training in righteousness" (2 Tim 3:16), thus according these Scriptures universal value. They judged them not only to be pointing to God's words and acts from the beginning of creation, but also to be an unfolding of God's continuing action in them and through them, centred on Jesus Christ.

We therefore need to look at the Bible not primarily as a book, but as a story. Firstly, we need to see it as God's story: his words and works; an account of his unfolding will and purpose in bringing "all things in heaven and on earth together under … Christ" (Eph 1:10). Secondly, as Lesslie Newbigin has put it, we need to see it as universal history,[8] because God's words and works span all time and space. Thus, although the Bible focuses attention on particular people in particular epochs in history, it spans all time: the past, the present and the future, beginning "in the beginning" (Gen 1:1) and reaching to the coming of "a new heaven and a new earth" (Rev 21:1). The subject of its message is not bound by chronological time. It is also not bound

---

8. "The Bible as Universal History" is the title of a chapter in Lesslie Newbigin, *The Gospel in a Pluralist Society* (London: SPCK, 1989), 89–102.

by culture, because its message is for all peoples, "all the world … all creation" (Mark 16:15) and "all peoples on earth" (Gen 12:3).

The most significant achievement in the pioneering work of missionaries is the translation of the Bible into the native languages of the people among whom they are called to serve. Lamin Saneh, in his book *Translating the Message*, has made the point that "missionary adoption of the vernacular … was tantamount to adopting indigenous cultural criteria for the message, a piece of radical indigenization far greater than the standard portrayal of mission as Western cultural imperialism".[9] It should not surprise us that the completion of the translation of portions of Scripture always propelled growth in the numbers of those accepting the message of the gospel as well as depth in commitment to their new-found faith. Unfortunately, the story of the process of translating the Bible into native languages is often credited to European or North American missionaries alone, yet part of the significance of the translation process is that it was one of the ways in which the recipients of the new message felt that the message was their own. In reading the Bible in the vernacular, they not only read about the history of Israel, but they also discovered in it the clue to their own history.

The story is told of a village community in central Africa in the late nineteenth century. A European missionary and his African colleague had been working painstakingly for many months translating the book of Genesis. On completion of their work they decided they would give to the chief the first printed version of Genesis in the mother tongue of the community. During the presentation the African colleague read Genesis to the chief. Slowly, he worked through the creation story, with its refrain "And God said, 'Let there be …'" (Gen 1:3, 6, 9, etc.). At the end of the reading the chief exclaimed, "God speaks my language!" To the amazement of the chief, each time God spoke, he spoke in his own language.

Thirdly, the Bible is the story of a community of faith that finds its ultimate significance in Jesus. Although the Bible gives specific accounts of diverse communities and their encounters with God in different times and places, and could therefore be characterized as many stories, it is also one story and one community, the story of the community of faith both in ancient times and in succeeding generations, who are all united in Christ. The Bible is therefore our story as it continues to unfold towards the final triumph of the

---

9. Lamin Saneh, *Translating the Message: The Missionary Impact on Culture* (Maryknoll, NY: Orbis, 1993), 3.

kingdom of God. We do not read the Bible simply as a description of the faith of those in its pages – a people living in a different time, culture and world; we read it as descriptive of our faith, as new generations of those who "believe [and are] saved" (Rom 10:9). Our connection with them is the relationship we share with Jesus that coheres with the biblical narrative – the story of *their* faith, which is also the story of *our* faith. Thus the Bible is not just the book we read; it is the place and story in which we live. We do not read it just to understand it, but rather to find our place within it, as we allow it to critique our story, reshaping it and realigning it.

Many studies on the church begin and end with the New Testament account, arguing that the Old Testament has nothing to teach about being and becoming church. Therein lies part of our error in the contemporary church. I believe that this has impoverished the church, because it truncates the story. This approach separates the story of Israel from the story of the church. One would have hoped that beginning with the New Testament would have forced the church to read the whole story, which begins with the Old Testament account. The value of having the Scriptures in one volume is that it communicates the fact that from Genesis to Revelation it is one unfolding story. The story of the Lord of the church does not begin with the New Testament but with the Old, because he is the Lord of the kingdom, by whom, for whom and in whom everything was created (John 1:1–3; Col 1:15–17). One of my hopes is that this book will help every reader appreciate the Bible as one story: our story, the story of all humanity, past present and to come; the universal story.

The People of God: The Continuing Story, Hebrews 11 – 12

Hebrews 11 – 12 is one of the few passages in the Bible that draw together the entire biblical narrative into one coherent account, taking the people of God as an interpretative thread through the entire story. It weaves together the themes of faith, community (both Old Testament and New Testament) and kingdom. It shows how God's unfolding purposes for humanity and all creation are realized fully in Christ and that these purposes are being worked out through his people throughout all the generations. What the author of Hebrews does in these chapters is retell the story of the people of God from ancient times to the first-century followers of Jesus, identifying characteristic features common to all the people of God, whatever their generation, wherever they are. The point here is that the story of any people of God in any generation is part of the story of the people of God in previous generations as well as the coming generations. Hebrews 11 – 12 provides a methodological approach for discourse on the nature and character of the "authentic church" of Jesus.

There are at least three features that Hebrews 11 – 12 identifies as characterizing the continuing story of the people of God. The first mark is faith. Commentators on the epistle to the Hebrews are agreed that the immediate audience to whom the message was addressed were suffering for their faith in Jesus. The purpose of the letter was to encourage the persecuted minority, the majority of them Jewish followers of Jesus in the diaspora, to persevere in their faith in Christ, because in Christ they were the true heirs of God's promise to Abraham. In Christ they were now the true descendants of the patriarchs and it was no wonder that, like them, they lived as wanderers. Citing the roll of honour, from Abel to Noah, Abraham to David and including all the prophets, who were "commended for their faith" (Heb 11:39), the writer encouraged them that they too would be commended for their faith and perseverance.

Thus Hebrews 11 summarizes the account of all the Old Testament heroes, from Abel in Genesis to King David and the prophets, in the phrase "by faith". Faith distinguished them from other people, both in life and in death, as the people of God, for "without faith it is impossible to please God" (11:6). The writer's argument was that Israel and its patriarchs were a people called out and called together, that through them God was fulfilling his purpose for all creation. The persecuted followers of Jesus were included in God's promises to the patriarchs. The patriarchs and the persecuted minority of followers of Jesus in first-century Palestine shared the same faith and destiny. In other words, the connection between Noah, Abraham, King David, Peter, Paul, John and those to whom their writings were immediately addressed in first-century Palestine and Asia was faith – a living relationship with God.

The author also wanted his readers to be encouraged by the fact that "none of them [patriarchs and ancestors] received what had been promised, since God had planned something better for us [them], so that only together with us [them] would they be made perfect" (11:39–40). The first-century believers were thus included in the promise and, by extension, those who share in the same faith in Jesus today, in the twenty-first century, are also included in God's promises and share the same destiny as the patriarchs. In a profound way, Hebrews 11 – 12 is saying that the "church", as the people of God, did not begin with the New Testament.

The second mark of the authentic people of God is community – a social entity distinguishable in its shared life, values and purpose. Hebrews 11 asserts that authentic faith is expressed in community – in relationship with others. It is faith that formed them into a community, and community formed their faith: belonging to God and to each other. They were all related to each other by faith – a communion or sharing in the faith. It was the common denominator of their lives: *they were all* commended by their faith, and so can rightly be called a "community of faith". They belonged together by faith. Since faith is a gift – it begins with God's initiative –we should also acknowledge that becoming a community of faith is a gift. It is God who creates the community of faith. However, God's initiative invites a response. The faith the people share is demonstrated in their response of obedience. Thus even for Israel, it was not enough that they were the biological heirs to Abraham; it was by the obedience of faith that they would inherit the promises of Yahweh's covenant with Abraham. Hence Abraham is referred to as the father of all those who come to God through faith in Jesus, for "if you belong to Christ, then you are Abraham's seed, and heirs according to the promise" (Gal 3:29). The basis of belonging together was their belonging to God, and that by faith. Abraham was therefore father of a community beyond his clan.

This communion of faith – the oneness of the people of God – has two axes to it: one relating to the passage of time, and the other relating to space or geography. The community spans all time; past, present and future. The "great cloud of witnesses" (Heb 12:1) is constituted by those from the past who have completed their earthly journey. They are witnesses cheering on those who are running now, persevering in order to receive, with all the others, the reward that awaits them in the future, "for only together with us would they be made perfect" (11:40). We who read Hebrews in the twenty-first century can also say of those to whom the epistle was addressed "that only together with us, would they be made perfect". Their story is our story and our story is in their story. Moreover, it is only "together with all the saints" that we shall "know this love [of Christ] that surpasses knowledge" (Eph 3:19).

My parents were first-generation believers. They were among the first people in our clan to accept the gospel of Christ. They both died in 2005. They made their home in a village in the south-west of Uganda, an eight-hour, 500-kilometre journey from Kampala, a route that is notorious for its accidents and which my family and I would regularly take to go to visit them. Each time my father prayed for us when sending us off on the return journey to Kampala, he would invoke the protection of God, beginning his prayers with "Oh God of Abraham, Isaac and Jacob, our God". Then he would recite the same prayer Moses prayed each time he and the Israelites set out from a place of rest on their arduous journey to the promised land:

> Rise up, O LORD!
>> May your enemies be scattered;
>> may your foes flee before you. (Num 10:35)

My father made the connection: that they who lived in Kiburara, their little village, were in communion with Abraham, Isaac, Jacob and Moses, who lived hundreds of years ago in the Middle East. He believed that just as God travelled with the patriarchs, so he would travel with us, protecting us from our enemies – the hazards of road travel in Uganda. He shared the same faith that the patriarchs were commended for.

But the community of faith also spans geography: it spreads all over the face of the earth, in all its diversities of race, tribe religion, class and so on. All are united in their faith in God, in Jesus Christ. In 1980 I travelled for the first time to Europe, to a conference of international students in Austria. I had never before been to such an international gathering of followers of Christ. I was enthralled by being in the company of followers of Christ from Latin America, Asia, the Middle East, the then communist lands of Eastern Europe and various parts of Africa. "Wow!" I thought to myself, "all these are my brothers and sisters in Christ!" Yes, his people are spread all over the face of the earth, "from every nation, tribe, people and language" (Rev 7:9) and generation!

The third mark of the authentic people of God that we learn from Hebrews 11 – 12 is pilgrimage. Pilgrimage gives character to the people of God, for faith and community are lived out in pilgrimage with God – that is, on a journey. We read:

> All these people were still living by faith when they died. They did not receive the things promised; they only saw them and welcomed them from a distance. And they admitted that they were aliens and strangers on earth. People who say such things show that they are looking for a country of their own. If they had been thinking of the country they had left, they would have had opportunity to return. Instead, they were longing for a better country – a heavenly one. Therefore God is not

ashamed to be called their God, for he has prepared a city for them. (Heb 11:13–16)

Pilgrimage emphasizes that the people of God live in hope, recognizing that theirs is an in-between life: one between the already and the not-yet. They are pilgrims because they are yet to reach home. The author of Hebrews says that the community of faith lived their lives "wandering". Their wandering was not, however, aimless; it is to be contrasted with settling or having arrived. Wherever they were, they were strangers and foreigners (11:13). The author of Hebrews explains that the reason the people of God did not settle was because they were looking for a country of their own. Each time they settled in a place it was temporary – "living in tents" (11:9). The goal of their journey – "looking for a country of their own ... a better country – a heavenly one" – would not allow them to settle. Even Abraham, after arriving in the country of promise, "made his home in the promised land like a stranger in a foreign country" (11:9), because the promised land was not ultimately home. This sounds contradictory; however, once we recognize that Abraham's call was not simply for the nation of Israel but for the blessing of all the nations, we understand why not even the promised land was home. Thus he looked towards the "city with foundations, whose architect and builder is God" (11:10). This is reminiscent of the garden of Eden, where God's dwelling was among his creation. They lived in hope: hope for the "better country", a recreated garden, their heavenly dwelling. This is what gave them courage to endure all the hardships on the way. "Wandering" was given meaning and purpose in their hope of their true homeland.

Thus the motif of pilgrim is a clue to "being authentic church". "Church" is not an end in itself; it is in the pilgrimage that God works out his purposes among and through his people. There is here a close connection between promise and hope. The pilgrim's life is anchored in the promise of "the better country". The promise keeps hope alive, a hope that keeps the pilgrim on the way. The promise is inclusive, not exclusive. It is missional. The promise to Abraham, to bless him and make him a "great nation", was given in order that he would be a blessing to all the peoples of the earth (Gen 12:2–3). As God revealed to Moses while on Mount Sinai, the nation of Israel was called "out of all nations" to be "a treasured possession" and was chosen and formed through the exodus to be a "kingdom of priests and a holy nation" (Exod 19. 3–6). Thus "none of them [patriarchs and ancestors] received what had been promised" because the promised included succeeding generations. God has an eternal and universal promise – for all people, for all time and for all creation. And the promise is sure, because "He who promised is faithful" (Heb 10:23).

The temptation of the pilgrim community is to domesticate the promise – to enjoy the blessing for its sake and their sakes, and to ignore or abandon its universal character. The temptation arises from at least two sources. Firstly, the pilgrim nature of life engenders a survival mentality that focuses energies on self-preservation. Secondly, the experience of blessings makes the people of God forget or abandon their pilgrim mode of life. They forget that the experience of the blessing is only a foretaste and a shadow of the promise. The author of Hebrews therefore points to the anchor of faith, indeed the eternal grounds for perseverance on the journey: Jesus, with whom they share the pilgrim life. Jesus was the pilgrim par excellence, who, for the "joy set before him, endured the cross, scorning its shame" and is now seated "at the right hand of the throne of God" (Heb 12:2). It is fixing their eyes on Jesus that will enable the pilgrims to overcome the temptation to domesticate the promise or even to give up in the face of discouragements and suffering. Our sufferings, like his sufferings, are part of the exercise of our faith, for even he, "Although he was a son, … learned obedience from what he suffered and, once made perfect, he became the source of eternal salvation for all who obey him" (Heb 5: 8–9). He is the pilgrim Saviour.

In Jesus, faith, community and pilgrimage meet. He is "the author and perfecter of our faith", and the one whom God "appointed heir of all things, … through whom also he made the universe. … the radiance of God's glory and the exact representation of his being, sustaining all things by his powerful word" (Heb 1:2–3). He is God's gift of eternal life; by his Spirit we are able to walk in obedience; and in him we are counted with the cloud of witnesses. In Jesus, God displays his purposes, as Paul affirmed: "… he made known to us the mystery of his will according to his good pleasure, which he purposed in Christ, to be put into effect when the times reach their fulfilment – *to bring unity to all things in heaven and on earth* under Christ" (Eph 1:9–10; italics mine).

It is important to note that the scope of God's purpose is "all things in heaven and on earth", the entire created order. Thus, according to his promise, although his church is imperfect and buffeted by the gates of hell, he will accomplish his purpose through it. Jesus' promise that the gates of hell will not prevail over his church still stands. We have that promise – for his church and now ours!

As we ponder these truths, may we constantly pray:

Build your church, Lord,
Make us strong, Lord,
Join our hearts, Lord,
Through your Son.
Make us one, Lord,
In your body,
In the kingdom,
Of your Son.[10]

Outline of This Book

As already indicated, Hebrews 11 – 12 provides us with a methodology for coming to grips with the mystery of God in the life of his people throughout the ages, down to our own times and generation. Our purpose is to try to tell the story – because it is one story, the story of the people of God. Our method, just like that in Hebrews 11 – 12, is to retell the story.

A word about narrative as a methodology is necessary at this point. The way we as humans experience the world and live our faith-life through events that happen, in particular places and times, is filtered through a learned framework of attaching meaning to those events. The way we apprehend the world, therefore, is primarily through description. The way we communicate the exercise of faith in those events is also by description. Bolaji Idowu, the pioneer African theologian, has asserted, "The cogent fact [here] is that no one has ever seen or touched 'faith'. Faith only becomes known as it realizes or actualizes itself in expressions. And expressions of faith by persons must reduce themselves into forms, which can be described in categories."[11]

Narrative is a way of describing the people, events, places and the network of relations and issues around them. The merit of narrative as a descriptive tool is its capacity to combine events and interpretation together. Stanley Hauerwas and Gregory Jones have made the case for narrative as a method: "Narrative is neither just an account of genre criticism nor a faddish appeal to the importance of telling stories; rather it is a crucial conceptual category for such matters as understanding issues of epistemology and

---

10. Dave Richards, "For I'm Building a People of Power".
11. E. Bolaji Idowu, *African Traditional Religion: A Definition* (London: SCM Press, 1973), 27.

methods of argument, depicting personal identity, and displaying the content of Christian convictions."[12]

That is what we hope is achieved in the following pages: bringing out the issues and truths as we retell the story. The story comes in three parts: the first part deals with the ancient people of God, Israel, born through Moses; the second part looks at the creation of the new Israel, the people of the new covenant in Christ, born through the Holy Spirit at Pentecost; and the third part looks at the life of the new community, the church, during the apostolic era. The dominant thrust of the story in part one is the people and promise of God through Moses; the thrust in part two is the people and the kingdom of God in Christ; and the thread in part three is the people of God in and by the Holy Spirit. In each of these sections, we are keen to trace the manifestation or lack of the three features that Hebrews 11 – 12 commends: faith, community and pilgrimage.

We start the story in Chapter 2 at the beginning, with Moses and the creation of the people of God, Israel, because it is with Moses that even the story of the Bible begins, and because it is through the lens of Moses that we read from Genesis through to the inheritance of the land of promise. Although there is no consensus on a Mosaic authorship of the first five books of the Bible among Old Testament scholars, our view is that there is enough internal and external evidence supporting it. Moses is the figure around which faith, community and pilgrimage are constructed for this ancient people. Chapter 3 takes the story from the occupation of the promised land through to the exile. The dominant motif is rebellion rather than faith, climaxing in the apostasy of Israel and its destruction. But the end of that chapter is the hope in the remnant, through whom the promise of the Messiah is fulfilled in Jesus the Galilean, born in Bethlehem of Judea.

Chapters 4 and 5 delve into the accounts by the evangelists, Matthew, Mark, Luke and John, and retell the story of Jesus creating a new community, climaxing with its "birth" at Pentecost. We will see that Jesus was not only the fulfilment of all that the ancient people hoped for – the promise of faith, the grounds of the hope of the community and its defining moment on its journey with God; it was his intention to create a new people of God, with a new covenant sealed with his blood on the cross, in whom and through whom he would bring everything under the rule of Christ, according to the

---

12. Stanley Hauerwas and Gregory Jones, eds., *Why Narrative? Readings in Narrative Theology* (Grand Rapids, Mich.: Eerdmans, 1989), 5.

eternal purposes of God. It was to be a community of love; called out and called together, to live in and out of that love, reflecting the holiness and justice of the kingdom of God.

Chapters 6 and 7 retell the story of the life and witness of the new community in Christ, the churches during the apostolic era: among the Jews and Gentiles in Jerusalem, Judea, Samaria and to the ends of the earth – the Gentile world. There is a dual thrust to the story: the internal life of the new community and its witness to the wider society of which it was a part. In both, what sustained the life of the community were the apostolic preaching and teaching and the Holy Spirit, the very factors that gave birth to the communities of Christ. Our story ends with the apostolic era, for that is how the biblical narrative ends; but of course it is not the end of the story of the people of God. It is our view, however, that for succeeding generations to claim authenticity as a people of God, they must be connected to that story in a way that is normative and definitive.

In the concluding chapter, we first return to where we started, Hebrews 11 – 12, drawing on the metaphor of "pilgrim" as an integrating motif and showing that the story is one. It is the story of one community, sharing the same faith throughout many generations, dispersed all over the earth. We highlight three marks – faith, love and hope – as the key features that mark out the new community in Christ as the people of God. These three are definitive as they are descriptive of the identity and missional life of the new community in Christ, from the New Testament times to date. It is these three that are the marks of authentic church. We characterize the church as the new pilgrim people of God. Just as the story of ancient Israel, as the people of God, was incomplete until the revelation of Christ, so it is with the story of the church. It is a participant, as it awaits and looks forward to the full consummation of God's kingdom, when it will be fully realized, in the "new heaven and [the] new earth, where righteousness dwells" (2 Pet 3:13).

2

Beginning with Moses: The Promise, the Covenants and the People of God

He said to them "How foolish you are, and how slow of heart to believe all that the prophets have spoken! Did not the Messiah have to suffer these things and then enter his glory?" And beginning with Moses and all the Prophets, he explained to them what was said in all the Scriptures concerning himself. (Luke 24:25–27)

By faith, Moses, when he had grown up, refused to be known as the son of Pharaoh's daughter....

By faith he left Egypt, not fearing the king's anger; he persevered because he saw him who is invisible. By faith he kept the Passover and the application of blood, so that the destroyer of the firstborn would not touch the firstborn of Israel.

By faith the people passed through the Red Sea as on dry land ...

By faith the walls of Jericho fell, after the army had marched round them for seven days. (Heb 11:24, 27–30)

Many aspects of the state of the contemporary church leave one baffled. Mark Labberton, in his book *The Dangerous Act of Worship*, says that the vast majority of the evangelical and Protestant churches in the USA would best be described as in a state of slumber. "The church is asleep. Not dead. Not necessarily having trouble breathing. But asleep. This puts everything that matters at stake: God's purposes in the church and the world."[1] Labberton's observations apply equally to the many churches in Africa, Asia and Latin America. If that is what is said about these otherwise vibrant and growing churches, as they are portrayed in many reviews of the state of the church worldwide, what are we to say of the pre-World War II thriving churches in Europe? They are no longer just asleep; many of them seem to have been anaesthetized to a state of unconsciousness.

The sense of despair that many feel concerning the future of the church in the twenty-first century is akin to the distress and despair felt by the first disciples after their teacher and master had been crucified. The story of the two who were going down to the village of Emmaus discussing the tragedy of his death captures that sense of gloom. They recounted to the stranger who joined them how "the chief priest and rulers had handed [Jesus] over to be sentenced to death, and they crucified him" (Luke 24:20–21), dashing their hopes that he would be the one to redeem Israel. So deep was their despondency that they could not recognize that the stranger was in fact the resurrected Jesus. Incognito, Jesus "… *beginning* with Moses and all the Prophets, … explained to them what was said in all the Scriptures concerning himself" (24:27, italics mine). The way to enable the disciples to gain the true perspective to the meaning and significance of the events of the weekend was to point them to where it all began – with Moses and the Prophets, and with the link between Moses and the crucified Jesus.

We too, like the two disciples on the road to Emmaus, are prone to losing perspective. Just as those disciples needed Jesus to begin with "Moses and all the Prophets" to help them make sense of who he was, so we too need to start there in order to make sense of his church and its future. We cannot adequately understand Jesus of Nazareth and his church – and indeed God's purposes in him for and through his church in the New Testament to the present century – without understanding God's action in and through Israel. The roots of the community of followers of Jesus lie in the story of Israel as

---

1. Mark Labberton, *The Dangerous Act of Worship: Living God's Call to Justice* (Downers Grove, Ill.: Inter-Varsity Press, 2007), 14.

a people of God. Thus the starting point for understanding the call of the people of God today, Christ's church, and the promise of its future is not with the Gospel record, but with Moses and all the Prophets, indeed with the story of Israel, the first people of God.

It is noteworthy that Jesus did not begin with Abraham but rather with Moses. It was Moses and his encounter with God in the burning bush while he tended the flock belonging to his father-in-law Jethro that was the starting point of Israel's corporate journey: a journey that formed them into a people of God.

Beginning with Moses: God's Revelation of Creation at Mount Horeb

Moses was born into a Levite family in slavery in Egypt. At that time the pharaoh of Egypt, for fear of the consequences of the growing Hebrew slave population, had passed a decree that every boy born to the Hebrews must be killed by being thrown into the Nile (Exod 1:22). The story is worth retelling as it is recorded in Exodus:

> Now a man of the house of Levi married a Levite woman, and she became pregnant and gave birth to a son. When she saw that he was a fine child, she hid him for three months. But when she could hide him no longer, she got a papyrus basket for him and coated it with tar and pitch. Then she placed the child in it and put it among the reeds along the bank of the Nile. His sister stood at a distance to see what would happen to him.
>
> Then Pharaoh's daughter went down to the Nile to bathe, and her attendants were walking along the river bank. She saw the basket among the reeds and sent her slave girl to get it. She opened it and saw the baby. He was crying, and she felt sorry for him. "This is one of the Hebrew babies," she said.
>
> Then his sister asked Pharaoh's daughter, "Shall I go and get one of the Hebrew women to nurse the baby for you?"
>
> "Yes, go," she answered. And the girl went and got the baby's mother. Pharaoh's daughter said to her, "Take this baby and nurse him for me, and I will pay you." So the woman took the baby and nursed him. When the child grew older, she took

him to Pharaoh's daughter and he became her son. She named
him Moses, saying, "I drew him out of the water." (2:1–10)

Although Moses was raised in Pharaoh's palace, he grew to discover
that he was not Egyptian but rather belonged to the slave Hebrew people.
I wonder how Moses came to know the story of the patriarchs – Abraham,
Isaac and Jacob. Could he have inquired of the elders, as he visited the labour
camps, how it came about that his people became enslaved? These elders
would have told him the story of how their ancestors migrated to Egypt and
then "multiplied greatly and became exceedingly numerous, so that the land
was filled with them" (Exod 1:7). They must have told him about Yahweh,
their God, and their hope that one day he would bring their servitude to an
end, remembering one of the parting messages of Joseph, that God would one
day take them "out of this land to the land he promised on oath to Abraham,
Isaac and Jacob" (Gen 50:24). It was a story that had been passed on from
generation to generation, over a period of at least four hundred years. Moses
must have been incensed and distressed by the account. The continuing
misery of his people must have caused him anguish. So when one day he saw
an Egyptian beating one of his own people he acted in defence of the Hebrew,
killing the Egyptian. Subsequently Moses realized that his life was in danger;
Pharaoh in fact tried to kill him. So he fled.

It was while a fugitive in Midian, as he was shepherding the flock of
his Midianite father-in-law, that he had an encounter with God that changed
the course of his life and that of the Israelites. Moses must have thought it
just a dream when God announced to him his intention to use him as his
instrument to lead Israel out of captivity in Egypt. How could this be? It had
been four hundred years of servitude and bondage. Moses may have been
afraid that four hundred years of slavery had clouded out of the minds and
experience of the Israelites the possibility of a God who cared and would fulfil
his promise to Abraham. Where was this "God of Abraham, the God of Isaac
and the God of Jacob" (Exod 3:6)? Generations had come and gone, and the
patriarchal era was so distant that the knowledge and worship of the God of
Abraham, Isaac and Jacob must have receded in significance. So he inquired
further of God: "Suppose I go to the Israelites and say to them, 'The God of
your fathers has sent me to you,' and they ask me, 'What is his name?' Then
what shall I tell them?" (Exod 3:13).

God said to Moses, "I AM WHO I AM. This is what you are to say
to the Israelites: 'I AM has sent me to you.'"

God also said to Moses, "Say to the Israelites, 'The LORD, the God of your fathers – the God of Abraham, the God of Isaac and the God of Jacob – has sent me to you.'

This is my name for ever,
    the name you shall call me
    from generation to generation." (3:13–14)

The Genesis narrative was God's answer to Moses. It is an exposition of the "I AM WHO I AM", his being and relationship with humankind and then with Israel.

Firstly, this narrative declared that he was the origin of all life and being; the beginning of all that is, as the eternal "I AM". The Genesis narrative begins with God: "In the beginning God…." (Gen 1:1). God was the only actor in the creation drama. At that point he alone was; all else was created out of nothing and formed – for "the earth was formless and empty, darkness was over the surface of the deep" (1:2). God brought into being that which was not, by his repeated command: "Let there be … and there was …" (Gen 1:3, 6–7, 9–12, 14–15). All creation owed its existence to him – he created it all out of nothing. The God who was taking action to liberate Israel from bondage was the God not just of the promise to Abraham but of all creation. Yahweh was not a provincial or tribal deity. He was unlike any of the gods of Egypt that Moses had grown up with in the courts of Pharaoh. Yahweh was the Creator God. God wanted Moses to understand that years of bondage and servitude could not thwart his promise to Abraham. That promise was itself rooted in the promise to creation, the promise made to Noah after the flood that "As long as the earth endures, seedtime and harvest, cold and heat, summer and winter, day and night will never cease" (Gen 8:22). God's purposes could not be frustrated by the passage of time or generations, because from eternity – before the beginning – he was God!

Secondly, the Genesis narrative declared that God's divine being was relational, in-community, in himself and with humankind and creation. He was unlike the distant, impersonal gods of the Egyptians – the gods of Moses' childhood and young adult years; he was not only God Almighty, the Creator, but also God-in-community. But it was his relationship with humankind that was definitive of his relationship with the rest of creation. The making of humankind was the one act in the whole creation drama that called for community action. While the rest of creation came into being with the command "let there be" followed by "And it was so", with the creation of humankind there was not only the divine community summons "Let us …", but also it was followed by a personal address of blessing: "Be fruitful and increase in number; fill the earth and subdue it. Rule over the fish of the sea and the birds of the air and over every living creature that moves on the ground" (Gen 1:26, 28).

Note also that whereas the other creatures were created "according to their kinds" (1:21, 24–25), humanity was made "in our [God's] image, in our likeness". Humankind was marked out of all creation as uniquely in relationship with God: "in his own image, in the image of God he created them; male and female he created them" (1:27). Human beings had something of the divine being. The Genesis 2 narrative captures the uniqueness of the making of humankind in a different way. Atkinson observed that even God is given a more intimate name in the act of forming the human: "In Chapter 1 he is 'God'. In 2:4b he is 'the LORD God', the word LORD representing God's covenant name: YAHWEH. Our focus is no longer the cosmic perspective of the One who made the stars. It is the intimacy of fellowship with the One who calls Man by his name."[2]

Hence – as the narrative continues – God "breathed into his nostrils the breath of life" (2:7). This was a relationship not of separate entities but rather of the genetic kind. We might say that humankind carries some of the "God-community genes". Humankind, unlike other parts of creation, enjoyed a relationship in which there was communication. "Human being" communes with "God-being", because of a shared "being": in community. Community was the social reality – the entity – created by communion. And because "God-being" was in community, only "in-community" could "human-being" be like God. It was no wonder that "human-being" was not complete until there was "another". The acknowledgement by God that "it is not good for the man to be alone" (2:18) was recognition of the incompleteness of "human-being" at this point in the creation drama. It is no wonder that it was only when there were both male and female that there was a celebration of "being":

The man said,

"This is now bone of my bones
    and flesh of my flesh;

---

2. David Atkinson, *The Message of Genesis 1–11* (Leicester: Inter-Varsity Press, 1990), 54.

she shall be called 'woman,'
> for she was taken out of man." (2:23)

"Human-being" is in community. John Mbiti, one of Africa's pioneer theologians, expressed this truth when reflecting on the primacy of the community motif in defining human identity in African primal societies. He stated that for the African human identity is summed up in the axiom "I am because we are; and since we are, therefore I am".[3] "Human-being" is in community, just as "God-being" is in community.

Although many theologians and commentators are eager to read into these narratives God being "Trinity-in-community", it is not only incredible within the framework of the biblical narrative, it is also unnecessary and shifts the focus away from the drama in the garden. "Human-being" as community originates in God. We learn that in the making of "human-being" God formed a being in his likeness – in-community. Just as "God-being" was in community, so "human-being" was also in-community, in a plural self: male and female. But it is not only communion with God that defines being human: there was also communion with the rest of creation. This was the essence of the garden of Eden: a glorious picture of creation-community abiding in its Creator. This brought pleasure and glory to the Creator.

Thus God confidently bequeathed to Adam and Eve the continuation of his work of creation with the mandate to "fill the earth and subdue it. Rule over [it]" (1:28). Again, the account in Genesis 2 expresses the same truth but differently. It gives the picture of the garden that God planted, after which he "took the man and put him in the Garden of Eden to work it and take care of it" (2:15). God's creative work was to continue in partnership with humankind, now as co-worker exploiting all its potential and caring for it. God's personal address "Be fruitful ..." assumes the possibility of response. Response entails choice. Choice is only possible where there is freedom; it is the exercise of the responsibility of freedom. God, in giving "every seed-bearing plant ... and every tree that has fruit with seed in it ... for food" (1:29) also placed limits on humankind. Thus we read, "And the LORD God commanded the man, 'You are free to eat from any tree in the garden; but you must not eat from the tree of the knowledge of good and evil, for when you eat of it you will surely die'" (2:16–17).

---

3. John Mbiti, *African Traditional Religions and Philosophy* (London: Heinemann, 1969), 108–9.

Freedom can also be said to be the celebration of relationship and the exercise of responsibility through obedience. The celebration of communion and community comes within set limits. Freedom is God's gift and invitation into relationship, partnership and communion. Obedience is humankind's response of continual gratitude and recognition that it is God who made all things (Gen 1:1). Thus the ecological order, life, harmony, growth and productivity would be maintained through humankind's exercise of responsible stewardship in the context of "being in union" (communion) with God. The communion of creation-community would continue to be enjoyed only in obedience. To be in God, in community with creation, is true worship of the Creator. That is the whole purpose of humankind: to glorify God – to display the wonder of his nature and character – and to enjoy him for ever.

The third reality that the Genesis narrative explained is the presence of evil; how is it that the picture of a garden in which communion and community thrive, with God as source and fountain as he intended it from the beginning, is not what we experience? I can imagine Moses receiving this glorious revelation of the things that were – a garden of blessing, community and worship. How could he understand the level of evil and bondage meted out by the Egyptians upon God's people? The Genesis narrative explained how such evil was introduced into creation-community in Genesis 3. Humankind trespassed the limits set by God. Adam and Eve believed the lie about God: that he could not be trusted; and about themselves: that they would be more than God intended them to be, like God, (yet they were already like God, made in his image!), "knowing good and evil". Hence when "the man and his wife heard the sound of the LORD God as he was walking in the garden in the cool of the day, … they hid from the LORD God among the trees of the garden" (3:8). Humanity became estranged from its Creator. Communion was replaced by estrangement.

But it was not simply communion with God that was impaired; the harmony in the entire created order was damaged. The growth and progress of the created order as intended by God was fractured by humankind's failure to "rule" in freedom and obedience; for instead of continuing on the journey of living within the limits set by the Creator, humankind turned for guidance to the very creation it was to rule. Instead of following God's clear instructions not to "eat from the tree of the knowledge of good and evil" (2:17), Adam and Eve succumbed to the lie of the creature, "that when you eat from it your eyes will be opened and you will be like God, knowing good and evil" (3:4). The tables were turned. Instead of subduing creation, they themselves were subdued. This is idolatry – serving the creature instead of the Creator, seeking to be what only God is. This was truly a mighty fall – a distortion in "human-being"! Consequently, community and harmony broke down, in both human community and all creation. The ground was "cursed", human biological processes were distorted, and discord between humanity and the rest of creation became part of the "new order" in creation (3:8–24).

Henceforth, there was an unhappy mixture of order and disorder, celebration and destruction, harmony and discord, obedience and disobedience, and good and evil. Conflict and violence were now to be part of human community, as exemplified by the story of Cain and Abel in Genesis 4. The dominant narrative becomes one of discord and rebellion in increasing measure, depicted in the enigmatic account of how "when men began to increase in number on earth and daughters were born to them, the sons of God saw that the daughters of men were beautiful, and they married any of them they chose" (6:1–2). Rebellion, disorder, discord and corruption were so rife that God became alarmed at "how great man's wickedness on earth had become and that every inclination of the thoughts of his heart was evil all the time" and he was grieved that he had created humankind! The account describes it thus: "Now the earth was corrupt in God's sight and was full of violence. God saw how corrupt the earth had become, for *all the people on the earth had corrupted their ways*" (6:11–12, italics mine). Egyptian ruthlessness and idolatry was simply an example of how corrupted, idolatrous and disobedient all the peoples of the earth had become.

Fourthly, the Genesis narrative explained that God's initiative to liberate Israel from bondage was consistent with his character and eternal purposes. He had already proved so with Noah and Abraham and he would remain true to his purpose – restoring creation-community for his pleasure and glory. Thus, although the dominant narrative is one of deformed humanity and community, there are anecdotes of obedience and harmony, signalling that all was not lost for humanity and creation. God was the liberator, working his creation purposes through those who chose obedience rather than disobedience. The direction of the narrative is towards the restoration of "human-being" and creation order. The hope lay with the remnant of humanity that continued the pilgrimage of obedience to God. Enoch was part of such a hope, for he "walked with God", and God was so pleased with him that he "took him away" (5:22). But it is Noah's story that is the first to demonstrate God choosing a particular people as the agency for his purposes.

Already we are beginning to see consistency in whom God called his, for it is said of Noah, just like Enoch, that he "walked with God" (6:9).

God's decision was to destroy all the people and the earth with a flood while preserving a remnant – Noah, his family, and remnants of all species of plant and animal life on earth – so that the created order and community might be restored and preserved. Noah "was a righteous man, blameless among the people of his time" (6:1). So God commanded Noah to build the ark; and "Noah did all that was commanded of him" (6:22; 7:5). In the ark, for twelve months, they lived together:

> Noah and his sons, Shem, Ham and Japheth, together with his wife and the wives of his three sons, entered the ark. They had with them every wild animal according to its kind, all livestock according to their kinds, every creature that moves along the ground according to its kind and every bird according to its kind, everything with wings. Pairs of all creatures that have the breath of life in them came to Noah and entered the ark. The animals going in were male and female of every living thing, as God had commanded Noah. Then the LORD shut him in. (7:13–16)

The ark was a kind of miniature "garden of Eden", a storehouse of the seeds of a new crop of life. We read that after the flood, the same command given to Adam and Eve was given to Noah and his sons: "Be fruitful and increase in number and fill the earth" (9:1). God established a covenant with Noah, as he had promised before the flood (6:18–19), and pledged:

> I now establish my covenant with you and with your descendants after you and with every living creature that was with you – the birds, the livestock and all the wild animals, all those that came out of the ark with you – every living creature on earth. I establish my covenant with you: never again will all life be cut off by the waters of a flood; never again will there be a flood to destroy the earth. (9:9–11)

As William J. Dumbrell, in his book *Covenant and Creation: An Old Testament Covenantal Theology*, explains, the covenant that God established with Noah was not new but a confirmation of what had been brought into existence by the act of creation.[4] Thus it was universal in scope, a covenant with "every living creature" as well as with Noah, his family and descendants. It was a symbol of God's intention to preserve humankind and the whole community of creation for a restored created order. It was a covenant for all his creation.

However, fallen humankind did not know any other way of "human-being" except the distorted version. Rebellion and disobedience, both characteristic of estrangement and broken community, continued, with consequences for all creation. It is significant that following the story of the flood we have the account of the building of the Tower of Babel, epitomizing the great heights and the solidarity of humankind's rebellion. It was the rebuilding of community without God, to "make a name for ourselves and not be scattered over the face of the whole earth" (11:4). The judgement of the flood had not eradicated rebellion and estrangement from creation. In response to Babel God scattered all the people over the earth – to preserve humankind according to the covenant made with Noah; but it was a distorted version of humanity.

In between the story of the flood and the story of Babel is the table of the nations in Genesis 10, outlining their dispersion "by their clans and languages, in their territories and nations" (10:20, 31). It concludes, "From these the nations spread over the earth after the flood" (10:32). At least two things can be inferred from this. Firstly, God was true to his promise to preserve human-community and creation. Secondly, the preservation of human-community was found in its diversity – the nations. Clearly God intended diversity not only in nature, but also among humans.

It has been suggested by some that ethnic diversity, as reflected in the proliferation of languages and cultures, was a result of the scattering after Babel. From this argument, based on Genesis 11:1 ("the whole world had one language and a common speech"), follows the idea that we cannot celebrate cultural and ethnic diversity because it is God's judgement against rebellious humanity. However, a careful reading of the text shows the opposite to be the case. The story of scattering in Genesis 10 precedes the story of Babel in Genesis 11, which suggests that the scattering was God's intention in order to preserve human-community and that the Tower of Babel was itself a resistance against this scattering. So we read of "the sons of Javan: Elishah, Tarshish, the

---

4. This is the main thesis of Dumbrell's argument in the chapter "The Covenant with Noah: A Recall to a Basic Pattern of Creation", in William J. Dumbrell, *Covenant and Creation: An Old Testament Covenantal Theology* (Exeter: Paternoster, 1984), 11–43.

Kittim and the Rodanim. (From these the maritime peoples spread out into the territories by their clans within their nations, each with its own language)" (10:4–5). Also we find that "Later the Canaanite clans scattered … by their clans and languages, in their territories and nations" (10:19–20). Ethnic, cultural and language diversity is a result of God's command to humankind in creation to "be fruitful and increase in number; fill the earth and subdue it" (1:28) re-established in the covenant with Noah.

It was those who moved eastwards, taking the advantage that they still spoke one language, who determined to resist the scattering and resolved to "build ourselves a city, with a tower that reaches to the heavens, so that we may make a name for ourselves and not be scattered over the face of the whole earth" (11:4). They sought to set themselves apart and consolidate their power in order to dominate other clans, families and nations. The consequence was that "the LORD scattered them from there over all the earth, and they stopped building the city. That is why it was called Babel – because there the LORD confused the language of the whole world. From there the LORD scattered them over the face of the whole earth" (11:8–9).

The scattering was carried out to preserve the blessing of ethnic, language and cultural diversity and to prevent the destruction of human-community that in effect was the project of what we may call the "Shinar community". For their project was to consolidate their ethnic and racial power and hegemony in order to dominate others. By Moses' time, this is what had been replicated in the bondage of Israel at the hands of the Egyptians.

Abraham: The Promise and the Covenant

God continued to reveal to Moses that it was with Abraham that the story of his people began. Abraham and his family were called by God in order to form a people through whom God's plan to preserve and restore harmony and community in creation, as in the garden of Eden, would be fulfilled. With the command to go and leave "your country" for a place that God would show him came the promise pledging protection and blessing for him and his descendants, as well as for the land and country to which he had migrated. God promised Abraham:

> I will make you into a great nation
>   and I will bless you;

> I will make your name great,
>> and you will be a blessing.
> I will bless those who bless you,
>> and whoever curses you I will curse;
> and all peoples on the earth
>> will be blessed though you. (12:2–3)

In Abraham, God started a new family line of succession, from all the families of the nations and for all the families of the nations and all creation. "In choosing the man, God is in fact choosing the seed yet to be. In demanding a break with the past, God is in this way bringing the future into the present."[5]

On the journey of Abraham's obedience, the covenant came after the promise, in Genesis 15–18. It confirmed the different aspects to the promise: posterity – that Abraham would become a great nation and that he would be the father of many nations; relationship – that God would bless him with a special relationship with himself; protection – "to be your God and the God of your descendants after you" (17:7); and land – the land of Abraham's sojourn as an inheritance. Abraham and his descendants' part was obedience, to "walk before me and be blameless", and as a sign of that commitment they were to circumcise every male (17:1, 10–14). Thus, although it was a done deal that "Abraham will surely become a great and powerful nation, and all nations on earth will be blessed through him" (18:18), it was incumbent upon Abraham and his descendants "to keep the way of the LORD by doing what is right and just so that the LORD will bring about for Abraham what he has promised him" (18:19). Moreover, in keeping the ways of the Lord the Abrahamic clan would distinguish themselves from all the other clans around them. All this would be worked out on the journey, as strangers and pilgrims, towards the promise.

It is important to note that God's covenant with Abraham presupposed and built on the one made with Noah, and that in both covenants it was God who took the initiative. However, while the covenant with Noah was for all the people and every living creature on earth, the one with Abraham entailed firstly a calling-out from among the people and secondly a promise that out of Abraham would emerge a new people, a new nation, through which all the peoples of the earth – and indeed all creation – would be blessed. Through Abraham God committed himself to restore (bless) that which he had

---

5. Dumbrell, *Covenant and Creation*, 58.

committed himself to preserve through the covenant with Noah. The calling of Abraham was therefore the beginning of the story of God's initiative to form a people to participate with him in his purpose to redeem humanity and all creation, that they might bring delight to God.

The progression is also significant: first a covenant with all creation through Noah; then a covenant with the one man, Abraham; then one family line (clan) – Abraham, Isaac and Jacob; and later, as we shall see, with the one nation, Israel – for all the nations. Each of the transitions was marked by a memorable symbol or event which was a sign or seal of God's reaffirmation and renewal of his covenant. The symbol or event was to serve as a perpetual reminder of God's intervening favour towards them. The rainbow was God's sign and memorial for the Noahic covenant; circumcision was the sign for the covenant with Abraham; and Abraham's painful and faithful obedience in going to sacrifice his son was a manifestation of confidence in God to fulfil his covenant. Notably, after God provided an alternative sacrifice to Isaac, as though to pat Abraham on the back with approval he restated and reaffirmed his promise to Abraham and his descendants: "… to bless you and make your descendants as numerous as the stars in the sky and as the sand on the seashore. Your descendants will take possession of the cities of their enemies and through your offspring all nations on earth will be blessed because you have obeyed me" (22:16–18).

The process of fulfilment of the promise for posterity was not primarily by blood heritage but rather on the basis of God's sovereign and providential choice. So although Abraham had two sons, Ishmael and Isaac, the line of promise was only that of Isaac – the miracle child, born even though Abraham was old and Sarah herself "past childbearing age" (Heb 11:11). Although Isaac's natural heir was Esau, the elder of his twin sons, God chose Jacob, the younger, while the twins were still in the womb. God revealed to Rebekah, "Two nations are in your womb, and the two peoples from within you will be separated; one people will be stronger than the other, and the older will serve the younger" (Gen 25:23).

Abraham's leaving his country, his people and his father's household and going to the land God would show him was the process of being formed into who God wanted him to become. God could have selected from among his people and kept his residence there, without asking him to leave physically. However, in leaving his people and country, journeying with God to a country and land that only God knew, Abraham's knowledge, confidence and faith in God would be deepened. The journey with God was essential for the nurturing of his faith. It was this journey with God that distinguished him and his family from the other families and nations of the world.

In this way God was superintending the fulfilment of his promises to Abraham, creating the new family line of succession. God would remind Isaac time and again, through the hazards of his nomadic life and famine in the land, that he would be true to the promise he made to his father Abraham, to bless him and increase the number of his descendants (26:2–5, 24). In a vision at Bethel God confirmed to Jacob that he was the inheritor of the promise of the covenant. God introduced himself as "the God of your father Abraham and the God of Isaac" and repeated the promise as he had done to Isaac (28:13–16). In the moment of crisis, when it looked as if God's promises would be thwarted by the family's flight to Egypt as a result of a severe famine, God spoke to Jacob and reassured him that he would make him into a great nation there. Thus the pattern of pilgrimage under the impulsion of a promise continued with Isaac and Jacob. God was henceforth known – and chose to be known – as "the God of Abraham, Isaac and Jacob". Then, in the burning bush, God was taking forward his work of redemption by calling Moses to be his instrument.

With all this that God revealed to him, Moses could be confident to go and face Pharaoh. It was part of God's purpose for his people and all creation, having begun with the act of creation itself and now being rooted in the covenant with Abraham, the Hebrew patriarch. He who had allowed their sojourn in Egypt was the one who would deliver them. God had showed Moses that what he was asking him to do was not to be achieved in his own strength and wisdom.

The Exodus, the Covenant and the Land of Promise: Creating a People of God

It was important that Moses understood the continuity of God's agenda. The sign that God had taken the initiative to fulfil his purposes for Israel would be that after he brought the people out of Egypt, they would do as he pleased, obeying him and ascribing to him the glory and praise that were due to him – indeed, they would worship him on that very mountain (Exod 3:12). Thus, when Moses embarked on his task and was met with a harsh response from Pharaoh and the pessimism of the Israelites, God referred him to his covenant as grounds for trusting him to accomplish his project of liberating Israel from bondage:

> I am the LORD. I appeared to Abraham, Isaac and Jacob as God Almighty, but by my name the LORD I did not make myself known to them. I also established my covenant with them to give them the land of Canaan, where they resided as foreigners. Moreover, I have heard the groaning of the Israelites, whom the Egyptians are enslaving, and I have remembered my covenant. Therefore, say to the Israelites: "I am the LORD, and I will bring you out from under the yoke of the Egyptians. I will free you from being slaves to them, and I will redeem you with an outstretched arm and with mighty acts of judgement. (Exod 6:2–6)

The act of delivering Israel and the journey to the land of promise were fulfilments of the promise to Abraham. Through the journey they would understand that they were one people, God's people. God therefore assured the Israelites, "I will take you as my own people, and I will be your God. Then you will know that I am the LORD your God, who brought you out from under the yoke of the Egyptians" (6:7). In their deliverance and pilgrimage they would know who they were as they grew to know who God was. While on the journey, as God acted on their behalf, protecting and blessing them, they would grow in their confidence in him as their God, and would worship and serve him. God wanted to liberate them from the slavery and bondage of Egypt as well as the bondage of servitude and worship of other gods that were no gods at all, and free them to obey and serve him. Hence God's persistence in demanding that Pharaoh "Let my people go, so that they may worship me" (7:16; 8:1, 20; 9:1, 13; 10:3). Just as God had called Abraham's family out, so he was calling a nation out of all the nations.

The climax of Israel's miraculous deliverance was the assembly at the foot of Mount Sinai, where they had a meeting with God and where God established a covenant with them as a nation. This was the sign that he promised Moses: to "worship God on this mountain" (3:12). When they were thus gathered, God addressed them as one people:

> You yourselves have seen what I did to Egypt, and how I carried you on eagles' wings and brought you to myself. Now if you obey me fully and keep my covenant, then out of all nations you will be my treasured possession. Although the whole earth is mine, you will be for me a kingdom of priests and a holy nation. (19:4–6)

It should be noted that the pledge that God gave to Moses for the people was delivered to the elders of the people (19:7; 24:9). The covenant was made with the nation and therefore it was delivered to the elders because it was their responsibility to hear and respond on behalf of all the people. It was critical that they develop their self-consciousness as one people.

At this point it is important to consider the nature of covenants. A covenant signals uniqueness and obligation. African peoples will appreciate this as covenants used to be commonplace in many traditional African societies prior to the advance of European and Arabic civilizations. When a head of a household developed a strong relationship with another with whom there was no blood kinship, the way to make the bond continue with posterity was by sealing it with a covenant, which entailed each of them taking a sip of the other's blood. The action of sharing blood not only sealed the special relationship between their households and their descendants, but also obligated members of the families to each other henceforth. Any breach of loyalty would bring wrath from the ancestors upon the offender.

Similarly, in the ancient Near East, the world of Old Testament times, covenants of all kinds were common as means of regulating behaviour between peoples, empires and vassal states. In ordinary life there were simple covenantal oaths in which promises were elevated to a solemn and binding form. International treaties were also made between empires and vassal states in which "the benefits, protection and services of the conqueror were granted in exchange for political and military loyalty and allegiance".[6] Such treaty covenants were sanctioned by threats of dire punishment from the gods or men, or both. Thus, although the Old Testament covenants did not conform wholly or neatly to the structure of those that were operative in the socio-political arena at the time, the language and concept of covenant were consistent with the culture of bonding and obligation.

Three key motifs constituted God's covenant with Israel. Firstly, they were God's people, and in a way that no other nation could claim. Although there is evidence in the biblical narrative that God was active in the histories of other peoples, as the prophet Amos was later to observe (Amos 9:7), Israel were uniquely his people. Their deliverance from Egypt and their journey thus far were forming in them a unique corporate identity as "his people". Their worship, reflected in their obedience and continued walking in the ways of

---

6. Christopher J. Wright, *Knowing Jesus Through the Old Testament* (Downers Grove, Ill.: InterVarsity Press, 1992), 77.

the Lord, would affirm that they were his "treasured possession" (Exod 19:5). Secondly, they were his for a purpose: a kingdom of priests, for the nations. Christopher J. H. Wright explains this:

> The function of priesthood in Israel itself was to stand between God and the rest of the people – representing God to the people (by their teaching function), and representing and bringing the people to God (by their sacrificial function). Through the priesthood, God was made known to people, and the people could come into acceptable relationship to God. So God assigns to his people as the whole community the role of priesthood for all the nations. As their priests stood in relation to God and the rest of *Israel*, so the whole community were to stand in relation to God and the rest of *the nations*.[7]

Thirdly, they were to be a holy nation. There are two aspects to this "holiness". The first aspect arises from the fact that they were "set apart" – "out of all nations" (Lev 20:24; Exod 19:5); and the second arises from their calling and ethical obligation as a unique people, "a kingdom of priests" (19:6). The exercise of their priestly role among the nations was conditional on their obedience. Walter Kaiser expresses it thus: "Israel was to be separate and holy; she was to be separate and as no other people on the face of the earth. As an elect or called people now being formed into a nation under God, holiness was not an optional feature. Israel had to be holy, for her God. Yahweh was holy."[8]

After the Israelites responded as one people to God's initiative and pledged to "do everything the LORD has said" (Exod 19:8), "Moses led the people out of the camp to meet with [their] God, and they stood at the foot of the mountain" (19:17). Now God could give to his people the content of their part of the covenant – the commandments and the laws.

It is noteworthy that after God confirmed his covenant with the people, symbolized in the sacrifices and sprinkling of blood on the people (Exod 24:3–8), he instructed Moses to make a sanctuary for him – the tabernacle – and with it paraphernalia to symbolize his presence among his people. The single most important fact of the Sinai experience and of the formation of

---

7. Wright, *Knowing Jesus Through the Old Testament*, 86.

8. Walter C. Kaiser, Jr., *Toward an Old Testament Theology* (Grand Rapids, Mich.: Zondervan, 1978), 11.

this nation was that God had come to "tabernacle" or dwell in their midst. Thus God declared, "Then I will dwell among the Israelites and be their God. They will know that I am the LORD their God, who brought them out of Egypt so that I might dwell among them. I am the LORD their God" (29:45–46). His people were those among whom God made his dwelling. As his people they were to live a life of obedience (worship); hence the commandments and the law were given.

The commandments and the law were given to a people already redeemed, rescued from the tyranny of Egypt (Exod 20:1–2) and whom Yahweh already referred to as "my people" (Exod 5:5; 6:7; 7:16; 8:1, 20; 9:1). The commandments were not the basis of their relationship but were given to clarify to Israel the nature of their worship, which was unlike the worship of other gods, and their ethical obligations as God's people, so that they were never in doubt as to what was expected of them. Obedience was worship; disobedience was equivalent to idolatry and would impair that relationship and invoke God's judgement. Israel's loyalty to God and obedience to the law was the evidence that they had a special relationship with him and was the means by which God would fulfil his purpose of bringing blessing to the nations. Thus in the future, when their descendants would ask them what was the significance of the commandments and laws, they were to explain that they had been given because God loved them and had redeemed them from slavery in Egypt (Deut 6:20–25) in order that he might fulfil his covenant with Abraham.

The two motifs of pilgrimage to the land of promise (exodus) and gathering (at Mount Sinai) were core to their "being and becoming" the people of God. They highlight the concrete ways in which Israel's relationship with God was to be lived out. On the journey to the land of promise they would exercise their trust and confidence in God and his promises through perseverance and obedience, demonstrating to surrounding nations the "finger of God" (Exod 8:19; 31:18; Deut 9:10). In the assembly God would speak to the community as one, and in turn the people responded in reaffirming and declaring their allegiance and loyalty to God in an act (ritual) of worship. God speaking, enunciating his will and purpose, and the people's response of repentance and a pledge to obedience were henceforth to define the framework of any gathering of God's people.

The exodus and the commandments were to serve as the motivation and rule of their corporate life as God's people among other peoples. Thus, on the eve of Moses' death he charged them:

> Remember how the LORD your God led you all the way in the desert these forty years, to humble and test you in order to know what was in your heart, whether or not you would keep his commands....
>
> When you have eaten and are satisfied, praise the LORD your God for the good land he has given you. Be careful that you do not forget the LORD your God, failing to observe his commands, his laws and his decrees that I am giving you this day. (Deut 8:2, 10–11)

Unfortunately, Israel did forget and was often disobedient and rebellious throughout the journey to the promised land. In times of difficulty and adversity on the way they grumbled against Moses and longed for the fleeting pleasures of Egypt. They wanted the "fish we ate in Egypt at no cost – also the cucumbers, melons, leeks, onions and garlic". "Why did we ever leave Egypt," they wailed; "If only we had died in Egypt!" (Num 11:6, 20; 14:2).

Moses was afraid that God's people would disobey and suffer the consequences – the curses. Therefore, in his farewell address he wanted to make sure that they understood their call:

> For you are a people holy to the LORD your God. The LORD your God has chosen you out of all the peoples on the face of the earth to be his people, his treasured possession. The LORD did not set his affection on you and choose you because you were more numerous than other peoples, for you were the fewest of all the peoples. But it was because the LORD loved you and kept the oath he swore to your forefathers that he brought you out with a mighty hand and redeemed you from the land of slavery, from the power of Pharaoh king of Egypt. Know therefore that the LORD your God is God; he is the faithful God, keeping his covenant of love to a thousand generations of those who love him and keep his commands.... Therefore, take care to follow the commands, decrees and laws I give you today. (Deut 7:6–9, 11)

Moses made it clear that the people of Israel were now God's people in God's mission to restore creation harmony and community for his pleasure and glory. A careful reading of the Old Testament shows that God was active in the histories of other peoples.[9] However, the people of Israel were unique in that it was God who formed them and called them as *one* people. It is not that God made an already existing people his own; through the exodus he brought them and formed them into a people to serve his purpose for the other peoples, nations and all creation.

However, Joshua, Moses' successor, had much trouble with them. They often forgot the significance and purpose of their liberation and journey and their calling as Yahweh's special people. They forgot the Lord their God and followed foreign gods, worshipping them. In forgetting the Lord their God they lost their distinctiveness as his people, thus compromising their identity. The roots of rebellion and disobedience lay in their failure to understand the meaning and implications of being God's people, and the calling to fulfil God's purpose (serving the Lord) through the journey to and possessing of the land of promise.

Joshua 24 is an important point in the story of Israel as the people of God. It marks the end of the main stage in Israel's occupation of the promised land, the land itself having now been distributed among the tribes. The final aspect of the patriarchal promise was fulfilled. Joshua took the opportunity to call the entire assembly to Mount Shechem and to remind them of, and challenge them to renew, their covenant. He set before them their only option: to live as the people of God, serving him with all faithfulness. He warned them that failure to do this would bring upon them disaster, now that they were God's people in their land. "The land becomes ... the holy land, Yahweh becomes the God of this particular country, Israel becomes the people of the land. Land, people and faith are henceforth bound together."[10]

God, His Purposes and His People

As we saw at the start of this chapter, for us who live with the dilemmas of twenty-first-century church it is possible to lose perspective, just as Cleopas and his friend on the road to Emmaus did. We, like them, need to be reminded, firstly, that the beginnings of the church do not lie with us, with the technology of our times, but with God himself, the one who revealed himself to Moses not only as the "God of Abraham, Isaac and Jacob" but also

---

9. Christopher J. H. Wright makes this observation in his *Knowing Jesus Through the Old Testament*, 34–54.

10. John Goldingay, *Theological Diversity and the Authority of the Old Testament* (Grand Rapids, Mich.: Eerdmans, 1987), 68.

as Creator of the universe. He has no equals or rivals. He is not a provincial tribal deity, like the gods of Egypt were. He is the great "I AM". He is God who was not only in the beginning, but was the beginning of all. He is the one who began all – he created all, out of nothing. This is our God and Saviour! He is not a Christian God or a particular church's God or a Jewish God; he is God and God alone. And he will bring his purposes to fruition.

Secondly, we too, like Moses despairing over the condition of the people of Israel, should remember that that which God began in restoring his creation-community, he will continue to do until it reaches its consummation in a new heaven and a new earth, a recreated and mature garden of Eden! Adam and Eve's banishment from the garden, which prevented them eating from the tree of life, was itself redemptive, ensuring that humanity would not be condemned to an eternity in the fallen state. Moses was added to the number of the chosen ones, after Enoch, Noah and Abraham, who "walked with God". Through Noah God had preserved creation; and Moses was the chosen instrument to bring to fulfilment the promise to Abraham, to create a people for God's name, through whom he would redeem humanity from rebellion and disobedience and restore the divine–human communion and creation-community.

Thirdly, God's way of assurance to his chosen ones – from Noah to Israel – of his determination to accomplish his purposes was by entering into covenants with those through whom he chose to work. Covenants with God, therefore, were simply acts of his love and mercy, for there is nothing that obligates him towards anyone for anything. But through covenant, God chooses to hold himself obligated to those he has chosen. He did it with Noah, with Abraham, and then with the people of Israel through the leadership of Moses. This is the continuing story of God choosing a people and then obligating himself to fulfil his purpose through them. But in Jesus we have a new covenant, sealed with his blood. Writing about the superiority of the new covenant over the covenant with Israel, the author of Hebrews said, "He [Jesus] did not enter by means of the blood of goats and calves; but he entered the Most Holy Place, once for all by his own blood, so obtaining eternal redemption…. For this reason Christ is the mediator of a new covenant, that those who are called may receive the promised eternal inheritance …" (Heb 9:12, 15).

Fourthly, just as Israel's identity was formed in gathering together (at Mount Sinai) and in the pilgrimage to the land of promise, so it is with us. We need to ponder the account of the journey of Israel and learn from it. As Paul admonished the Corinthian believers:

> For I do not want you to be ignorant of the fact, brothers and sisters, that our ancestors were all under the cloud and that they all passed through the sea. They were all baptised into Moses in the cloud and in the sea. They all ate the same spiritual food and drank the same spiritual drink; for they drank from the spiritual rock that accompanied them, and that rock was Christ. Nevertheless, God was not pleased with most of them; their bodies were scattered in the wilderness…. These things happened to them as examples and were written down as warnings for us, on whom the culmination of the ages has come. (1 Cor 10:1–5, 11)

The two motifs – gathering and pilgrimage – are critical in defining and shaping how we live as the people of God today. As we saw in Chapter 1, the root of the word translated "church" is "assembly" or "gathering". We should "not give up meeting together, as some are in the habit of doing" (Heb 10:25). But it is not just the act of gathering that is important; it is what we do and what happens when we gather. Just as the people of God assembled at Mount Sinai to hear the will and mind of God, so too, when we gather, it is that we may together hear God and respond to him, pledging and committing ourselves to obey him, as they did. Sadly, many of our gatherings on Sundays or on other days in the week have been turned into rituals of worship or, as some call it, "a time for worship", when a few songs are sung and prayers are offered. Surely God does not deserve just two of the 168 hours in a week as "the time for worship"! He deserves our worship all the time.

Hence the significance of the journey, because it is on the journey that our worship is manifested. Not only is the exodus a part of our own story, since it is part of the story of our redemption in Christ, but it also defines the way of living as the people of God today. As Paul reminded the believers in Corinth, we need to remember that we live in an earthly tent and are looking forward to the "building from God, an eternal house in heaven, not built by human hands" (2 Cor 5:1). We should ascribe to him honour and glory in the tent of our living: in all we say and do; awake or asleep; at home, at work or at church. The time when we gather together is for renewing ourselves to worship him 24/7! A lot of the malaise and slumber in the churches today can be traced to the loss of consciousness of the pilgrim nature of our lives, individually and corporately.

Fifthly, from Abraham to Moses and from Moses to Joshua it is evident that God chose to be identified with a particular people – one nation – to make himself known to them and, through them, to reveal himself to all nations. God's promise through Moses to Israel in slavery in Egypt, to redeem them "with an outstretched arm and with mighty acts of judgment", and to journey with them throughout their pilgrimage to the land he promised, had a purpose: that they might know him (Exod 6: 6–7). Thus they were to be identified with him and he with them. The God of the promise is not just any "god". As Goldingay expresses it:

> Yahweh himself enters a new sphere of activity. The God of the clan becomes the God of history and the God of politics, battling with the Egyptian pharaoh and defeating him. He meets the needs of his people in a new mode of life, though this involves him in taking on one nation's side against another in a way he has not done before. He gains new status as the lord of nature at whose bidding seas part and come together again, as the warrior whose fury brings a shiver even to the hearts of those he aids, as the master of the elements whose coming makes Sinai tremble.[11]

He chose to be known as the God of Abraham, Isaac and Jacob – a pilgrim God for a pilgrim people.

Pilgrimage had a purpose. The particular story of Israel was linked with God's universal purposes. Israel's story was only part of the wider story of God's redemptive purposes unfolding in the history of a people he chose for the blessing of all the people and indeed creation. To be God's people meant a commitment to being an instrument on behalf of the nations within the universal scope of Yahweh's Lordship. Niles has expressed it thus: "The God who chose Israel out of the nations and gave it a distinctive history remained also and always the God of the nations too."[12] Israel's unique historical experience laid upon them a moral responsibility and a missionary task.

---

11. Goldingay, *Theological Diversity and the Authority of the Old Testament*, 65.
12. D. T. Niles, *Upon the Earth: The Mission of God and the Missionary Enterprise of the Churches* (London: Lutterworth Press, 1962), 250.

The tragedy of the account, however, is that the people of Israel failed to grasp that their history was not "an end in itself or for the sake of Israel alone, but rather for the sake of the rest of the nations of humanity".[13] They failed to possess their inheritance as a light to the nations. Instead, they sought to be like the other nations. Yahweh became, in their perception, simply the God of Israel, whose responsibility was to protect their fortunes.

The same is true today of many communities that claim to be churches. The way they speak about God might give the impression to an outsider that the God they worship is one of them, as though God was a Christian among them, protecting the fortunes of the church. Many so-called churches have lost the vision of their calling to follow Jesus and proclaim the good news of the kingdom of God beyond their boundaries. But just as God gave Israel and its leaders warnings and ample opportunities for repentance and turning to him, so he does the same for us today. When they did not heed the warnings, God gave them up.

13. Wright, *Knowing Jesus Through the Old Testament*, 36.

3

Israel, the Monarchy and Exile: God's Rebellious People

He has shown you, O mortal, what is good.
    And what does the Lord require of you?
To act justly and to love mercy
    and to walk humbly with your God. (Mic 6:8)

Therefore, since we are receiving a kingdom that cannot be shaken, let us be thankful, and so worship God acceptably with reverence and awe, for our "God is a consuming fire". (Heb 12:28–29)

In 2004 I went to Rwanda with Bishop Yokana Mukasa (retired Diocesan Bishop of Mityana, Uganda), at the invitation of the Anglican Church of Rwanda's Archbishop Emmanuel Kolini, to lead at a retreat of bishops and their wives. The purpose of the retreat was for those present to reflect on their lives and ministries in the context of the pain and trauma unleashed by the genocide; to seek healing and renewal for themselves; and to seek the mind of the Lord on how the church could become a beacon of healing and reconciliation among the people of Rwanda.

Being among my brothers and sisters that week I could see that the differences that divided Banyarwanda were still alive in the consciousness of the bishops: for although their flocks were all Banyarwanda (literally, "the people of Rwanda") and Anglicans, some were Abahutu and others Abatutsi; and some came from the north and others from the south. Clearly the Church's self-identity was still marked by ethno-regional tensions. The leadership and membership of this church in Rwanda could not yet think of themselves simply as "belonging to *Eglise Episcopale au Rwanda*" but only as "coming from" a particular ethnic and regional background. This was a Church whose foundations were in the East African Revival movement.

The following is part of a journal entry I wrote at the end of my visit:

> It is 7:30 a.m., Saturday 13 March 2004. I am starting this journal while sitting in the lounge of Kigali International Airport. This year marks the 10th anniversary of genocide in Rwanda.
>
> As I leave Rwanda I have a heavy heart. 1994 is not yet history. I am astounded at how, in spite of the passing of a decade, the pain and trauma are as real as though it happened yesterday. And I fear it will remain, possibly until the current generation passes. The country and its people do not yet seem to have the emotional strength to cope with the aftermath.
>
> Psychologists tell us that in coping with grief and loss we go through at least four stages: shock and numbness; denial; acceptance; and resolution. It seems most of Rwanda and her people are still struggling with stages one and two. As one listens to stories about how different people and institutions are coping with the mayhem and tragedy of ten years ago, understandably it seems they are yet to accept that it all happened.
>
> How can one accept that a man hacked to death his own children and wife for "possessing the wrong blood in them", because the mother was of a different ethnic heritage; that government officials sounded the drums of ethnic cleansing in a country of a people who speak the same language; that church buildings were turned into killing fields? How could a country that was purported to be the most Catholic nation in the world descend to such levels of darkness?

How could it be? How could the church in Rwanda have failed to stand up to the evils in the society leading to the genocide? It is easy from the outside to ask such judgemental questions. Yet if we and our communities look closely at ourselves we see the same issues where we are. So instead of pointing the finger at our brothers and sisters in Rwanda, we need to rephrase the question: How could we? What went wrong with us? The story of Israel helps us in this quest, at two levels. Firstly, it helps us because it is part of our story. As we noted in the previous chapter, the apostle Paul affirmed that the story of Israel and that of the followers of Jesus find a meeting point in Christ, because they "drank the same spiritual drink; for they drank from the spiritual rock that accompanied them, and that rock was Christ" (1 Cor 1:4). Any community, therefore, which considers itself part of Christ will take seriously the story of Israel as part of its own story.

Secondly, we can learn from Israel's disobedience. The story of Israel's pitfalls and the consequences is instructional. As Paul wrote, "These things happened to them as examples and were written down as warnings for us, on whom the culmination of the ages has come" (1 Cor 10:11). The author of Hebrews referred to the patriarchs of Israel, the prophets and all the people who hoped in God as a "cloud of witnesses" (Heb 12:1). Therefore we need to engage with the story of Israel's pilgrimage with God to enrich our own pilgrimage with Christ in our time and age.

Living in the Land of Promise: The Rebellious People of God

As we saw in the previous chapter, the exodus which climaxed in the gathering at Mount Sinai was the defining event in forming the identity of the Israelites as God's people. From this time onwards God was not just the God of Abraham, Isaac and Jacob, but also "God who brought them out of Egypt" (in keeping with Exod 3:12 we read: Exod 16:6; Lev 11:45; 25:38; 26:13; Num 15:41; Deut 6:12). The God of the Abrahamic clan became the God of their story – past, present and future – as it unfolded. Ferguson has put it well: "The combined expression 'I am your God' and 'You are my people' (Deut 26:17–18; 29:12–13; Jer 7:23; 11:4; 24:7; 31:33; Hos 2:23) served as something of a covenant formula to describe the intimate relationship between God and his chosen people."[1]

There is no doubt that in forming Israel into a nation, God intended it to be a nation among nations – with territory and social, economic, political, military and judicial institutions. But the historical origins in Abraham's

---

1. Everett Ferguson, *The Church of Christ: Biblical Ecclesiology for Today* (Grand Rapids, Mich.: Eerdmans, 1996), 72.

call, the people's deliverance from slavery in Egypt, the covenant at Sinai, the wandering in the desert and the gift of the land had formed them into *God's* nation, one through whom all the nations of the earth would be blessed. God had revealed himself to them in a special way so that they might be his witnesses to the nations around them. The covenants of Moses and Joshua, at Sinai and Shechem, reaffirmed this.

Unfortunately, with the deaths of Joshua and of all his generation "who had seen all the great things the LORD had done for Israel", "another generation grew up, who knew neither the LORD, nor what he had done for Israel" (Judg 2:7–10). Disobedience and idolatry became part of their lifestyle. The writer of the book of Judges summarizes the tragic account of Israel's disobedience and God's continual struggle with them: "Then the Israelites did evil in the eyes of the LORD and served the Baals. They forsook the LORD, the God of their fathers, who had brought them out of Egypt. They followed and worshipped various gods of the peoples around them. They aroused the LORD's anger because they forsook him and served Baal and the Ashtoreths" (Judg 2:11–13).

The problem was not just that these succeeding generations abandoned "the ways of the LORD". More significantly, they were losing their corporate consciousness as the people of God, on a pilgrimage with a purpose.

But God was intent that his purposes for his people and through them for the nations and creation would not be thwarted. So he continually raised up judges from among them, to ensure that justice prevailed among and for his people, lest they should degenerate completely and become like the nations around them. But that did not end their disobedience. The author of Judges summarizes well their vicious circle of life – of disobedience, judgement, repentance and restoration:

> In his anger against Israel the LORD handed them into the hands of raiders who plundered them. He sold them into the hands of their enemies all around, whom they were no longer able to resist. Whenever Israel went out to fight, the hand of the LORD was against them to defeat them, just as he had sworn to them. They were in great distress.
>
> Then the LORD raised up judges, who saved them out of the hands of these raiders. Yet they would not listen to their judges but prostituted themselves to other gods and worshipped them. They quickly turned from the ways of their ancestors,

who had been obedient to the LORD's commands. Whenever the LORD raised up a judge for them, he was with the judge and saved them out of the hands of their enemies as long as the judge lived; for the LORD relented because of their groaning under those who oppressed and afflicted them. But when the judge died, the people returned to ways even more corrupt than those of their ancestors, following other gods and serving and worshipping them. (Judg 2:14–19)

The rejection of Yahweh as their God was a reflection of their distorted view of their identity. It was as though all that history, the wandering and the covenants, was wasted on them. Once they occupied the land, it became an end in itself. They fashioned themselves after their neighbouring nations and even worshipped their gods.

Their demand for a king, "such as all the other nations have" (1 Sam 8:5, 20), epitomized their disorientation. The problem with their request was not the king as such. It was evident that Samuel's sons were mismanaging the nation and therefore there was a need to put in place better leadership and administrative structures; a monarchy was one possible option. God does not seem to have been wholly opposed to the idea of a king. In fact, he actually intended the nation to have a king at some point, as directed by Moses in Deuteronomy 17:14–20. The problem was the motive for desiring a king: that they "shall be like all the other nations". Walter Kaiser expresses it thus:

Samuel's opposition, as was true of Yahweh as well, was a condemnation of the people's spirit and motives for requesting a king: they wished to be "like all the nations" in having a king (8:5, 20). It was also a tacit statement of disbelief in the power and presence of God: they wanted a king to go before them and fight their battles (v20).[2]

Hence God's indictment: "It is not you [Samuel] they have rejected, but they have rejected me as their king. As they have done from the day I brought them up out of Egypt until this day, forsaking me and serving other gods, so they are doing to you" (1 Sam 8:7–8). The desire to be like the other nations was tantamount to rejecting Yahweh.

---

2. Walter C. Kaiser, Jr., *Toward an Old Testament Theology* (Grand Rapids, Mich.: Zondervan, 1978), 145.

I have pondered over the way in which churches become part of, and in some cases the architects of, racial and ethnic conflicts in North America, South Africa, Rwanda, Kenya, Congo – in fact, everywhere in the world, at different times. It is the same folly as that of Israel: losing the defining identity as the people of God in the world and becoming like all the other people among whom racial, ethnic or tribal identities trump all other identities. Once that has happened, there is nothing that stops the church from living and behaving like the world. We need to hear afresh God's indictment against Israel: it is not just that the church is lost in the world; it is that the church has lost its grounding in God, thus losing its identity.

But God is true to his name as he revealed it to Moses: "The LORD, the LORD, the compassionate and gracious God, slow to anger, abounding in love and faithfulness, maintaining love to thousands, and forgiving wickedness, rebellion and sin" (Exod 34:6–7). He is patient with us, just as he was with Israel; and he did not let their waywardness thwart his plans. He established the nation with the three complementary institutions of the priesthood, prophets and kings. The priests were intermediaries between God and his people, to steward the "cult" (worship) according to the pattern established on Sinai. The prophets received and declared the will of God for his people and his creation. The kings guided and guarded the nation and his people, for his will and purpose.

It was David's ascension to the throne that marked the fulfilment of what God intended Israel to become in order to be a blessing to the nations. Israel now occupied all the land promised to Abraham; they had become a great nation, enjoying rest from the neighbouring enemy nations as well as a relationship of favour and protection from God. The ark of the covenant, symbolizing God's presence with his people, was in Jerusalem, the capital. As with the other high points in the journey of God's people, this one was also marked by a covenant, as recorded in 2 Samuel 7. Although the word "covenant" does not appear, the structure and content of the promise was covenantal. God spoke to David through the prophet Nathan:

> The LORD declares to you that the LORD himself will establish a house for you: when your days are over and you rest with your ancestors, I will raise up your offspring to succeed you, your own flesh and blood, and I will establish his kingdom. He is the one who will build a house for my Name, and I will establish the throne of his kingdom for ever. I will be his father,

and he shall be my son. When he does wrong, I will punish him with a rod wielded by men, with floggings inflicted by human hands. But my love will never be taken away from him, as I took it away from Saul, whom I removed from before you. Your house and your kingdom will endure for ever before me; your throne shall be established for ever. (2 Sam 7:11–16)

As with the covenant with Abraham, God tied his promise to the house of David and the continuation of the throne of Israel, for the blessing of all the nations (Ps 72:17). The promise included a son and heir, a great name and a special relationship of blessing. As in every covenant, the responsibility of the beneficiary was stipulated. It was the same fundamental demand for loyalty and obedience from David's offspring. Disobedience would invite punishment, "with a rod wielded by men".

The language of "kingdom" was prominently factored into the unfolding of God's purposes for his people. However, the numerous uses of the words "for ever" indicate that as with other promises, the scope of the Davidic kingdom was universal, for all time and eternity, establishing "the throne of his kingdom for ever". David's reign was a sign of a greater reign.

As the story unfolds it becomes clear that the immediate reference to "offspring" was Solomon, for indeed Solomon glorified and consolidated the empire that David had built. The completion and dedication of the temple in Jerusalem was the highest point in the establishment of the kingdom, the enduring symbol to Israel of God's presence (1 Kgs 6 – 9). But Solomon also "did evil in the eyes of the LORD; he did not follow the LORD completely, as David his father had done" (1 Kgs 11:6). He had seven hundred wives and three hundred concubines, who turned his heart after other gods. True to his word, God punished him "with a rod wielded by men". External enemies of the kingdom emerged, as well as internal rivalries and rebellion. The kingdom split into two, with only the two tribes of Benjamin and Judah remaining loyal, with Jerusalem as the capital (the kingdom of Judah); the other tribes formed a breakaway kingdom of Israel to the north, with Samaria as the capital. This was only the beginning of disaster for the entire nation of Israel. The beginning of the divided kingdom marked the beginning of the end for the new nations of Judah and Israel.

Although in the Davidic covenant the responsibility of obedience for the fulfilment of God's purpose lay primarily with Solomon, by extension it lay also with his successor kings. The prophets and priests were also accountable for warning the kings and people about the consequences of disobedience, but the ultimate responsibility for ensuring that the reign of Yahweh was upheld in Israel lay with the kings. Even when the prophets spoke "the word of the LORD", the kings had the choice whether to take heed or not.

It is very depressing to read the record of the kings of Israel and Judah after the death of Solomon. With only a few exceptions, from Jeroboam in Israel and Rehoboam in Judah, the first kings of the separated kingdoms, we find what seems to be a chorus with the same refrain: "... became the king of Israel [or Judah] and reigned ... number of years. He did evil in the eyes of the LORD and ..." The rest of the story amplifies the record, setting out the magnitude of their evil in comparison with previous kings and contrasted with David (see 1 Kgs 15:3, 25–26, 34; 16:25, 30). They did not heed the word of warning and rebuke from the prophets. In fact, they even killed many of the Lord's prophets and priests.

The prophets pointed out three evils that signified their betrayal of their history as God's covenant people, bringing God's judgement on the nation. Firstly, social corruption and systemic injustice were rife, manifested in the rich dispossessing the poor, the neglect of the oppressed, orphans and widows, and the entrenchment of systems that favoured those in the religious and political establishment. Isaiah denounced ceremonial worship as meaningless and distasteful to Yahweh. What the Lord demanded of kings and his people was to "stop doing wrong. Learn to do right; seek justice. Defend the oppressed. Take up the cause of the fatherless; plead the case of the widow" (Isa 1:16b–17). Micah reminded Israel what it meant to be God's people:

> He has shown you, O mortal, what is good.
>   And what does the LORD require of you?
> To act justly and to love mercy
>   and to walk humbly with your God. (Mic 6:8)

The second evil was that of idolatry, which in fact was the root of the first evil: the worship of foreign gods and the desecration of holy places. Amos, in Samaria, attacked the thriving idolatrous religious practices at Bethel and Gilgal as unacceptable, a sham and a mockery of Yahweh – practices that ignored the gross injustices and the plight of the poor in society. Such religion Yahweh declared an abomination and he warned of impending disaster.

Hosea's bitter experience of marriage to an unfaithful and adulterous wife was parabolic, reflecting Israel's betrayal of Yahweh in turning to worship

Baal and other foreign gods; but it also communicated Yahweh's unflinching commitment to "allure her; … speak tenderly to her" (Hos 2:14) and restore Israel to himself. Continued idolatry would invite God's judgement.

The third evil is highlighted by the story of Jonah: Israel's refusal and failure to declare God's glory among the nations. God sent Jonah to preach repentance to a traditional enemy of Israel. In Jonah's view, however, Yahweh belonged to Israel and served Israel's purposes. In this instance he reckoned that the only right thing to do to Nineveh was to punish it. He could not conceive of Yahweh giving Nineveh the chance to repent, because Yahweh was the God of Israel. Yahweh had thus been reduced to a provincial or dynastic deity, like the gods of their neighbouring nations. And yet God had shown them that he was God who reigns over the nations, the King over the whole earth (Ps 47). Instead of declaring the works of the Lord to the nations his people had followed the detestable ways of those nations. God acted decisively in the case of Jonah, who was drowned in the sea and swallowed by a big fish. He then submitted to God and went and preached to the Ninevites. Likewise, God would act to show Israel that he was sovereign over them and over all the nations, and that he desired that his glory be declared to all the nations. Failure to heed this command would result in God handing Israel over to their enemies.

During this period the expression "the day of the LORD" – hitherto an everyday term meaning the time when God manifested his sovereignty and power in creation and over evil – took on greater significance. The prophets Isaiah, Amos and Joel warned that instead of "the day of the LORD" being simply the dawn of a new day, bringing light, favour and blessing from the Lord, it would be a day of gloom and darkness, "a cruel day, with wrath and fierce anger – to make the land desolate and destroy the sinners within it" (Isa 13:9). It would be a day of judgement against Israel. The kings and leaders of Israel had led God's nation and people astray. Instead of embodying God's reign of justice, mercy and the fear of the Lord, corruption and injustice held sway. They fashioned themselves according to the life and worship of their neighbours and did the things God had forbidden them to do. The author of 2 Kings wrote, "They followed worthless idols and themselves became worthless" (2 Kgs 17:15). Israel was cast off. They lost their standing as the people of God. They were no longer one nation, God's people. As the prophet Amos had warned, neither the election itself, the exodus, nor the land was any guarantee of immunity from God's judgement. By their disobedience they had disqualified themselves from the promises of the covenants: land, blessings of protection and greatness. Israel was deceived in assuming that even when they disobeyed God they would still be protected. As a nation, Israel committed apostasy. They would suffer the consequences.

I shudder as I reflect on churches in contexts in which they wield socio-economic and political power and privilege, particularly in Africa, Latin America and North America. I find that such churches often lose their cutting edge and get conformed to the society around them, worshipping its idols and participating in its greed. They coexist with, and in some cases enhance, the levels of social injustice in their societies. These churches are said to be strong, thriving and powerful, and yet the levels of social injustice are growing. Doesn't that say something about whom they serve and worship? Just as in Israel there was a lot of religion, so these churches are packed with programmes and activities. Yet God's verdict on such churches stands: they are idolatrous. I wonder whether part of the ethical and missionary malaise may be due to a misconception of the kind Israel suffered as a strong people and kingdom.

However, there was a remnant in Israel: a people whose vision for life was still controlled by the covenants and promises of Yahweh. They were in the minority and their voice was often silenced – whether they were leaders or ordinary people. Increasingly, errant and false priests and prophets outnumbered the prophets and priests who served the Lord. To this remnant and any of the people who would repent and disassociate themselves from the evils of the nation, God promised that on the day of the Lord, in calling on his name, they would be saved.

In fact, as the prophets warned of impending judgement they spoke of the destruction of the nation as the only way to save the purposes of God from the captivity of Israel. Thus it would be the remnant that would inherit all the ancient promises given to Abraham and David. The only hope of the people of God lay in the destruction of the apostate nation of Israel. Out of the remnant would come the one who would establish the throne of David for ever, characterized by righteousness and peace. Isaiah's prophetic vision of the hope of the people of God in the remnant is compelling. He spoke of the remnant as a stump that remains after a tree has been felled. From that stump God would raise a ruler, anointed by his Spirit:

> A shoot will come up from the stump of Jesse;
>   from his roots a Branch will bear fruit.
> The Spirit of the Lord will rest on him –

the Spirit of wisdom and of understanding,
the Spirit of counsel and of power,
the Spirit of the knowledge and fear of the LORD –
and he will delight in the fear of the LORD. (Isa 11:1–3)

Unlike the evil rulers of the apostate nation,

He will not judge by what he sees with his eyes,
or decide by what he hears with his ears;
but with righteousness he will judge the needy,
with justice he will give decisions for the poor of the earth.
He will strike the earth with the rod of his mouth;
with the breath of his lips he will slay the wicked.
Righteousness will be his belt
and faithfulness the sash round his waist. (11:3b–5)

The hope of harmony of creation also lay in the destruction of the apostate nation and the raising of the "Branch" of the lineage of David. For under his reign:

The wolf will live with the lamb,
the leopard will lie down with the goat,
the calf and the lion and the yearling together;
and a little child will lead them.
The cow will feed with the bear,
their young will lie down together,
and the lion will eat straw like the ox.
The infant will play near the cobra's den,
and the young child put its hand into the viper's nest.
They will neither harm nor destroy
on all my holy mountain,
for the earth will be filled with the knowledge of the LORD
as the waters cover the sea. (11:6–9)

This is a vision of not simply a restored people, but a restored creation – a kind of renewed garden of Eden! Therefore the destruction of Israel was the "day of the LORD", for it was the day that would display his sovereign initiative to reveal his control of history and of all time; of his people and of all people; and indeed of all creation.

Exile: The Promise of a New Covenant

The "day of the LORD" came first to the northern kingdom, Israel. The author of Kings summarizes the story thus:

> When he tore Israel away from the house of David, they made Jeroboam son of Nebat their king. Jeroboam enticed Israel away from following the LORD and caused them to commit a great sin. The Israelites persisted in all the sins of Jeroboam and did not turn away from them until the LORD removed them from his presence, as he had warned through all his servants the prophets. So the people of Israel were taken from their homeland into exile in Assyria, and they are still there. (2 Kgs 17:21–23)

Samaria, the capital, was overthrown and the kingdom of Israel destroyed. Its king, princes and leaders were deported to Assyria. The king of Assyria repopulated Israel's towns and villages with migrants from the territories of Assyria. They took over the entire kingdom and intermarried with the Israelites who remained.

One would have thought that the leadership of Judah would have got a cue from the fall of Samaria, but unfortunately, about 130 years later, "… even Judah did not keep the commands of the LORD their God. They followed the practices Israel had introduced". Sadly, the entire people were apostate. "Therefore the LORD rejected all the people of Israel; he afflicted them and gave them into the hands of plunderers, until he thrust them from his presence" (2 Kgs 17:19–20). God used the rising star to the east – the Babylonian Empire, under the reign of Nebuchadnezzar, that had overrun the Assyrian Empire. Nebuchadnezzar invaded the land, initially imposed upon Judah vassal status, but then, upon the rebellion of the king of Judah, attacked Jerusalem, broke down its walls, "set fire to the temple of the LORD, the royal palace and all the houses of Jerusalem. Every important building he burned down" (2 Kgs 25:9). The bulk of the population, except the poorest, were carried off in captivity to Babylon. The monarchy was ended. As Wright puts it, "The destruction was total: the city, the temple, and everything in them went up in smoke. The bulk of the population, except for the poorest in the land, were carried off to captivity to Babylon. The unthinkable had happened.

God's people were evicted from God's land."[3] They had been evicted because they were no longer as one nation God's people.

The people God held responsible for the apostasy of the nation were the leaders of Israel: the kings, prophets and priests. As the African proverb says, "A fish begins to rot from the head:" the decline and destruction of a society begins with the drifting and loss of direction by its leaders. That is the root of the story of genocide in Rwanda. The problem was never the three ethnic groups that constituted Rwanda: Abahutu, Abatutsi and Abatwa. It was rather the utter failure of the leadership – colonial and post-colonial, political, missionary and church – to create a sense of national consciousness. In fact, colonial leadership entrenched political–social injustice along ethnic lines, as a way of subduing and subjugating the Banyarwanda. Unfortunately, it was not always the case that the European missionary pioneers challenged the oppressive policies and unjust practices of the colonists; nor did their successors, the African church leaders, challenge the post-independence African political leaders who deepened the cleavages. Once the colonial and post-independence governments provided an enabling environment for missionary church enterprise and growth, it seemed not to matter too much to the mission and church leaders what kind of socio-economic and political structures were developed. Genocide in Rwanda was the consequence.

The Israelite survivors in exile lamented their situation. Psalm 137 expresses the anguish, distress and bewilderment of the people:

> By the rivers of Babylon we sat and wept
>   when we remembered Zion.
> There on the poplars
>   we hung our harps,
> for there our captors asked us for songs,
>   our tormentors demanded songs of joy;
>   they said, "Sing us one of the songs of Zion!"
> How can we sing the songs of the LORD
>   while in a foreign land?
> If I forget you, Jerusalem,
>   may my right hand forget its skill.
> May my tongue cling to the roof of my mouth
>   if I do not remember you,

---

3. Christopher J. H. Wright, *Knowing Jesus Through the Old Testament* (Downers Grove, Ill.: InterVarsity Press, 1992), 18.

> if I do not consider Jerusalem
>   my highest joy. (Ps 137:1–6)

The lament was not simply the anguish of being in a foreign land, but rather the loss of identity. How could they be God's people without God's protection and the land that he had promised to their forefathers? How could God's people sing the Lord's song in a strange land? How could they worship the Lord without the temple? Wright expresses their predicament thus: "The people of God were not only no longer a state; they were scarcely a nation. As a tiny remnant, they learned once again how to live like their forefathers, as strangers in a strange land, in the very land indeed from which their forefathers had departed in obedience to God's call. Now they were back there under God's judgement."[4]

They could not understand how they were no longer God's people as a nation. Was there a future for Israel? Had God failed them? Had God forgotten Israel?

God had not forgotten Israel; Israel had forgotten their God. In fact it was precisely because he cared for Israel, and indeed for all humanity and creation, that he had given them over to their enemies, in order that his purposes might be fulfilled. The hope for Israel and for all peoples and nations lay with the remnant in exile. They were the community through whom the promise of the nations would be fulfilled. Though now like a valley of dry bones, as God revealed to Ezekiel, they would in his time be brought back to the land. While in exile they were to live as a people of hope. Thus, through Jeremiah, God admonished them to integrate with the societies among whom they lived; to "Build houses and settle down; plant gardens and eat what they produce. Marry and have sons and daughters; ... Also, seek the peace and prosperity of the city to which I have carried you into exile. Pray to the LORD for it, because if it prospers, you too will prosper" (Jer 29:4–7).

The first half of the book of Daniel recounts how some integrated and sang "the songs of the LORD while in a foreign land". The example of Daniel and his friends Hananiah, Mishael and Azariah, and how God used them to move Nebuchadnezzar to decree the recognition of Yahweh in the entire kingdom of Babylon, stands out. Nebuchadnezzar's successor, Belshazzar, also decreed the worship of Yahweh. This says something of what Israel could

---

4. Christopher J. H. Wright, *Walking in the Ways of the Lord: The Ethical Authority of the Old Testament* (Downers Grove, Ill.: InterVarsity Press, 1995), 234.

have achieved in becoming a blessing to the nations if they had fulfilled their part of the covenants.

The nation was destroyed but not God's purpose nor his people. The message of the prophets during the time of exile (Isa 40 – 66; Ezekiel and Jeremiah) was that the demoralized remnant were God's people and that God would pursue his purposes through them to fulfil his covenants with Abraham, the nation of Israel and King David. They were to be a community of promise. Ezekiel's vision of the dry bones communicates the miracle that would take place (Ezek 37). God himself would bring back to life the dead and the buried. "I will save them from all their sinful backsliding, and I will cleanse them. They will be my people, and I will be their God" (Ezek 37:23b).

In Isaiah 40 – 55 the description of the servant is the key motif that designates the remnant community as the people of God. Unlike the former servant, the nation of Israel, in which injustice, corruption and idolatry reigned, the servant of the Lord would "bring justice to the nations" and establish "justice on earth…. to open the eyes that are blind, to free captives from prison and to release from the dungeon those who sit in darkness" (42:1, 4, 7). The servant's obedience would bring peace and justice to the weak, dispossessed and oppressed. The servant would achieve this, not through the conquest and domination of other peoples, but rather through suffering (52:13 – 53:12).

But the promise to the remnant was different from previous ones. It was new. The remnant were to look forward, not to the renewal of previous covenants, but to a *new* covenant, recorded in its fuller version in Jeremiah 31 (with aspects of it in Isa 40 – 55).

> "The days are coming," declares the LORD,
>   "when I will make a new covenant
> with the people of Israel
>   and with the people of Judah.
> It will not be like the covenant
>   I made with their ancestors
> when I took them by the hand
>   to lead them out of Egypt,
> because they broke my covenant,
>   though I was a husband to them,"
>   declares the LORD.

"This is the covenant that I will make with the people of Israel
after that time," declares the LORD.
"I will put my law in their minds
and write it on their hearts.
I will be their God,
and they will be my people.
No longer will they teach their neighbour,
or say to one another, 'Know the LORD,'
because they will all know me,
from the least of them to the greatest,"
declares the LORD.
"For I will forgive their wickedness
and will remember their sins no more." (Jer 31:31–34)

God made it clear that this was a new covenant unlike any of the previous ones made with their forefathers (the covenants with Noah, Abraham and Israel). At least three features distinguished it as superseding those that came before it. Firstly, its promise combined features of all previous covenants: it included the guarantee of the regularity and unfailing consistency of God's nature and character (Jer 31:35–37), as did the Noahic covenant; it was universal in scope – for Israel and for the blessing of the nations, as with the covenant with Abraham (Isa 42:6); and it established King David's throne for ever. In other words, the new covenant would be the consummation of all the previous covenants. By their obedience, the restored people of God would become a light to the nations, as described by Isaiah: "Listen to me, my people; hear me, my nation: instruction will go out from me; my justice will become a light to the nations" (Isa 51:4).

Secondly, obedience and knowledge of God would no longer need to be taught but rather would come from the heart, for the law would be in their minds and engraved on their hearts. God's people would have a new heart and a new spirit. "I will remove from you your heart of stone and give you a heart of flesh. And I will put my Spirit in you and move you to follow my decrees and be careful to keep my laws" (Ezek 36:26–27). Ezekiel's language is reminiscent of the communion between God and humankind at the beginning of creation, when God "breathed into his nostrils the breath of life, and the man became a living being" (Gen 2:7). However, this time it would be a new creation, with a new heart having removed the heart of rebellion and disobedience: a new experience of forgiveness.

Thirdly, this new covenant was distinguished by the suffering servant, a theme which, as noted above, is best developed in Isaiah. This was a reference to their corporate entity but finally would be seen in a single individual who embodied the whole remnant community. The servant of the new covenant would be afflicted, not for his disobedience but for "our iniquities", "our transgressions" (Isa 53). The response of obedience would entail suffering. In other words, God's purposes for Israel and all creation would be achieved through the servant's acceptance of affliction and suffering.

These three features of the new covenant were not tantamount to a promise of the restoration of the nation state or monarchy of Israel, although the prospect of a newly gathered and reunified nation is implied in the prophecies of Jeremiah and Isaiah. Clearly the land would be restored to them, as would be the temple and the law, but they would have a different standing in the scheme of God's purposes. A restored nation state was never the ultimate goal of God's election of Israel; rather it was that Israel would be the channel of blessing to all the nations of the earth and ultimately the restoration of creation-community.

The story of Israel is replicated in the story of the church down the ages. Whenever the church has lost its purpose in the world it was simply a matter of time before it degenerated in its life and simply became a reflection of the world. Pastor Rick Warren's book *The Purpose Driven Church* has merit in that it reminds the church that it is here for a purpose. Although I do not agree with him that you can reduce "being church" to the five purposes he states, he is right to challenge every community of believers to seek to be true to God's purpose for the church.

Although we cannot say for sure at what point Israel as a nation lost its consciousness as a people elected by God for a mission, the clue was in their demand for a king "such as all the other nations have" (1 Sam 8:5, 20). It was this orientation of accommodation that was the beginning of their end. It was the opposite of the pilgrim mode. That is why the exile was redemptive, because it was the remnant that restored to Israel the orientation of their calling as God's people, to "sing the songs of the LORD" among foreign nations. As Goldingay has remarked, "The calling of the people of God is the calling of the servant; the calling of the servant is a call to die. That is the exile's deepest insight on what it means to be the people of God."[5]

---

5. John Goldingay, *Theological Diversity and the Authority of the Old Testament* (Grand Rapids, Mich.: Eerdmans, 1987), 76.

After Exile: The Community of Promise

The exile lasted about fifty years from the time of the destruction of the temple in 587 BC. The books of Ezra and Nehemiah recount the story of the return of some of the exiles and the rebuilding of the temple and the wall of Jerusalem, climaxing in their dedication. They were now a people without national sovereignty, yet back home, with the promise of the new covenant.

The Bible does not tell us much about how they were ruled and how they lived after their return, except what we glean from the post-exilic prophets, Haggai, Zechariah and Malachi. About seventy years had passed from the time of the destruction of the temple to the completion of its rebuilding, fulfilling the prophecy of Daniel (Dan 7). Goldingay identified four main features of the life of the remnant community living as the people of God post-exile. Firstly, they were a worshipping community, acknowledging that God was still present with and active among his people. The rebuilt temple and cult were the focal points of their restored identity. Israel's worship would also declare to the nations God's purposes through his people, as Ezekiel had prophesied: "the nations will know that I the LORD make Israel holy, when my sanctuary is among them for ever" (Ezek 37:28).

Secondly, they were a waiting community, looking to the future when God would bring to an end this "God-forsaken order of history in judgement and salvation",[6] waiting for another day of the Lord, a day of salvation. The people of Israel were henceforth to define themselves not just by the redemption from bondage in Egypt but also by the hope of the promise. Hope of the fulfilment of God's promise was at the core of the messages of the prophets. The scope of the promise was always universal. It was their inspiration behind the purity of their worship. All would not end in gloom and despair but in the triumph of God. Malachi captures this in these words:

> "Oh, that one of you would shut the temple doors, so that you would not light useless fires on my altar! I am not pleased with you," says the LORD Almighty, "and I will accept no offering from your hands. My name will be great among the nations, from where the sun rises to where it sets. In every place incense and pure offerings will be brought to me, because my name will be great among the nations," says the LORD Almighty. (Mal 1:10–11)

---

6. Goldingay, *Theological Diversity and the Authority of the Old Testament*, 78.

Indeed, "Yahweh's success was as extensive geographically as was the circuit of the sun, and his places of worship were to be located not just in Jerusalem but 'in every place' men and women would offer 'pure offerings' ... God's name would be 'great and highly exalted among the Gentiles.'"[7]

The prophets of the periods immediately before the exile, during the exile and after spoke of the promise and hope of Israel and the nations in different ways. The first was the "son of man" figure of Daniel's prophecy (Dan 7), the one who was "given authority, glory and sovereign power; all peoples, nations and men of every language worship him" (Dan 7:14). The universal extent of his reign would be unmistakable. Moreover, his kingdom would surpass that of David because "his dominion is an everlasting dominion that will not pass away, and his kingdom is one that will never be destroyed" (7:14).

The second picture of the hope of Israel was the "anointed one", the Messiah, also of Daniel's vision (9:25–26), who would come and bring a climax to God's purpose, which is summed up in the words "to finish transgression, to put an end to sin, to atone for wickedness, to bring in everlasting righteousness, to seal up vision and prophecy and to anoint the Most Holy Place" (9:24). The notion of "anointed one" in Israel's history had come to be associated with King David; he was the prototype of the "anointed". It is appropriate, then, to associate the "anointed one" of Daniel's vision with the anointed prince in Ezekiel's prophecy (Ezek 34:24), the one who would be the bearer of the covenant of peace. Israel's hope therefore lay in the coming of the Messiah.

The third picture was the suffering servant of Isaiah 40 – 55, which we referred to above and which could be understood as referring both corporately to the remnant community after the exile and also to an individual in the line of succession to the Davidic throne. The servant had a mission to accomplish the restoration of the servant Israel and to call them back to God. It was this servant who was anointed and was portrayed as the successor to all the covenants of Israel, "to be a covenant for my people and a light to the Gentiles" (Isa 42:6). The universal purpose of the election of Israel was to be achieved through the mission of this servant.

The fourth picture was the shepherd of Ezekiel's prophecy in exile (Ezek 34), whose mission was to rescue his sheep, Israel, from the greed and corruption of the shepherds who had devoured the sheep instead of protecting and feeding them. His people were "my sheep, the sheep of my

---

7. Kaiser, *Toward an Old Testament Theology*, 258.

pasture, and I am your God" (34:31). God pledged to exercise his rights over and responsibility towards Israel just as a shepherd cares for his sheep, by placing over them "one shepherd, my servant David, and he will tend them; he will tend them and be their shepherd" (34:23).

Thirdly, the wait for the promise was to motivate Israel to be an obeying community, with a new devotion to the law of the Lord. Ezra had set them an example. He "had devoted himself to the study and observance of the Law of the LORD and to teaching its decrees and laws to Israel" (Ezra 7:10). It was the disobedience of the law that had led to the catastrophe of the exile. As we read the prophets we also get the sense that the remnant community was also, fourthly, a questioning community, wrestling with doubt and uncertainty, bewildered by their history. The visions and oracles of the post-exilic prophets were in part a response to this. Haggai was responding to the question of the glory of the rebuilt temple in comparison with the former one built by Solomon; Zechariah spoke concerning the validity of previous covenants and the future of Jerusalem; and for Malachi the question seemed to be "Where is the God of justice"? Although all the pre- and post-exile prophets declared that the God of Israel would restore to Israel land and the lost glory, they also pointed beyond that to a time when, in the words of Isaiah and Habakkuk, "the earth will be filled with the knowledge of the LORD as the waters cover the sea" (Isa 11:9; Hab 2:14). God would fulfil his promise to Israel for the nations.

The People of God: The Remnant

That the destruction of Israel and the exile was the redemption of God's purposes is a sobering thought. Goldingay has observed that in the patriarchal period the people of God were the pilgrim clan of Abraham,[8] given a new identity by the act of God's election. During the period from Exodus to Judges the oppressed minority in Egypt were liberated to become a liberating people under God's rule in a pagan city-state culture of Canaan. Then "they opted for monarchy, survived Saul, served David, suffered Solomon, split in two and finally sank respectively into oblivion and exile".[9] During that period the people of God were identified with the nation state of Israel. Wright observes

---

8. Goldingay, *Theological Diversity and the Authority of the Old Testament*, 59. Also Wright, *Walking in the Ways of the Lord*, 215.

9. Wright, *Walking in the Ways of the Lord*, 225.

that "the origins of the idea of a faithful remnant probably go back as far as this. It was not the state of Israel that constituted the true people of God, but a minority of 'true believers' within it".[10]

During the period of exile, the people of God constituted a suffering minority in a hostile environment – a persecuted remnant. "As a tiny remnant, they learned once again to live like their forefathers, as strangers in a strange land, in the very land indeed from which their ancestors had departed in obedience to God's call."[11] Israel-in-exile rediscovered their true identity and how to live as the people of God: worshipping, waiting, obeying and questioning.

It was this remnant who, on their return from Babylon to Judea, were the community with a clear sense of distinct ethnic and religious identity, "a restored community, a community of faith, and a community of promise"[12] looking forward to a new future from God.

Here may be the silver lining in the story of the decline of the church in history, and more recently the decline of the historic churches in Europe – the churches that sent missionaries to Africa, Asia and Latin America in the eighteenth and nineteenth centuries. God admonished the remnant to stop mourning their exile, to celebrate God where they were and to look forward to the promise, and this metaphor of exile may be an appropriate way of thinking about those contexts where the institutional church has declined in its vitality or where, though structurally present, true communities of believers have been relegated to the margins of the church. When I first visited Denmark in May 2007 I was puzzled by the fact that while around 85 per cent of the population would call themselves Christian and belonged to the state church, the country and its people prided themselves on calling their society secular. I recall asking a pastor how big her church was. She told me that there was a membership of 13,000 people. I inquired further how many came to Sunday worship services. She said that on average there were between fifty and sixty people.

Yet it is often the case that churches in contexts where the believers are persecuted or are at the fringes of socio-economic and political power – a kind of exile living – have a clear sense of their vocation in Christ. I was in secondary school and at university in Uganda during the Idi Amin regime in

---

10. Wright, *Walking in the Ways of the Lord*, 230.
11. Wright, *Walking in the Ways of the Lord*, 234.
12. Wright, *Walking in the Ways of the Lord*, 238.

the 1970s; the church in Uganda seemed to be at its healthiest at that time. The Amin regime was repressive. Islam was declared the quasi-established religion of the country and Christianity was stripped of its socio-economic and political privilege that it had enjoyed under previous regimes. In my view there has been no other time in the recent history of the church in Uganda when the churches' social conscience was so alive to the gospel and its implications. It culminated with the martyrdom of Janan Luwum, then Archbishop of the Church of Uganda. It is no surprise that this act strengthened the church further, as the Lord of the church said, "Blessed are those who are persecuted because of righteousness, for theirs is the kingdom of heaven. Blessed are you when people insult you, persecute you and falsely say all kinds of evil against you because of me. Rejoice and be glad, because great is your reward in heaven, for in the same way they persecuted the prophets who were before you" (Matt 5:10–12). Followers of Jesus in contexts where they are maligned and persecuted have the opportunity to bear witness to the love, power and presence of Christ among them as the people of God.

4

Jesus, the Fulfilment of the Promise: Creating New Community

I am coming to you now, but I say these things while I am still in the world, so that they may have the full measure of my joy within them. I have given them your word and the world has hated them, for they are not of the world any more than I am of the world. My prayer is not that you take them out of the world but that you protect them from the evil one. They are not of the world, even as I am not of it. Sanctify them by the truth; your word is truth. As you sent me into the world, I have sent them into the world. For them I sanctify myself, that they too may be truly sanctified.

My prayer is not for them alone. I pray also for those who will believe in me through their message, that all of them may be one, Father, just as you are in me and I am in you. May they also be in us so that the world may believe that you have sent me. I have given them the glory that you gave me, that they may be one even as we are one – I in them and you in me – so that they may be brought to complete unity. Then the world will know that you sent me and have loved them even as you have loved me. (John 17:13–23)

In the past God spoke to our ancestors through the prophets at many times and in various ways, but in these last days he has spoken to us by his Son, whom he appointed heir of all things, and through whom also he made the universe. The Son is the radiance of God's glory and the exact representation of his being, sustaining all things by his powerful word. After he had provided purification for sins, he sat down at the right hand of the Majesty in heaven. (Heb 1:1–3)

My first visit to Jerusalem was in June 2008. The occasion was the Global Anglican Future Conference (GAFCON), a meeting of Anglican bishops, their spouses and select priests and lay leaders which had been called by a group of archbishops and bishops. Among other things the conference was meant to provide opportunities for fellowship and care for those who had decided not to attend the Lambeth Conference (the conference hosted every ten years by the Archbishop of Canterbury for bishops and their spouses in the Anglican Communion). It was called in part as a protest against the failure of the Archbishop of Canterbury to discipline the Episcopal Church in America and the Anglican Church in Canada that had violated resolutions agreed at the previous Lambeth Conference barring the ordination of practising gay priests and bishops and the blessing of same-sex marriages. The archbishops and bishops who called for GAFCON resolved that they could not sit at the same communion table at Lambeth with those who had blatantly gone against the teaching of the Bible. The choice of Jerusalem was deliberate. According to the conveners there was no better place to meet at a critical time for the future of the Anglican Communion than in the Holy Land. It was billed as a pilgrimage to the places of the biblical story to renew our faith and commitment. But the leaders also wanted to make a point: that their stand was orthodox, true to the biblical and historical faith.

I had always had mixed feelings about "pilgrimages to the Holy Land". On the one hand, I longed for the opportunity to feel and touch the soil and see the people and places of the drama of our faith – the land where Jesus Christ was born, ministered, died, rose again, ascended into heaven, and where the gift of the Holy Spirit was poured out. On the other hand, I felt uneasy about it, as it seemed to be a concept informed by notions of holiness that posit Jerusalem as the "Mecca" of Christians. This uneasiness was deepened by readings of Scripture that suggest that the destiny of the church and the nations today depends on the destiny of the Jewish people and the modern nation state of Israel. It did not help that my first visit to this region was as part of a meeting that was convened to make a point!

In the end I was glad I visited and would want to visit again – but not for a pilgrimage or another GAFCON. It was the fact of being in the place where the biblical drama unfolded. This enriched my appreciation of the biblical narrative. However, there was another side to it. Visiting biblical and historical sites in Jerusalem, and listening to the tour guides, I was amazed at how central Jewish nationalism was to the politics and economics of the current state of Israel. This was brought home to me by one tour guide who seemed to speak with conviction and faith as she explained to us the Jesus story. I asked her about her personal faith journey. She shared with me how she had grown up in Russia as a migrant and belonged to the Orthodox Church. On returning home after the war and victory of the state of Israel in 1967 she converted to Judaism, the national religion. She no longer believed that Jesus was the Messiah and had risen from the dead. For her, there was no continuity between Judaism and Christianity. However, as a tour guide who was selling a service, it was to the advantage of the business of the tour company for her to tell the story of Jesus and the early followers as though it was true. In fact, she mentioned to me that the largest group among her clientele were Christians.

There is a spectrum of perspectives and theological positions on the question of the continuity and discontinuity between Israel of the Old Testament and the faith of the Jews, the current nation state of Israel, and the New Testament church. The question here is not about the right of a people to nationhood and the justice for all the nations and peoples of the world; it is about the destiny of the nations of the world, indeed the purposes of God for all creation. I have asserted that we need to engage with the story of ancient Israel and its pilgrimage because it is part of the story of the church, the community that Jesus brought into being. This should not be construed to mean that the contemporary Jewish faith is a sister, albeit elder, to the Christian faith and that today's followers of the Jewish faith, like my tour guide, and followers of Jesus are alike the people of God. If by "people of God" we mean created by God, yes; in that sense all human beings are the people of God. But if by "people of God" we mean a people elected by God through whom he wants to fulfil his will and purposes, no. The Old Testament story was certainly incomplete and looked forward to the fulfilment of all that was promised.

The foundation of the New Testament is that the hope of the faith of ancient Israel was fulfilled in Jesus. That is what the early disciples of Jesus found in him: the fulfilment of all that the prophets foretold concerning the

Messiah. However, in Jesus there was more than the prophets could fully comprehend: something new and better, something that "Since ancient times no one has heard, no ear has perceived, no eye has seen" (Isa 64:4) had come. The old gave birth to the new. As we saw in Chapter 2, the defining event for the old was Sinai in the desert. However, as the author of Hebrews points out, "none of them [patriarchs and ancestors] received what had been promised [because] God had planned something better for us so that only together with us would they be made perfect" (Heb 11:39–40). In Jesus a new people of God was created. Let us consider the story more closely.

Jesus: The Fulfilment of the Promise to Israel

The period between the last post-exile prophet of Israel, Malachi, and the appearance of John the Baptist (otherwise called the inter-testamental period), can be likened to the period when the children of Israel were in slavery in Egypt. So much had changed for Israel, mostly for the worse. From the benevolent rule of the Persians they were thrust into oppression by the Greeks when the Persian Empire was overrun by Alexander the Great. Instability and internal conflict in the Greek Empire, precipitated by internal weaknesses due to its vastness, gave rise to a Jewish nationalist movement. This brought for a time the quasi-independence of Israel, but that too was cut short by the rise of the Roman Empire with its use of brute force. The sequel of political upheavals and intermingling with other cultures, particularly their encounter with Greek thought and culture, had a massive impact on Israel's faith-consciousness. It was a time of uncertainty.

What did it mean to be the people of God in such a context of turmoil? Many movements and parties emerged providing different answers to this predicament, each representing a distinct response to the older traditions and the newer political and religious realities. Among them were Pharisees, Sadducees, Herodians, Zealots and Essenes. They were different attempts at preserving what they perceived to be their identity as the people of God. They represented varying models of expectation of the promise and hope of Israel that was still in their collective memory.

It was into this context that Jesus was born in Bethlehem of Judea. He grew up in Nazareth and spent most of the last three years of his life around the Sea of Galilee, preaching and teaching and performing signs and wonders of all kinds – exorcisms and healing of diseases. He spent his last months in Judea, was accused by the Jewish religious establishment of being a heretic and impostor, and was killed as a criminal by the Roman Empire by being hanged on a cross. For many in Palestine he was just one of a large number of messianic figures that had arisen. Others wrote him off as a Samaritan, a lunatic or "possessed by Beelzebub … the prince of demons" (John 8:48; Mark 3:22). However, there were others who followed him from the time he began his public ministry in Galilee and Jerusalem and who recognized in him the one of whom the prophets had spoken. They recognized that he was the fulfilment of the promise to Israel: the Messiah, the Son of David, the Son of Man of Daniel's vision, the suffering servant of Isaiah's prophecy, the Son of God. The final evidence for them that he was surely the one was that he rose from the dead on the third day after he was crucified by the Romans. After that, he appeared to them and was among them for forty days, eating and drinking with them. They reported that before he was taken away in the clouds he commanded them to continue to tell the good news of the kingdom of God.

Of the four evangelists, Matthew was certainly the most conscious to show Jewish backgrounds to the entire life and account of Jesus. Introducing the subject of his narrative in the first chapter Matthew made it clear that it was about "Jesus Christ the son of David, the son of Abraham" (Matt 1:1). Yet even in the other three Gospels there is no doubt that Jesus of Nazareth was the fulfilment of all the covenants. Although Mark and John focus on the divine identity – for Mark he is "Jesus Christ, the Son of God" (Mark 1:1) and for John he is "the Word [that] was with God, and … was God" in the beginning (John 1:1–2) –they immediately link him to John the Baptist, who was himself linked to Isaiah's prophecy of the "voice of one calling in the wilderness, 'Prepare the way for the Lord, make straight paths for him'" (Mark 1:3; see also John 1:19–26). Luke is very explicit in his genealogy: "the son, so it was thought, of Joseph", Jesus was "the son of David, … the son of Abraham, … the son of Adam, the son of God" (Luke 3:23–38).

The two extended birth narratives of Jesus in Matthew and Luke, though distinct in detail and emphasis, make it clear that the baby boy's identity had at least three facets to it. Firstly, in relation to God he was a son in a unique way: "a child through the Holy Spirit", "from the Holy Spirit", "Immanuel … God with us", "Son of the Most High" and "the Son of God" (Matt 1:18, 20; Luke 1:30–32, 35). Secondly, in relation to the house of Israel, he was the fulfilment of all the covenants: inheriting "the throne of his father David", reigning "over the house of Jacob for ever", "a ruler who will be the shepherd of my people Israel", "a Saviour … Christ the Lord" (Luke 1:32–33; Matt 1:6;

Luke 2:11). In other words, Jesus was *born* king and Messiah. Jesus' lineage in the Davidic dynasty has already been established by the genealogies. His kingly and messianic status was not conferred on him later; it was his from birth.

Thirdly, and very explicitly, in relation to the nations and all creation the baby boy would be the promised blessing, since at the heart of the covenants of Israel lay God's purpose to bless the nations and all creation. It is John the evangelist who is most explicit about the cosmic implications of the birth of Jesus as the "true light that gives light to everyone" (John 1:9). John makes the connection even more clearly when introducing John the Baptist. Of him he writes that he was not simply preparing the way for a Jewish Messiah, but rather "He came as a witness to testify concerning that light, so that through him *all* might believe. He [John] himself was not the light; he came only as a witness to the light. The true light that gives light to *everyone* was coming into the world" (1:6–9, italics mine). John the Baptist introduced Jesus to his disciples as the "Lamb of God who takes away the sin of the *world*!" (1:29, italics mine). Thus in Jesus was all that the prophets had spoken about: the promise and hope of Israel, the Son of David, the Messiah, the shepherd and the servant, the Saviour of the world.

It is not just that others recognized in Jesus of Nazareth the promised Messiah; his words and deeds portray a self-consciousness as the one of whom the prophets spoke. It is instructive that although he did not explicitly refer to himself as the Messiah, when he was thus addressed he accepted it and clarified that his messianic mission would be achieved through suffering. During his first recorded public appearance in his home synagogue in Luke, after reading the passage from Isaiah the prophet looking forward to the coming of the Messiah, he boldly declared, "Today this scripture is fulfilled in your hearing" (Luke 4:19). When the Samaritan woman he met at the well said to him, "I know that Messiah … is coming" (John 4:25), Jesus was unambiguous in his response: "I, the one speaking to you – I am he" (John 4:26). Another incident where it is clear that Jesus identified himself as the Messiah was at Caesarea Philippi, when he asked his disciples who the public that had seen his ministry thought he was.

> They replied, "Some say John the Baptist; others say Elijah; and still others, Jeremiah or one of the prophets."
> "But what about you?" he asked. "Who do you say I am?"

Simon Peter answered, "You are the Messiah, the Son of the living God."

Jesus replied, "Blessed are you, Simon son of Jonah, for this was not revealed to you by flesh and blood, but by my Father in heaven." (Matt 16:14–17)

Jesus clearly acknowledged Peter's declaration as coming from God. Later, during Jesus' trial, while appearing before the Roman governor Pilate to answer accusations of plotting to overthrow the Roman establishment, he accepted the reference to him as king but clarified that "My kingdom is not of this world. If it were, my servants would fight to prevent my arrest by the Jews. But now my kingdom is from another place" (John 18:36).

Jesus: The Presence of the Kingdom of God

Jesus as the fulfilment of ancient Israel's promise is the point of continuity between Israel as a people of God and the church. But the community that Jesus was bringing into being was not simply a continuation of the old or even a renewal of the old; it was to be a new people, in continuity with the old but reflecting something that had not yet been revealed in the world: the kingdom of God. Jesus' mission was the kingdom of God. In him the kingdom of God had come. He was its revelation.

All four narratives of the inaugural events of Jesus' public life and ministry agree on two things that Jesus did. Firstly, he stated his passion, mission and message in terms of the kingdom of God. Secondly, he identified himself as the one embodying the kingdom of God and its message. Matthew tells us that in Capernaum, "From that time on Jesus began to preach, 'Repent, for the kingdom of God is near'" (Matt 4:17). What he began then, he continued to do – announcing the kingdom of God. Unlike Matthew, Mark does not give a specific location where Jesus began his kingdom mission. He simply records that "Jesus went into Galilee, proclaiming the good news of God. 'The time has come,' he said. 'The kingdom of God has come near. Repent and believe the good news!'" (Mark 1:14–15). Luke records the beginning of Jesus' ministry in his home village of Nazareth in Galilee, in the local synagogue, when Jesus took the reading from Isaiah (Luke 4:17–19). Although Luke's record does not use the language of "kingdom", Jesus' hearers would have understood the reference to "the year of the Lord's favour" as an indication of God's purpose to re-establish his rule over Israel. The Isaiah passage was pregnant with kingdom-of-God language. In reading it, Jesus was announcing that the time the prophets of old spoke about was being fulfilled in him.

John's narrative of the beginning of Jesus' public ministry is set in Jerusalem during the season of the Passover. John notes how in Jerusalem Jesus did many things that caused the onlookers wonder and amazement. One of those onlookers, Nicodemus, a devout Jew belonging to the sect of the Pharisees, followed him and privately inquired of Jesus who he was. Jesus clarified to him that his mission and message were about the kingdom of God. He told Nicodemus, "Very truly I tell you, no one can see the kingdom of God unless they are born again" (John 3:3, 5). For Jesus, his purpose, life and teaching as a fulfilment of God's promise and hope of Israel were summed up in the phrase "the kingdom of God has come".

Although the Gospel narratives record Jesus' announcement of his kingdom mission at the beginning of his public ministry as an adult, this mission was at the core of his being from birth. Luke tells the story of how at the age of twelve, following Jewish custom, Jesus went with his parents to Jerusalem for the Feast of the Passover. After the Feast was over, while his parents were returning home the boy stayed behind in Jerusalem. The family must have been part of a crowd because Jesus' parents were at first unaware that he was not in their company. So they began frantically looking for him among their relatives and friends and found him three days later in the temple courts, sitting among the teachers, listening to them and asking them questions. "His mother said to him, 'Son, why have you treated us like this? Your father and I have been anxiously searching for you.'" His answer reveals something of his childhood passion: "Why were you searching for me?" he asked. "Didn't you know I had to be in my Father's house?" (Luke 2:43–49). God's house and business were his preoccupation and passion right from his childhood.

Thus, when he began to teach and preach at the age of thirty, the age at which tradition and custom allowed one to be a teacher, he had one message: the kingdom of God. Matthew tells us that he "went throughout Galilee, teaching in their synagogues, preaching the good news of the kingdom" (Matt 4:23). John Stott observed that the Sermon on the Mount in Matthew 5 – 7 "describes what human life and human community look like when they come under the gracious rule of God". It portrays "the repentance (*metanoia*, the complete change of mind) and the righteousness which belong to the kingdom".[1] When he was asked by one of the disciples "to teach us how to pray, as John taught his disciples", he told them that whenever they prayed they should ask the Father for his kingdom to come (Luke 11:1–2). Matthew's account of this teaching, the prayer of which is now commonly called "the Lord's Prayer", is put in the section on the discourse on prayer. While chiding those who pray "babbling like pagans", labouring to tell God what they want and need, Jesus told his disciples not to be like them. Unlike the pagans, who dwelt on their needs and wants, his disciples were to desire first and foremost the kingdom of God.

However, what Jesus meant by the kingdom of God was not what his disciples, the Jewish religious leadership or the people understood. At that time the Jewish people were faced with a crisis, the breakdown of Jewish community – a phenomenon that had been going on for about six centuries, since the time of the divided kingdom. The climax of the destruction of Jewish community was the destruction of the city and the temple of Jerusalem by the Babylonians, the two defining pillars of Jewish community. Thus, one of the hopes of the Jewish people was that the expected Messiah would restore Jewish community, autonomy and supremacy to how it had been in the days of King David. For the Jewish people and even the Jewish religious establishment the messianic project was a nationalist one. The kingdom of God meant the restoration of Israel. Throughout the three years of his ministry Jesus was faced with and confronted this paradigm, declaring that it was a misunderstanding and misrepresentation of God's purpose for Israel and the nations. It was not for the restoration of the kingdom of Israel that the Messiah had come, but for the kingdom of God.

The challenge of understanding the kingdom of God remains to this day, two thousand years after it was revealed by Jesus. Our understanding of the biblical vision of the kingdom of God is clouded by notions of kingdom in our various histories. For many in contemporary times, "kingdom" evokes ideas of something archaic, oppressive and often involving brutal force. I recall a lady protesting in a meeting over the use of the term "kingdom of God" in explaining the mission of Jesus. Her argument was that "kingdom" conjured up the idea of oppression, domination and opulence at the expense of the poor. In Uganda, when one speaks about a kingdom the mental model for many is that of the ancient kingdom of Buganda, whose vestiges still

---

1. John R. W. Stott, *Christian Counter-Culture: The Message of the Sermon on the Mount* (Bible Speaks Today; Leicester: Inter-Varsity Press, 1978), 18.

remain to this day: a centralized, hierarchical and dominant structure of government. At the height of its dominance, prior to the advent of British colonists at the end of the nineteenth century, the kingdom of Buganda was the most powerful of all kingdoms in the region that later constituted Uganda. At the top, and indeed at the centre, of the kingdom was the Kabaka (king of Buganda), the most powerful person and "the symbol of social, political, economic and, to some extent, religious power".[2] Wilson Mutebi expressed what the Kabaka was to Buganda at the time:

> The whole land of Buganda belonged to him and all its inhabitants. He was called *Namunswa* (the queen ant) to indicate his importance. He was referred to as *Ssabalongo*. This is the title of a man who has had twins more than once, and it is the greatest title any man can get in Buganda. It was given to the Kabaka to indicate that no person could be greater than him.
>
> He was called Mukama (Lord), Ssabasajja (greatest of all men), Mpologoma (Lion), Ssegwanga (Cock), Magulunyondo (metal legged). He was also called Ssabataka which means the head of all clans in Buganda.[3]

The problem with this model of kingdom is not the absolute power vested in the king, but rather that such power is vested in and wielded by mortal and sinful rulers who use it to control and dominate, and sometimes enslave, others. The language of kingdom therefore carries with it these connotations of domination and abuse of power.

Such were the mental models that dominated the culture of Palestine at the time of Jesus' life on earth, too. The Roman kingdom had dominated them for years. For many, their idea of the rule of the "Lion of Judah" was one under which Rome would be overthrown and Jerusalem's dominance be re-established. A further problem that these models present is that they lay more emphasis on the sphere and realm where the reign is exercised than on the nature of the reign itself. Jesus was well aware that such were the notions of kingdom in the minds of his hearers as he announced the good news of the kingdom of God.

---

2. Abdu B. K. Kasozi, *The Spread of Islam in Uganda* (Nairobi: Oxford University Press, 1986), 17.

3. Wilson Mutebi, *Towards an Indigenous Understanding and Practice of Baptism Amongst the Baganda, Uganda* (Kampala: Wavah Books, 2002), 21.

The kingdom of which Jesus spoke was unlike that of Israel, Rome or Buganda. The word translated "kingdom" in the Gospels is the Greek word *basileia*. When Jesus used this term, the dominant meaning he poured into it was the order of "kingly rule", "sovereignty" or "kingship", that is, the right of a king to reign. The idea of kingdom as territory or location was secondary. Indeed, some New Testament scholars have suggested that only 15 per cent of Jesus' use of the term "kingdom" had any reference to domain or community over which the rule of God would be exercised.[4] The expression "kingdom of God" is about God's sovereign and dynamic rule. It has to do with God's right to reign over all creation as its Creator.

I recall a time when my wife and I were visiting the parish of Christ Church Anglican in Overland Park, Kansas, USA. On a visit with the senior minister of the parish and his wife to one of the shopping malls in the area we stopped at a fast-food restaurant to pick up some lunch. The mission statement of the restaurant, which was stamped on the serviettes we were given with the lunch, caught my eye: "It is all about you." I realized that the simplest way to express what the kingdom of God is about is this: it is all about God! Jesus, as the unique, complete and final revelation of God, is the embodiment of the kingdom of God. Indeed, "there is no way to know the Kingdom except by learning the story of this man Jesus. For his story defines the nature of how God rules and how such a rule creates a corresponding world and society".[5] His life and work in first-century Palestine demonstrated God's dynamic rule. Jesus described his mission as reflecting God's nature, character and will. The three main attributes that are seen in Jesus – love, holiness and justice – reveal who God is.

It is the Gospel of John that is explicit in reflecting Jesus, his life and ministry, as the incarnation of God, whose nature is love. Firstly, John states that Jesus is God revealing himself in the world: "the Word [that] was with God" in the beginning and "was God ... became flesh and made his dwelling among us. We have seen his glory, the glory of the one and only Son, who came from the Father, full of grace and truth". "No one has ever seen God, but the one and only Son, who is himself God and is in the closest relationship with the Father, has made him known" (1:1–2, 14, 18). Secondly, John tells us that Jesus is the manifestation of God's love: "For God so loved the world that

---

4. Arthur F. Glasser, *Announcing the Kingdom: The Story of God's Mission in the Bible* (Grand Rapids, Mich.: Baker Academic, 2003), 221.

5. Stanley Hauerwas, *The Peaceable Kingdom: A Primer in Christian Ethics* (Notre Dame, Ind.: Notre Dame University Press, 1981), 45.

he gave his one and only Son, that whoever believes in him shall not perish but have eternal life" (3:16). As he approached his death on the cross, Jesus explained to the disciples that his death was the expression of the extent of his love, by which he glorified the Father (13:1, 31–32). In fact, Jesus is not just the expression of God's love; he is God's love embodied.

The motif of the holiness of God being manifested in Jesus' life and ministry is expressed in the metaphor of light contrasted with darkness, which represents evil. Jesus was the light that came into the world.

> This is the verdict: light has come into the world, but people loved darkness instead of light because their deeds were evil. Everyone who does evil hates the light, and will not come into the light for fear that their deeds will be exposed. But whoever lives by the truth comes into the light, so that it may be seen plainly that what they have done has been done in the sight of God. (3:19–21)

John records that Jesus himself declared, "I am the light of the world. Whoever follows me will never walk in darkness, but will have the light of life" (8:12). These words evoked a hostile response from the Pharisees because they knew he was ascribing to himself a quality that was only accorded to God.

Jesus manifested God's justice in two ways: firstly, in being the embodiment of justice and the just rule of God. It was the rule of justice to which Isaiah's prophecy looked forward that Jesus proclaimed as being fulfilled in him when he took the reading in the synagogue in Nazareth:

> … the scroll of the prophet Isaiah was handed to him. Unrolling it, he found the place where it is written:
>
> "The Spirit of the Lord is on me,
>   because he has anointed me
>   to proclaim good news to the poor.
> He has sent me to proclaim freedom for the prisoners
>   and recovery of sight for the blind,
> to set the oppressed free,
>   to proclaim the year of the Lord's favour."
>
> Then he rolled up the scroll, gave it back to the attendant and sat down. The eyes of everyone in the synagogue were

fastened on him. He began by saying to them, "Today this scripture is fulfilled in your hearing." (Luke 4:17–20)

The "year of the Lord's favour" that Jesus proclaimed to be fulfilled in his coming was the year when justice would reign: for the poor, the prisoners, the blind and the oppressed – all those on the margins who bore the full brunt of oppression of the powerful and unjust structures of society. For "A bruised reed he will not break, and a smouldering wick he will not snuff out, till he has brought justice through to victory" (Matt 12:20).

The second way in which the justice of God was revealed in Christ was in judging evil. It is because God is love that he is holy; and because he is holy he judges evil, and Jesus is the manifestation of God's judgement on evil. Jesus proclaimed that in him the judgement of God had come into the world, not to judge the world, but to judge the evil in the world (John 12:47). He related easily with those who had suffered in an unjust society, notably women, who were often despised in Jewish society. Many of the miracles were signs indicating what justice under the rule of God looks like. His teachings, in particular through his many parables, addressed the just judgement of the kingdom of God. "Moreover, the Father judges no one, but has entrusted all judgement to the Son, that all may honour the Son just as they honour the Father. Whoever does not honour the Son does not honour the Father, who sent him" (John 5:22–23). Thus Jesus warned of the final day of judgement for a world that rejects him and continues in evil (John 12:36).

The life that Jesus gives – life under God's rule, in God's love, holiness and justice – is life in its fullness: abundant (John 10:10). Its fullness has at least two dimensions. Firstly, it is complete and lacking in nothing, in that it is God's life that he gives; for to know Jesus is to know God. Secondly, it is eternal, for God is eternal. "This is eternal life: that they know you, the only true God, and Jesus Christ, whom you have sent" (John 17:3). It is life in God, God's life in and among those under the reign of God, a reign of love, justice and holiness.

So the kingdom that Jesus preached, taught and demonstrated was first and foremost the expression of the sovereign love of God. It was because of love and for love that Jesus came. Love was the motivation and purpose for his revelation.

His miracles of healing, exorcisms and raising the dead were signs of the love of God for humankind and all he created, authenticating Jesus as the bearer of the good news of the kingdom – bringing reconciliation, justice and restoration to creation. They were signs pointing to the reality of the kingdom as already present in their midst. Thus, when the disciples of John confronted Jesus with the question as to whether he was the Messiah, his reply was that they should ponder the import of his miracles of healing and his preaching of the gospel to the poor. The miracles were also an assault on the powers that are opposed to the kingdom of God. So, when he was accused by the teachers of the law from Jerusalem of being possessed and being used by Beelzebub, the prince of demons, he explained to them that the rule of God was active in deposing the powers of evil.

> "How can Satan drive out Satan? If a kingdom is divided against itself, that kingdom cannot stand. If a house is divided against itself, that house cannot stand. And if Satan opposes himself and is divided, he cannot stand; his end has come. In fact, no one can enter a strong man's house without first tying him up. Then he can plunder the strong man's house. (Mark 3:23–28)

The exorcisms were simply a preliminary assault. The actual triumph over the powers would be accomplished by tying the strong man – Satan, the prince of evil. Jesus was pointing to his death on the cross as the place for the final triumph over these powers.

His death on the cross was not the curse that he should avoid at all costs, as Peter's rebuke seemed to imply, having declared him to be "the Messiah, the Son of the Living God" (Matt 16:16, 21–22). According to Peter the cross could not be the way of the kingdom that God promised would be ushered in by the Messiah. But for Jesus, just as Isaiah had prophesied concerning the suffering servant of the Lord (notably in Isa 53), "the Son of Man [Christ] must suffer many things and be rejected by the elders, the chief priests and the teachers of the law, and … he must be killed and after three days rise again" (Mark 8:31). By his death on the cross Jesus tied up the strong man, the evil one, and all his powers. The cross was the ultimate expression of the nature and character of God. The cross was the meeting point of love, holiness and justice. God so loved the world that Jesus died on the cross. The cross was also necessary because a holy God had to judge all that is in opposition to his will (sin) and save the sinner and the world under sin. For at the cross the act of disobedience in the garden of Eden was reversed by Jesus' total obedience to the Father, as Paul wrote: "For just as through the disobedience of the one man the many were made sinners, so also through the obedience of the one man the many will be made righteous" (Rom 5:19).

So Jesus sternly rebuked Peter, "Get behind me, Satan! ... You do not have in mind the concerns of God, but merely human concerns" (Mark 8:33). Satan, the enemy of the kingdom of God, was using Peter. Jesus had to complete the work of binding the powers and freeing the captives.

Thus by his death on the cross he triumphed over the powers in opposition to the kingdom of God, fulfilling his mission as the Christ of God. Hauerwas expresses it thus:

> The cross was not something accidental in Jesus' life, but the necessary outcome of his life and of his mission. His death is of decisive significance, not because it alone wrought salvation for us, but because it was the end and fulfilment of his life. In his death he finished the work that it was his mission to perform. In this sense the cross is not a detour or a hurdle on the way to the kingdom, nor is it even the way to the kingdom; it is the kingdom come.[6]

The cross was the decisive event by which the kingdom of God was inaugurated. Wright summarizes God's action in the cross of Christ as dealing with the guilt of human sin; defeating the powers of evil; destroying death; removing the barrier of enmity and alienation between Jew and Gentile; and healing and reconciling God's creation.[7] Ironically, the crown of thorns that was placed upon his head in scorn was his crowning as the King.

The resurrection was confirmation that the cross had accomplished the overthrow of the evil powers and the work of redemption. It was therefore necessary that the risen Jesus was seen by his disciples to attest that all that he had proclaimed and promised was true. Thus, after his resurrection, when he appeared to his disciples over a period of forty days, he continued with the message of the kingdom of God (Acts 1:3). His ascension and exaltation to the right hand of the Father was confirmation that the work of ushering in the kingdom was accomplished. At Pentecost, as he had promised, the Holy Spirit was given as the eternal presence of the Father and the Son among his people, mediating the triune love.

---

6. Hauerwas, *The Peaceable Kingdom*, 48.

7. Christopher J. H. Wright, *The Mission of God: Unlocking the Bible's Grand Narrative* (Downers Grove, Ill.: IVP, 2006), 312–13.

Jesus and His Disciples: Creating a Community of the Kingdom of God

Jesus not only proclaimed, taught, demonstrated and lived the kingdom of God, he also challenged his hearers to seek it; he invited them to "enter" it. In all four Gospels, the narratives of his inauguration of his public ministry, he called his hearers to repentance. The reign of God demanded repentance. Repentance, a radical turning away from self, all rebellion and all other forms of idolatry and evil, and turning all to God and his reign of love, holiness and justice, was the first sign that a person or people were submitting to the kingdom of God. Mark and Luke are the more explicit in making the connection between Jesus announcing the good news about the kingdom of God and the invitation to follow him. In Mark we read:

> After John was put in prison, Jesus went into Galilee, proclaiming the good news of God. "The time has come," he said. "The kingdom of God has come near. Repent and believe the good news!"
>
> As Jesus walked beside the Sea of Galilee, he saw Simon and his brother Andrew casting a net into the lake, for they were fishermen. "Come, follow me," Jesus said, "and I will send you out to fish for people." At once they left their nets and followed him. (Mark 1:14–18)

Entering the kingdom entailed repentance. Following was the act of repentance and submitting themselves to God's rule. In following Jesus they were receiving the offer of salvation and the forgiveness of sin and were signing up to be with him and do whatever he did. Another way of translating Jesus' invitation "Come, follow me and I will send you out to fish for people" is "Come, as you follow me I will send you out to fish for people". It was in following that they would submit to his rule and in submitting that they would taste and announce the good news of his rule, thus "fishing for people"; without following, they could not fish for people.

The idea of a group of pupils or learners spending time together with a teacher (rabbi) to interpret the law of Moses and the prophetic writings had developed among the Jews during the time after exile. The term "disciple" referred to one who was committed to the interpretations of the Scriptures and religious tradition given by the rabbi and who lived by them. Through the process of learning that would sometimes include a set meeting time and such pedagogical methods as question-and-answer sessions, instruction, repetition and memorization, disciples would become increasingly devoted to their master and the master's teachings. The vision and goal of the disciples was to become like the teacher in every way. In time, as the disciples became like their master, they would pass on the tradition to others.

Jesus' call to repent and follow him was an invitation to become like him, being formed by him into a people of the kingdom of God. Just like him, his disciples' passion, mission, life and identity derived from the kingdom of God. Their lives were to exemplify the values of the kingdom as a blessed and righteous people, laid out in the so-called "Sermon on the Mount" in Matthew 5 - 7, a treatise on how the kingdom community behaves and what it looks like. Whenever they prayed they would say "Our Father ... your kingdom come, your will be done on earth as it is in heaven" (Matt 6:9–10). Thus, wherever they went they were to announce that "the kingdom of God is near".

A look at those whom he gathered reveals something of the nature and character of the new community he was bringing into being, those who are under God's dynamic rule. There were fishermen such as Simon Peter, Andrew, James and John; there was Simon, who was part of the Jewish party of Zealots, a nationalist movement among the Pharisees fighting for the liberation and re-establishment of the nation of Israel (Luke 6:15). Then there were the women. Of all the Gospel writers, Luke is the one who gives greatest prominence to some of the women disciples: "Mary (called Magdalene) from whom seven demons had come out; Joanna the wife of Chuza, the manager of Herod's household; Susanna; and many others", who also provided material support for him (Luke 8:2–3). The Gospel of John has a record of some of the other women: the Samaritan woman (John 4:7–42), and Mary and Martha, Lazarus' sisters (John 11:1–44). In addition there is another category simply referred to as "tax collectors and sinners" (Matt 9:10–11; Mark 2:15–16; Luke 5:29–30; Luke 15:1). In this group were people like Matthew and Zacchaeus, both wealthy people and considered sinful by the Jewish community. The other "sinners" would have been prostitutes. Jesus' disciples were a diverse group.

It is understandable that the leadership of the Jewish religious establishment – the priests, Pharisees and teachers of the law – were puzzled by Jesus and could not easily characterize the rag-tag group that he allowed to be in his company as disciples. Neither he nor his disciples fitted with their interpretation of the Scriptures concerning the Messiah or the messianic community. A respectable rabbi, according to their traditions, would not choose his disciples from social outcasts and those who were religiously despised, such as the prostitutes, tax collectors, Samaritans and women. Thus, although some Jewish leaders believed in him, they were in the minority and many remained secret disciples "for fear they would be put out of the synagogue" (John 12:42). The Jewish establishment therefore took it upon themselves to guard the purity and integrity of their traditions by getting rid of him. They maligned him as an impostor, a lunatic, a lawbreaker and heretic, and his disciples as ignorant, irreligious and deceived. But many of those who accepted him, who believed in his name, were those on the margins, despised and even ostracized by the mainstream. It was to these that he gave the right to become children of God (John 1:12).

It should trouble us today that the people who least understood Jesus and his mission, who rejected him and worked night and day to eliminate him, were the religious establishment of his day: the chief priests, priests, Pharisees, experts and teachers of the law of Moses. They are today's ecclesiastical bureaucrats: archbishops, bishops, clergy and pastors are the chief priest and priests; Bible-believing evangelicals are the Pharisees of the time; and theologians of all shades are the teachers of the law. Jesus had warned them, as he does church leaders today, that unless they changed and became like little children they would never enter the kingdom of heaven, for the greatest in the kingdom of heaven are those who humble themselves like children (Matt 18:2–3).

It was the appointment of the twelve apostles that constituted the foundation of the new community. All three narratives of their appointment, in Matthew, Mark and Luke, distinguish them from the calling of the other disciples. The apostles had already been called first to be disciples. In Mark and Luke's narratives their appointment was preceded by Jesus' withdrawal to the mountain. After this he "appointed the twelve" (Mark 3:14), or as Luke puts it, "chose twelve of them" (Luke 6:13), whom he designated apostles, out of the larger group of his disciples. Mark makes the purpose clear: "that they might be with him and that he might send them out to preach and to have authority to drive out demons" (Mark 3:14–15).

The calling of the apostles should thus be understood in the context of their first call as disciples. In fact, it is more accurate to describe apostleship as an appointment rather than a call. Luke's account in 6:12–16 clearly says that Jesus "called his disciples to him and chose twelve of them, whom he also designated apostles". The English word "apostle" comes from the Greek term *apostolos*, which means a messenger, envoy or ambassador. Related to the verb "to send", it refers to one who is "sent" on behalf of another. The

Twelve therefore were to live out their discipleship as apostles, with a unique place and role among all the disciples. Their assignment as disciples was that of apostles.

The distinction between calling and assignment is important. Calling is assumed in assignment: it is about being and belonging to Jesus, in God's mission and his kingdom. Assignment is about the location and role within God's mission and kingdom, the particular journey of disciple that is marked out, the particular cross that the disciple must take up in following Jesus. It is in this sense that the apostles could be seen as prototype disciples, because to everyone Jesus calls, he assigns a task; everyone who follows has a particular journey with Jesus, growing to know him more on that journey as they live out their discipleship. Everyone Jesus calls, he calls to follow him in God's mission; and everyone who follows him he assigns a part in God's mission of redemption, restoration and renewal of all creation. But he does not give us these assignments because Jesus could not accomplish his work without us: it is rather that in being his disciples and acting in the roles he assigns us we grow to know him; and as we grow to know him we bring him honour and glory. The disciple's journey is about knowing him and glorifying him.

The Twelve had an assignment: a unique place and role among all the disciples. It is Matthew who outlines in detail the nature of their apostleship (Matt 10:1–42). A comparison with the sending of the seventy-two in Luke 10:1–16 reveals that the seventy-two and the Twelve shared the same calling to announce the kingdom of God and the same cost of following Jesus. The main difference is that while the seventy-two were commissioned to go to "every town and place where he was about to go", the Twelve were restricted to the Jews. They were not to go among the Gentiles or enter any town of the Samaritans, but only to the lost sheep of Israel (Matt 10:5–6). Some commentators have actually suggested that the number seventy-two was the number of the nations of the then known world; the number twelve is reminiscent of the twelve tribes that constituted the nation of Israel. They were now to be the foundation of the new people of God. Giles writes:

> The appointment of the twelve was thus a symbolic prophetic action. It announced that Jesus was recreating Israel. As the nucleus and foundation of restored Israel, the twelve were the patriarchs of a reconstituted people of God; but as a circumcised group, with whom only some identified, they were also a warning to recalcitrant Israel. In a sense the twelve

were witnesses to both the salvation and judgement now close
at hand for the historic people of God, the Jews.[8]

The Twelve therefore marked the transition between the old and
the new; from the twelve tribes of ancient Israel to a new Israel that would
embrace all the nations. Jesus made this point to the Samaritan woman at the
well when he said:

> Woman ... believe me, a time is coming when you will
> worship the Father neither on this mountain nor in Jerusalem.
> You Samaritans worship what you do not know; we worship
> what we do know, for salvation is from the Jews. Yet a time
> is coming and has now come when the true worshippers
> will worship the Father in the Spirit and in truth, for they
> are the kind of worshippers the Father seeks. God is spirit,
> and his worshippers must worship in the Spirit and in truth.
> (John 4:21–24)

In Jesus, the time had come when the true worshippers would worship
the Father neither in Jerusalem nor on Mount Gerizim of the Samaritans, but
"in the Spirit and in truth, for they are the kind of worshippers the Father
seeks" (4:23). Unlike the community of Israel, whose identity was informed
by memory of the exodus and the revelation at Mount Sinai, the worship of
the new community of the Messiah would be animated by the real presence
of God: for "God is spirit, and his worshippers must worship in the Spirit and
in truth".

Jesus made it clear that his sheep were not only of the house of Israel.
Speaking to his Jewish disciples he said:

> I am the good shepherd; I know my sheep and my sheep know
> me – just as the Father knows me and I know the Father – and
> I lay down my life for the sheep. *I have other sheep that are not
> of this sheepfold. I must bring them also.* They too will listen
> to my voice, and there shall be one flock and one shepherd
> [italics mine]. (John 10:14–16)

With the Twelve Jesus was establishing the foundation for the gathering
of all his flock; through them "the other sheep" would hear his voice and

---

8. Kevin Giles, *What on Earth Is the Church?* (London: SPCK, 1995), 32.

follow him. The Twelve were the reconstituted house of Israel, the new people of God, that would fulfil the calling to be "a light for the Gentiles" (Isa 49:6).

Thus in Jesus all that God purposed in and through Israel was being fulfilled. In him a new community was coming into being that would fulfil all that God intended through ancient Israel – declaring his glory to the nations. The Mount Sinai gathering, the defining moment of ancient Israel as the people of God, a gathering of one nation, prefigured the gathering in Christ for all the nations, which was made possible by his death on the cross. What the covenant at Mount Sinai was for ancient Israel, the cross was for the new people of God.

Thus the idea that the destiny of the new people of God, his church, and the nations depends on the destiny of today's nation state of Israel must be rejected as a distortion of the truth. On the contrary, the destiny of the Jewish people and indeed all the peoples of the world has been secured by Jesus' death on the cross, his resurrection and ascension, and the outpouring of the Holy Spirit at Pentecost. It is not today's nation state of Israel that is the clue to history, but Jesus of Nazareth.

5

Jesus, His Disciples and Pentecost: The Birth of the New Community

They devoted themselves to the apostles' teaching and to fellowship, to the breaking of bread and to prayer. Everyone was filled with awe at the many wonders and signs performed by the apostles. All the believers were together and had everything in common. They sold property and possessions to give to anyone who had need. Every day they continued to meet together in the temple courts. They broke bread in their homes and ate together with glad and sincere hearts, praising God and enjoying the favour of all the people. And the Lord added to their number daily those who were being saved. (Acts 2:42–47)

Therefore, holy brothers and sisters, who share in the heavenly calling, fix your thoughts on Jesus, whom we acknowledge as our apostle and high priest. He was faithful to the one who appointed him, just as Moses was faithful in all God's house. Jesus has been found worthy of greater honour than Moses, just as the builder of a house has greater honour than the house itself. For every house is built by someone, but God is the builder of everything. "Moses was faithful as a servant in all God's house", bearing witness to what would be spoken by God in the future. But Christ is faithful as the Son over God's house. And we are his house, if indeed we hold firmly to our confidence and the hope in which we glory. (Heb 3:1–6)

The Christian church is visible all over the world today. It is made visible by physical structures of all shapes and sizes – cathedrals, churches (the buildings where Christians gather for worship services); its congregations and gatherings – throughout the week, climaxing on the "Sabbath" (for some Friday, others Saturday and the majority Sunday); its institutions – theological training centres, schools and hospitals; its social-service infrastructure – health centres and other community-outreach projects; its leadership structures and clerical hierarchies – popes, metropolitans, apostles, bishops, priests, pastors and evangelists; and its activities and programmes – youth, women, men, choirs, radio and television stations. The institutional dimension of the church is visible through institutional forms.

Sometimes I have wondered what a visitor from a context where church is not visible in such forms, but rather is on the fringes of society, makes of this. What is it about this image that will encourage such a person to want to get to know more about a church? Suppose our visitor is encouraged to go beyond the forms; what will he or she see inside – sitting through the weekly worship service; sitting in the various committee meetings; attending any of the activities on offer; visiting any of the social service programmes, a school or health centre? I imagine our visitor finding the bishop, an apostle, evangelist, vicar, senior pastor or elder and asking them to describe what is at the heart of who they are, what makes them church, distinct from other institutions. Our visitor cares less about the titles because they have no meaning or significance in his or her world. I would want to eavesdrop on this conversation: to hear the leader describe what makes their church different from the world around. Sometimes one wonders what would remain of the churches if the structures were taken away.

Jesus and his disciples had none of these things. Jesus did not start a new synagogue for himself and his disciples, and yet he constantly urged them to remember that though in the world they were not of the world, for they did not belong to the world but to him. He did not institute a "new Sabbath" to replace the "old Sabbath", and yet he often gathered his disciples together to teach them the "secret of the kingdom of God" (Mark 4:11). He did not create any hierarchy among them to replace the old hierarchy of chief priest, priests and Levites – for all were simply disciples; and yet he designated some as apostles (Mark 3:14). There were no new parties or sects to replace the Pharisees and Sadducees, for his disciples included people from all sects, backgrounds and classes – even tax collectors and sinners! Who, then, were they? What did the community look like? What was it that distinguished them from the world around them? How were they to continue after he had gone? We consider these questions in some detail in this chapter.

The Disciples of Jesus: Becoming the Community of the Kingdom of God

We have already seen how Jesus had all sorts of people in his company. Not everyone in his company was his disciple. There were always crowds following him. What distinguished the disciples from the crowds and the seekers was that the disciples had fashioned their lives along that of Jesus. His disciples dedicated their lives to knowing him and learning from him. John Stott, in his work *The Message of the Sermon on the Mount*, observed that that sermon's main emphasis is that Jesus' true followers, the citizens of the kingdom of God, were to be entirely different from others – the crowds, pagans and religious people; the scribes and Pharisees; the Jews and Gentiles. "They were not to take their cue from the people around them, but from him [Jesus], and so prove to be genuine children of their heavenly Father."[1] They were to as be distinct from the world as salt is from food and light from darkness. The one who declared himself to be the light of the world charged them: "You are the salt of the earth … You are the light of the world" (Matt 5:13–16). The impact of their witness to the world would not be achieved in withdrawal, but like salt in food and light expelling darkness, it was through their presence, a savouring presence, and by the proclamation of the gospel of the kingdom that they would prevent moral decay and expel the darkness of evil in the world.

The incident recorded in Mark 4:35–41, with Jesus in the boat when the disciples encountered a violent storm, is instructive. While the storm was rocking the boat Jesus was in the stern sleeping. It troubled them that he should be sleeping while the boat was about to sink. When they woke him up

---

1. John R. W. Stott, *The Message of the Sermon on the Mount* (Bible Speaks Today; Leicester, Inter-Varsity Press, 1978), 18.

he "rebuked the wind and said to the waves, 'Quiet! Be still!' Then the wind died down and it was completely calm". Jesus then asked them, "Why are you so afraid? Do you still have no faith? They were terrified and asked each other, 'Who is this? Even the wind and the waves obey him!'" (Mark 4:39–41). Jesus' question and the disciples' response encapsulate the focus of the disciples on the journey following Jesus. Faith in Jesus, growing to know who Jesus really was and therefore to believe, trust and fashion their entire lives after him: that is what it was about. Since Peter and the rest of the apostles were to model discipleship, their first responsibility was "to be with him" (Mark 3:13). In being with him they would grow to know him and the kingdom of God of which he was the bearer.

Thus, just as they had heard him preach the good news and point to himself, they too pointed others to him. The narrative of the call of Levi in Mark 2:13–17 illustrates this. First Jesus preached and taught the crowds; then came the invitation to follow him, and in this case Levi (also called Matthew) was singled out. Levi responded. The next thing Levi did was to invite Jesus to a party at his house that he hosted for his fellow tax collectors and friends. He wanted his colleagues and friends to hear Jesus. Jews considered tax collectors to be the worst of sinners because by collecting taxes for the Roman Empire they were colluding with their oppressors. The Pharisees were unhappy that a rabbi of Jesus' standing should be seen in such company, but even more importantly, that among his disciples were people with a history like that of Levi. But for Jesus, Levi was the kind of company he delighted in – sinners who had turned to him and invited him to be among others. Disciples were those for whom proclaiming the wonders of God in Jesus became their life. It is what their Master did, so they did it too, with one difference: their Master was the good news, and their job was to point others to him.

The distinction between disciples, seekers and the crowd is very helpful as we think of many of our churches today. Wherever Jesus is he pulls crowds even today. (That is not to say that wherever crowds are, there is Jesus!) It is therefore important, in the way we structure community life, to provide space for all, as Jesus did. He had time for the crowds: preaching, healing and feeding them; then time with the seekers, individually and in homes; and he spent time teaching his disciples as they followed him, hearing and seeing him, and doing as he did. Effective teaching and preaching turns crowds into seekers or sends them away. It is troubling how the preaching of repentance (turning all to Jesus) has diminished in much of evangelism and discipleship today. Take for example what happens at mass gospel rallies (called "crusades" in most parts of Africa). It is astonishing to see how over the last three decades preaching repentance has given way to preaching miracles and prosperity. The emphasis has been put on what people can get from God, a human-centred gospel – which of course is no gospel at all – rather than the challenge to turn their lives and everything to God. Jesus was not calling them to come to him for things, but rather just to follow him.

The call to discipleship was a call to enter the kingdom and participate in its life, which among other aspects entailed proclaiming it to others. The Gospels are emphatic that as we follow Jesus we declare the good news of the reign of God in all we are and do. Sharing the good news about Jesus is integral to being a disciple. In other words, one cannot say that one is a disciple and not share the gospel with others. The act of proclaiming the gospel deepens the disciples' appreciation of its power, thereby bringing growth. We must therefore reject as unbiblical the separation of discipleship from witnessing for Christ. We are witnesses by how we live, what we say and what we do – declaring the praises of him who called us out of darkness into his marvellous light (1 Pet 2:9–11).

There are two occasions on record when Jesus actually sent the disciples to do as they had seen him do: announce the good news of the kingdom of God, demonstrate its presence through signs and wonders, and invite their hearers to enter by repentance (Luke 9:2; 10:1–24). They were his mouthpieces. It was to them that the "mystery" or "secret" of the kingdom of God had been given (Mark 4:11; Matt 13:11; Luke 8:10). He told them, "Whoever listens to you listens to me; whoever rejects you rejects me; but whoever rejects me rejects him who sent me" (Luke 10:1, 8, 16). Thus although they were apart from him, they were "following him" in his mission, announcing the good news of the kingdom. Upon their return from the mission to the towns and villages of Judea the seventy-two were filled "with joy and said, 'Lord, even the demons submit to us in your name'" (Luke 10:17). Their joy was in participating together with Jesus in announcing that "the kingdom of God is near". Although Jesus did not deny the reason for their joy, he pointed beyond their apparent achievement to their identity. The greater reason for rejoicing was that they were now members of the kingdom; their names were listed in the community of the kingdom, "written in heaven" (Luke 10:20).

But the disciples were not to declare the wonders of God merely by words, signs and wonders; it was the outflow of the love of Jesus among them that was to be the most potent witness to the kingdom. Jesus commanded them to love one another with the love with which he had loved them;

for by this, "everyone will know that you are my disciples, if you love one another" (John 13:35). As the community of the kingdom of God they were a community of love: being nurtured on the love of their Master and displaying it among themselves for one another's benefit. Jesus used the metaphor of the shepherd and the flock to describe the nature and nurture of the new community. He likened the disciples to the sheep.

The analogy of a shepherd with his sheep has deep roots in the Old Testament. David the shepherd boy was the one chosen to be king over Israel. King David acknowledged that the Lord was the true shepherd (Ps 23). In Ezekiel 34 God chastised the leaders of Israel as irresponsible and greedy shepherds over his flock. The analogy also appears in three Gospels – Matthew 26:31; Luke 2:8, 12:32; and John 10. Of these three, it is John the evangelist who gives us Jesus' extended use of the metaphor. There are three parts to the picture in John: the shepherd, the sheep and the sheepfold. The sheepfold in mind is a typical first-century Palestine sheep enclosure which had only one gate that served as the entrance and exit (more or less like the African *kraal).*

The metaphor affirms at least three things about Jesus and the new community he was bringing into being. Firstly, Jesus is the gate – the sole gate for the sheep. The sheep go in and out of the sheepfold through him. The only way any sheep become part of the flock is through him; it is only those who enter through him who will be saved (John 10:9). He is the only way appointed by God. Beside him there is no other. He categorically stated that those who came before him, claiming to be the Messiah, as well as anyone else who claimed to be the gate were "thieves and robbers". Moreover, those who were authentic messengers of God pointed away from themselves to him who was yet to be revealed. Jesus was the Anointed One of the promise and hope of Israel.

Secondly, he is the shepherd of the sheep. He is the one who calls them out, leads them, nurtures them and keeps them. The sheep belong together because they belong to him, following him. He knows the sheep by name. The sheep listen to his voice and follow him because they know his voice (John 10:4–5). Like any good shepherd (and unlike the thief who comes to steal and destroy), he leads them to the most sumptuous pastures – pastures of his love. The nurture of the community is his, for he came "that they may have life, and have it to the full" (John 10:10). The shepherd and his sheep are one family; they share a common language, the language of their shepherd, the language of love, the language of the kingdom of God. They have a common purpose, dictated by their shepherd who leads them: to display the love of the Father. This is the community of the kingdom – called out and called together, one people.

Thirdly, he is more than an ordinary good shepherd; he is the owner of all sheep. He is not a watchman or hired shepherd; he is the shepherd and owner at the same time.

> I am the good shepherd. The good shepherd *lays down his life for the sheep*. The hired hand is not the shepherd and does not own the sheep. So when he sees the wolf coming, he abandons the sheep and runs away. Then the wolf attacks the flock and scatters it. The man runs away because he is a hired hand and cares nothing for the sheep.
>
> I am the good shepherd; I know my sheep and my sheep know me – just as the Father knows me and I know the Father – and I lay down my life for the sheep. I have other sheep that are not of this sheepfold. I must bring them also. They too will listen to my voice, and there shall be one flock and one shepherd. The reason my Father loves me is that I lay down my life – only to take it up again. No one takes it from me, but I lay it down of my own accord. I have authority to lay it down and authority to take it up again. This command I received from my Father. (John 10:11–18, italics mine)

Jesus is not the ordinary owner, either. He loves his sheep so much that he will "lay down his life for the sheep" (10:11, 15, 18) – a clear reference to his death on the cross by which he would redeem his flock. Thus he assured his "little flock", his disciples, not to worry or be afraid, "for your Father has been pleased to give you the kingdom" (Luke 12:32).

Jesus made it clear that the work of building the community would not be complete during his earthly mission because he had "other sheep that are not of this sheepfold", meaning that there were others who were not of Jewish stock. The two types – those inside the sheepfold, his Jewish followers, and those not yet in, the Gentiles – were separated by the barrier of ethnicity and time. Note firstly that these "others" were his too, and it would be Jesus who would bring them in also, clearly an allusion to the fact that Gentiles are part of his mission. Secondly, they too would listen to his voice, and "there shall be one flock and one shepherd". This is a radical departure from the old covenant with Israel, which was constituted by one nation, the Jews. Now, in Jesus, the distinction Jew and Gentile would no longer count. The two would become one in a unity that would transcend ethnicity, geography and time. Together, Gentile and Jew would be one flock, drawn together in the love of God, a new humanity following the one shepherd. This unity, grounded in the self-giving love of Jesus, would be the distinguishing mark of the new community.

Jesus also made it clear that the fullness of the reign of God was yet to come. On the one hand, the kingdom of God was already present, having fully entered history through him. On the other hand, the final consummation awaited not only the drawing in of all the flock, but also the complete and final victory of love, holiness and justice, when all evil and rebellious powers will be removed. Jesus used many parables to teach this. One of the most penetrating for understanding the already-but-not-yet character of the kingdom of God is that of the wheat and the weeds (Matt 13:24–30, 36–43). A man sowed wheat seeds in his field; when they sprouted, weeds also appeared. This perplexed the servants, who inquired of their master the origin of the weeds. "An enemy did this," he replied. The servants then asked if they should pull out the weeds so that the wheat might grow unencumbered. But the owner of the field told them not to, lest by "pulling up the weeds, you may uproot the wheat with them". Their roots were intertwined, so the owner directed the servants to "Let them both grow together until the harvest", at which time they would first "collect the weeds and tie them in bundles to be burned; then [they would] gather the wheat and bring it into my barn". By this parable Jesus clarified to his disciples that the work of the reign of God will only be fully realized when evil and rebellion against God's reign is finally judged, and the people of God through the ages inherit the kingdom (Matt 25:34).

Each time I read this parable I am reminded that the wheat and weeds are not just two distinct people or communities: one for the kingdom, the other rebellious and evil. The parable is also about me. I have both realities within me: one seeking, longing for and living in God's kingdom; the other rebelling, desiring my own way, my pleasure and the pleasures of the world. But the parable is also about any community that seeks and longs to see the kingdom in its life and witness. Both realities exist. My constant prayer is this: Lord, may the wheat outgrow and choke the weeds, rather than vice versa! Thanks be to God for his Word and Spirit that continually sanctify his people! How I long for the harvest!

Community in the Holy Spirit

The Gospel of John places the narrative of Jesus' discourse on the distinctiveness of the new community with only the apostles, during what we have come to know as "the last supper", in chapters 13 to 17. This further illustrates the foundational nature of the apostolic assignment. But as elsewhere in the Gospels, whatever Jesus spoke to the inner circle of the apostles he intended for all his disciples. It is with the apostles that he became very clear about the imminent betrayal by one of them and his consequent death on the cross. He told them plainly that evening that the time for his departure from the world had come. This signifies the centrality and foundation of the discourse.

When Jesus began to speak about his imminent departure from them, they were perplexed. How could the Messiah depart, especially in the violent way Jesus was describing? How were they to continue without him? Jesus assured them that his departure would be good for them on two counts. Firstly, he would go to prepare a place for them, where they would be with him for ever; and secondly, he would ask the Father to send to them "another advocate", a comforter, to be with them for ever. This comforter was the "Spirit of truth" that would enable them to experience God in his fullness (John 14:17). He explained to them that since he and the Father were one, the Spirit would be the exact presence of the Father and the Son in them. He reaffirmed to them thus: "I will not leave you as orphans; I will come to you. Before long, the world will not see me any more, but you will see me. Because I live, you also will live. On that day you will realise that I am in my Father, and you are in me, and I am in you" (14:18–21). So they did not need to be afraid because by his Spirit he would be more fully present among them than he had been while he was with them in the body. After his death he would be *in* them (not just *with* them). That is why those who were not part of his flock –the world – could not accept him, "because it neither sees him nor knows him" (14:17). Just as he set them apart from the world as his own, so the presence of the Holy Spirit set them apart as his own. The new people of God were to be community in and by the Holy Spirit. The new community, now living in between the times of the inauguration of the kingdom by Jesus and its final consummation, would continue to experience the redemptive reign of God through the Spirit.

One can appreciate the difficulty of the disciples in understanding what Jesus was saying because it was totally outside their experience. So Judas (not Judas Iscariot) asked, "But, Lord, why do you intend to show yourself to us and not to the world?" To this Jesus answered, "Anyone who loves me will obey my teaching. My Father will love them, and we will come to them and make our home with them" (14:22–23). It was only those bonded together by his love, reflected in a life of obedience, who would be part of this new community of the Holy Spirit. It was the Spirit who would enable them to fathom the depths of God himself, revealing to them "that I am in my Father, and you are in me, and I am in you"; and by the Spirit they would be sealed as his own because through him they would become the dwelling place of God (14:20, 23), a dual dwelling: God dwelling in them and they dwelling in God! Something that hitherto had been impossible would be made a reality by the Spirit. Thus, instead of their being sad and afraid, Jesus told them to rejoice: "You heard me say, 'I am going away and I am coming back to you.' If you loved me, you would be glad that I am going to the Father, for the Father is greater than I" (14:28).

Community in the Spirit, a dwelling of God in God! We must accept this to be a mystery, beyond human comprehension and only to be appreciated in experiencing its depth and splendour. We can illustrate it like this. I am always fascinated by the vastness of the ocean. If you take a bucket and dip it in the ocean, it will be true to say that the ocean is in the bucket, because the ocean waters are truly in the bucket. The greater truth, however, is to say that the bucket is in the ocean! God, by his Spirit, is the dwelling place of the people of God; and just as fish cannot survive out of the ocean, so there can be no community of Christ except in the Spirit.

This is part of the point of the metaphor of the vine and the branches in John, which is sandwiched between chapters 14 and 16 and which speaks about the Holy Spirit continuing the presence of Jesus. Jesus used this metaphor to explain the nature of the bond of new community in the Holy Spirit.

> I am the vine; you are the branches. If you remain in me and I in you, you will bear much fruit; apart from me you can do nothing. If you do not remain in me, you are like a branch that is thrown away and withers; such branches are picked up, thrown into the fire and burned. If you remain in me and my words remain in you, ask whatever you wish, and it will be done for you. This is to my Father's glory, that you bear much fruit, showing yourselves to be my disciples. (15:5–8)

Jesus was saying to them, firstly, that just as the branches are united by being on the same stem, so the bond of community depended not on them but on him. He would maintain it himself, by the Holy Spirit. He was also saying, secondly, that just as the branches have no life apart from the main stem, so they too would only be part of God's sheepfold if they remained in him. Thirdly, he said that the only way to be productive in the kingdom was by remaining in the love of the Father and the Son; this is what the Holy Spirit mediates, for the Holy Spirit is the presence of the Father and the Son. Hence the fact that apart from him they could do nothing! It was the presence of the Holy Spirit among them that authenticated them as his people. His people had to totally and consciously depend on him; and this dependence would engender unity.

The bond in the Holy Spirit was a bond of love. Just as the bond between the Father and the Son is a bond in love and of love, so it was to be between the disciples. He admonished all whom he gathered as his own to let his love reign in and among them. In an acted parable he had just demonstrated to them the extent of his love by washing their feet, including the feet of the one who was his betrayer. Washing their feet symbolized his death on the cross that was to come – the ultimate act of his love for them and the world. They too were to love one another with the love with which he had loved them: "A new command I give you: love one another. As I have loved you, so you must love one another. By this everyone will know that you are my disciples, if you love one another" (13:34–35). But it was the Holy Spirit who would reveal and actualize the love of the Father and the Son. Jesus affirmed that "On that day [when the Holy Spirit has come] you will realise that I am in my Father, and you are in me, and I am in you" (14:20). The same love that the Father had for the Son would be mediated to the disciples by the Holy Spirit. Through the Holy Spirit, the disciples were to share in the eternal love that is the nature of God. It was by loving one another with his love that they would demonstrate the good news of the rule of God in the world. As a community they would display the love of God in the world.

The bond in the Holy Spirit was also a bond in the truth. Jesus referred to the Holy Spirit as the Spirit of truth. It was the Holy Spirit who would guide them into all the truth, by taking from Jesus and the Father and revealing it to the disciples. Jesus had already told them that he was "the way and the truth and the life" (14:6). Jesus knew that it was not possible for the disciples to comprehend who he truly was and what God was doing in him. It would be the work of the Holy Spirit to continue the work of revelation. Jesus said that it was "from me that he will receive what he will make known to you. All that belongs to the Father is mine. That is why I said the Spirit will receive from me what he will make known to you" (16:14–15). Jesus assured them, "All this I have spoken while still with you. But the Advocate, the Holy Spirit, whom the Father will send in my name, will teach you all things and will remind you of everything I have said to you" (14:25–26). Thus those who had been appointed apostles were assured that the Holy Spirit would equip them to fulfil their assignment as the foundation of the new community.

The Spirit was also to be the marker distinguishing them from everyone else in the world, because the "world cannot accept him, because it neither sees him nor knows him" (14:17). Time and time again Jesus reminded his disciples that while they were in the world they were like sheep among wolves (often referring to Jewish religious leaders), experiencing tribulations and persecutions. It was by their obedience to his commands, by the power of the Holy Spirit, that they would continue to be set apart by him as his own. This separation from the world was both the fruit of the work of the Spirit and the grounds of their witness to the kingdom of God before the world and it was therefore definitive of their identity as the new community. Jesus prayed earnestly for his disciples to always know that they were a called-out people, continuing his mission of drawing others into the kingdom through love. He prayed that while they remained in the world they would be protected from the greed and idolatry that characterize the world, enabled by his word. He also commissioned them to be his witnesses in the world, just as the Father had sent him to the world.

> I am coming to you now, but I say these things while I am still in the world, so that they [those who have believed in him] may have the full measure of my joy within them. I have given them your word and the world has hated them, for they are not of the world any more than I am of the world. My prayer is not that you take them out of the world but that you protect them from the evil one. They are not of the world, even as I am not of it. Sanctify them by the truth; your word is truth. As you sent me into the world, I have sent them into the world. (17:13–18)

The expression "world", as it is used in John 17, is a complex blend of at least four meanings. Rene Padilla, the Latin American theologian, has noted three.[2] The first meaning is the world in its created form – the world

---

2. Rene Padilla, *Mission Between the Times: Essays on the Kingdom* (Grand Rapids, Mich.: Eerdmans, 1985), 2–8.

as "the sum total of creation, the universe, 'the heavens and the earth' that God created in the beginning and that one day he will recreate". The second is the "world in its present human existence, the space–time context of man's life", the arena of life and activity, the people, their culture, professions and all other endeavours. These two are the "worlds" where Jesus himself lived and in which his followers would also live, with the rest of humanity; it was this "world" to which Jesus referred when he prayed, "My prayer is not that you take them [my followers] out of the world but that you protect them from the evil one" (17:15).

The third is the "world" hostile to God and enslaved by the powers of darkness, the adverse spiritual agencies and forces at work in people and through people, in institutions and professions. There is also a fourth meaning of "world": lifestyles, worldviews and attitudes shaped by human self-centredness and greed; it is manifested in acts of lust and in injustice, inequity, witchcraft, sorcery, hatred, murder, violence and all manner of perversions. The people and institutions whose characters and lives reflect these traits are "worldly". It was the third and the fourth types of "world" from which Jesus was apart and from which his disciples were also to separate themselves. He warned them that they should not be surprised when this world hated them because they did not belong. The motif of distinctiveness – that Jesus' community was to be apart from this anti-God world – defined the character of their witness to the world, in the following ways.

Firstly, their distinctiveness in the world was to be evident through their unity. This oneness in his love was so central to Jesus' vision of his community that he made it the leitmotif of his prayer for them, those who followed him, and "also for those who will believe in me through their message, that *all of them may be one*" (17:20–21, italics mine). The essential characteristic of community of all his disciples, at that time and in the future, and of the nature of their witness, was their unity. They were to be seen to be a people bound to one another in love, the same love that bound the Father with the Son. His relationship with his Father was the fountain of their bond and oneness and would remain essential to their witness to the kingdom of God, as he clarified:

> … that all of them may be one, Father, just as you are in me and I am in you. May they also be in us so that the world may believe that you have sent me. I have given them the glory that you gave me, that they may be one as we are one – I in them and you in me – so that they may be brought to complete

> unity. Then the world will know that you sent me and have
> loved them even as you have loved me. (17:21–23)

Thus their unity engendered by the flow of Jesus' love among them would be the sign of God's rule in the world.

Secondly, their distinctiveness would be sustained by their obedience to God's word; and this was to be enabled by the Holy Spirit. Thus, while in the world their chief preoccupation was obedience to the word that had been spoken to them and would be revealed to them by the Spirit. By their obedience they would continue to live as those under the reign of God, loving one another as their master loved them; proclaiming the gospel of the kingdom, as one community, a light to the world; and showing mercy to those on the margins of society – feeding the hungry, giving water to the thirsty, offering hospitality to strangers, clothing the naked, and visiting the sick and those in prison (Matt 25:31–46).

In relationship to the world, then, we could say that Jesus' portrait of this community was threefold: in the world; not of the world; and for the world. In his prayer Jesus acknowledged that:

- He, Jesus, was the embodiment of God's gift of eternal life;
- Those he called his were given to him by the Father – his people were God's people;
- Their identity, like that of Jesus, originated in God and his mission – they were all sent;
- God's mission predated the revelation of Christ;
- Their identity, like his, was only in community – in unity;
- Their mission was in continuity with Jesus' mission;
- They could only achieve his mission in community – in unity.

John records how, when he commissioned them, sending them into the world as the Father had sent him, "he breathed on them and said, 'Receive the Holy Spirit. If you forgive anyone's sins, their sins are forgiven; if you do not forgive them, they are not forgiven'" (20:22). They could proclaim forgiveness only in the power of the Holy Spirit. So he told them to "wait for the gift my Father promised, which you have heard me speak about…. in a few days you will be baptised with the Holy Spirit" (Acts 1:4–5). It was the baptism of the Holy Spirit that would make all that Jesus promised concerning his disciples and his continuing mission a reality. With the coming of the Holy Spirit would be the universalization of the gospel of the kingdom of God, "in Jerusalem, and in all Judea and Samaria, and to the ends of the earth" (Acts 1:8).

Pentecost: The Inauguration of Community in the Holy Spirit

So when the Holy Spirit came on the day of Pentecost it was precisely as Jesus had promised his disciples. Luke records that about 120 of them had been meeting together, in prayer, waiting in obedience to Jesus' instruction for them to stay in Jerusalem (Acts 1:4, 15). Among them were the eleven apostles plus Matthias, who had just been elected to replace Judas Iscariot, "along with the women and Mary the mother of Jesus, and … his brothers" (Acts 1:14). "All of them were filled with the Holy Spirit and began to speak in other tongues as the Spirit enabled them" (2:4).

Jerusalem was a hive of activity at the time. It was full of pilgrims from all over the known world who had come to celebrate the Jewish feast of Pentecost – "Parthians, Medes and Elamites; residents of Mesopotamia, Judea and Cappadocia, Pontus and Asia, Phrygia and Pamphylia, Egypt and the parts of Libya near Cyrene; visitors from Rome (both Jews and converts to Judaism); Cretans and Arabs" (2:9–11). They were perplexed by what they saw and heard from the 120 Galileans. They could hear them declaring the wonders of God in their own languages – languages used across the Roman Empire!

"Peter stood up with the Eleven …" (2:14) on the massive steps to the entrance of the temple and explained that it was the exalted Christ who, having "received from the Father the promised Holy Spirit", had "poured [it] out" upon his followers (2:33). What they were seeing was the realization of the promise of God: that Jewish history found meaning and fulfilment in the person and work of Jesus of Nazareth; and that the Holy Spirit had now been given as testimony that Jesus was "both Lord and Messiah" (2:36). It was what the prophets had foretold: that the long-awaited Messiah would pour out his Spirit on all people and "everyone [irrespective of nationality] who calls on the name of the Lord will be saved" (2:16, 21). Just as Jesus promised, once the disciples proclaimed Christ and him crucified, plainly and clearly, the Holy Spirit did the work of convicting and convincing. The hearers "were cut to the heart and said to Peter and the other apostles, 'Brothers, what shall we do?'" (2:37). Peter, like Jesus, stated that the appropriate response to God's work in Christ was repentance; God would complete his work of giving new life to them. They too would be filled with the Holy Spirit. Luke records that about three thousand of them accepted the message and "were added to their number that day" (2:41).

With the advent of the Holy Spirit at Pentecost God's redemptive activity shifted from working through the particular people and nation of Israel to working among all peoples and nations, "all whom the Lord our God will call", as Peter proclaimed (2:39). The universalization of the gospel of the kingdom of God was immediate upon the coming of the Holy Spirit. At Pentecost the new community, the community of the kingdom of God, was inaugurated – ushered into the world, embodying the presence of Christ in the world, living by His word and his Spirit. C. Norman Kraus puts it thus: "What happened at Pentecost was the formation of a new covenant community of the Spirit."[3]

The description of the community of the 3,120-plus disciples is amazing. The coming of the Holy Spirit had drawn this great number of disciples in one day, more than Jesus had gathered in his three years of public ministry, and they shared their life together.

> They devoted themselves to the apostles' teaching and to fellowship, to the breaking of bread and to prayer. Everyone was filled with awe at the many wonders and signs performed by the apostles. All the believers were together and had everything in common. They sold property and possessions to give to anyone who had need. Every day they continued to meet together in the temple courts. They broke bread in their homes and ate together with glad and sincere hearts, praising God and enjoying the favour of all the people. *And the Lord added to their number daily those who were being saved.* (2:42–47, italics mine)

They belonged together and to one another. They were not just a group but a community. The word "community" is, however, inadequate, because it can be applied generally to describe any group that has something in common. The believers in Jerusalem were bonded together as a family. The idea of a people from dissimilar backgrounds, bound together on a different basis from that of geography and race, or natural and legal ties, was not novel in those times. The Greek term *koinonia*, which is translated as "fellowship", signified voluntary partnership or sharing around a particular interest,

---

3. C. Norman Klaus, *The Community of the Spirit: How the Church Is in the World* (Scottdale, Pa.: Herald Press, 1993), 18.

vocation or commitment[4] and was in common use. What was novel was the nature and basis of their *koinonia*.

When we look closely at Luke's account of the "fellowship", what is distinctive is that whatever they did together was assigned to the agency of the Holy Spirit. Their *koinonia* was the work of the Holy Spirit. The four things around which their shared life revolved – their regular gathering together; the teaching of the apostles; the breaking of bread and prayer; and the sharing of their needs and material possessions – were possible because the Holy Spirit was at work among them, focusing their devotion to Jesus. It was the teaching and the breaking of bread that defined who they were – a community whose foundations were in the person of Jesus. In the breaking of bread, a meal that they ate together to remember the last supper with Jesus on the eve of his crucifixion, they re-enacted the story of his death on the cross, the defining moment of the Christ as Lord and Saviour.

They loved one another in such as way that they shared with and depended on one another in all things. They cared for one another so much that "there was no needy person among them" (4:34), because those who had property sold it and brought the proceeds to be distributed to those who were needy among them. The critical point here was not the selling of possessions because there is no suggestion that communal ownership of property was compulsory or the norm for communal life. Writing about this Luke says "No one claimed that any of their possession was their own, but they shared everything they had" (4:32). Clearly, they had possessions individually. The selling of property and putting it at the disposal of the community was voluntary. The important point is rather the attitude of mutual dependence that they had towards one another, and the way in which they put their resources at each other's disposal. This attitude was the work of the Holy Spirit. Darrel L. Guder writes, "At Pentecost, with the outpouring of the Holy Spirit, promise becomes actuality. God's promised reign of love and hope, compassion and reconciliation, harmony and justice, is incarnated in a new humanity, a people commissioned to represent the gospel of peace to the alienated and hostile powers of the world."[5]

Their life together was the work of the Holy Spirit among them, the outpouring of the love of God – the love with which Jesus had loved them. It

---

4. Robert Banks, in his book *Paul's Idea of Community* (Peabody, Mass.: Hendrickson, 1994), 6–8, makes this point in his discussion on the Graeco-Roman idea of community.

5. Darrell L. Guder, ed., *Missional Church: A Vision for the Sending of the Church in North America* (Grand Rapids, Mich.: Eerdmans, 1998), 145.

was startling to the onlookers, filling them with awe and wonder. It was this shared life as a community in the Holy Spirit that was the witness to those among whom they lived. They were a community of the kingdom of God.

Surely the Holy Spirit continues to do the same to this day! He continues to work among all who truly seek the kingdom of God and his righteousness. George Ladd has summarized the relationship between the church and the kingdom in five postulates: (1) The church is not the kingdom; it is only the people of the kingdom. (2) The kingdom creates the church; had it not come into the world by the mission of Jesus, there would never have been the church. (3) The church witnesses to the kingdom through proclaiming God's redeeming acts in Christ, both past and future. (4) The church is the instrument of the kingdom in that the works of the kingdom are performed through its members as through Jesus himself. (5) The church is the custodian of the kingdom; through its proclamation of the gospel throughout the world, God will decide who will enter the eschatological kingdom and who will be excluded.[6] This is a very good checklist for any community that calls itself church, and a helpful guide in evaluating its commitment and faithfulness to the kingdom of God.

The faithfulness of a church as a community that claims to gather and scatter under the name of Christ should be judged on the basis of the standard of the kingdom of God. Andrew Walls, in his review of K. S. Latourette's work *A History of the Expansion of Christianity*, suggested that one of the contributions by Latourette to understanding the expansion of Christianity was to subject the story of the church to what he called "the kingdom test". He made the point that, although the presence of a community that claims to gather regularly in the name of Jesus may be a sign of the influence of Christ in society, the claim cannot be taken at face value.

> The kingdom shines in the church and exerts its energy within and beyond it, yet cannot be identified with it. The kingdom of God, the gospel tells us, is sprouting seed, growing in secret and suddenly bursting into flower. The kingdom of God is fermenting yeast that stirs things up so that a little of it transforms three whole measures of meal. The kingdom of God is declared when demons are cast out by the finger of

---

6. George E. Ladd, *Jesus and the Kingdom of God: The Eschatology of Biblical Realism* (New York: Harper and Row, 1964), 111–19.

God. The kingdom of God has drawn near in the presence of Christ with his acts of mercy and power.[7]

All churches need to submit themselves to the kingdom test. Walls warns that "the presence of the church … is no guarantee of the continuing influence of Christ. The church without the signs of the kingdom becomes a countersign of the kingdom, hiding Christ instead of revealing him to the world".[8] Sadly, there are too many churches which, instead of pointing to the kingdom of God, are countersigns, hiding Christ.

Paul helps us understand what the presence of the kingdom of God looks like. Addressing the conflict in the fellowship of believers in Rome over clean and unclean food, he reminded them to focus on what mattered most for their community life: the kingdom of God. He then explained to them that "the kingdom of God is not a matter of eating and drinking, but of righteousness, peace and joy in the Holy Spirit" (Rom 14:17). Righteousness is a quality of being in right relationship with God, one's neighbour and God's creation, a right relationship with a just God that is evident in just relationships. Peace is a quality of harmony and well-being of individuals and communities. Joy is a state caused by a full enjoyment of life as intended by God – a life of dignity in community and communion with others and God's creation. These three – righteousness (justice), peace and joy – are the test of any community that makes a claim to the presence of Christ within it by the Holy Spirit. In the following chapter we will look more closely at the nature of community in the Holy Spirit, as we follow the story of its growth and spread in Jerusalem and beyond.

---

7. Andrew F. Walls, *The Cross-Cultural Process in Christian History* (Maryknoll, NY: Orbis, 2002), 14.

8. Walls, *The Cross-Cultural Process in Christian History*, 15.

6

In Jerusalem, Judea, Samaria, and to the Ends of the Earth: Acts of the Holy Spirit

In my former book, Theophilus, I wrote about all that Jesus began to do and to teach until the day he was taken up to heaven, after giving instructions through the Holy Spirit to the apostles he had chosen. After his suffering, he presented himself to them and gave many convincing proofs that he was alive. He appeared to them over a period of forty days and spoke about the kingdom of God. On one occasion, while he was eating with them, he gave them this command: "Do not leave Jerusalem, but wait for the gift my Father promised, which you have heard me speak about. For John baptised with water, but in a few days you will be baptised with the Holy Spirit."

Then they gathered round him and asked him, "Lord, are you at this time going to restore the kingdom to Israel?"

He said to them: "It is not for you to know the times or dates the Father has set by his own authority. But you will receive power when the Holy Spirit comes on you; and you will be my witnesses in Jerusalem, and in all Judea and Samaria, and to the ends of the earth." (Acts 1:1–8)

You have not come to a mountain that can be touched and that is burning with fire; to darkness, gloom and storm; to a trumpet blast or to such a voice speaking words that those who heard it begged that no further word be spoken to them, because they could not bear what was commanded: "If even an animal touches the mountain, it must be stoned." The sight was so terrifying that Moses said, "I am trembling with fear."

But you have come to Mount Zion, to the city of the living God, the heavenly Jerusalem. You have come to thousands upon thousands of angels in joyful assembly, to the church of the firstborn, whose names are written in heaven. You have come to God, the Judge of all, to the spirits of the righteous made perfect, to Jesus the mediator of a new covenant, and to the sprinkled blood that speaks a better word than the blood of Abel. (Heb 12:18–24)

My heart started pumping faster than usual when the captain informed us that we had started our descent to the airport. It was my first visit to a country where Christians were in the minority and where those who boldly shared their faith were persecuted. Then I remembered I had a huge Bible in my case. At that moment, I thought what a liability big Bibles can be! You cannot hide them. I remembered reading in *God's Smuggler* how, as Brother Andrew was crossing the border into the then communist Yugoslavia, he prayed that Jesus, who can open the eyes of the blind, would this time blind the eyes of the customs agents to the Bibles he was carrying in his car.[1] I thought to myself that such a prayer was useful, so I prayed that the customs officers would not see my Bible. What a relief when I finally went through immigration and customs without any problem. To my greater relief my friend Daniel was there waiting for me. For a while I didn't notice him because he was sitting on one of the benches reading his Bible (the flight had been delayed)! We hugged each other and praised the Lord. We had both longed for this day.

Then he started telling me how difficult things were for Christians in the country. The government in power had a deliberate strategy to wipe out the church and had developed a sophisticated spy network. There were

---

1. Brother Andrew with John and Elizabeth Sherrill, *God's Smuggler* (London: Hodder and Stoughton, 1967), 113.

informers everywhere, including most taxi drivers. Then we got into a taxi and Daniel started chatting with the driver. Daniel spoke the local language well. For the next half hour it was as though I was not there. I thought to myself, "Daniel should be showing me things" – except that there was not very much to see. The terrain was desert. Then I saw him pull a New Testament out of his briefcase. It looked used. He picked out the loose papers and handed them to the driver. They both looked happy, but I was concerned. I remembered what he had told me: that most taxi drivers were informants. Why, then, was he not more careful? When we got to our destination, they smiled goodbye to each other after Daniel paid the fare. My first question to Daniel was, "Was your name written in the New Testament you gave him?" Just as I feared, it was. But Daniel assured me that it was fine. What courage and boldness!

For the next week that I was in the country I was constantly amazed by the joy, boldness and perseverance of the believers as I heard and saw them speak about Jesus together. They were not afraid to do this whenever there was an opportunity, privately and publicly, irrespective of the cost. I felt ashamed that in my country, where Christians are in the majority and there is no persecution, we did not speak about Jesus as often. Were we the same Christians? Why, then, were we so different? As I read the Acts of the Apostles, I wonder whether it was written in answer to similar questions that Theophilus, the one to whom Luke addressed the Gospel of Luke and the Acts of the Apostles, may have asked.

Luke introduced the account which we know as the Acts of the Apostles by first reminding Theophilus what his earlier account was about: a record of what "Jesus began to do and to teach" (1:1); he was alerting Theophilus to the fact that what was to follow was what Jesus continued to do. Luke's point was that Jesus' life and work were not limited to the record in the Gospels but continued after his resurrection and ascension. The Holy Spirit was to be the continuing presence of Jesus in the world and among his disciples, the outworking and fulfilment of God's mission of making the kingdom of God a reality, drawing people into it and redeeming, restoring and renewing creation. Luke wanted Theophilus, as he read the story, to look out for the Holy Spirit, the primary actor in the story. Indeed, as many scholars of the New Testament have suggested, the Acts of the Apostles would be better entitled "The Acts of the Holy Spirit" in and through the disciples, "in Jerusalem, and in all Judea and Samaria, and to the ends of the earth" (1:8). The coming of the Holy Spirit at Pentecost was the beginning of the disciples' mission.

In Jerusalem

The story of the believers (as the disciples of Jesus are called in the book of Acts) in Jerusalem is covered in Acts 1 - 9:31. As we have already seen it began on the day of Pentecost, when the Holy Spirit came and filled all the disciples of Jesus that were gathered, inaugurating a new community.

In the power of the Holy Spirit the apostles proclaimed the message of the kingdom of God as they had leant and seen it in Jesus. We have already noted how in response to the wondering and murmurings of the crowds on the day of Pentecost, Peter, "with the Eleven" (2:14), clarified and proclaimed that it was the exalted Jesus who had poured out his Spirit. Peter's address then, and those given later to the onlookers after the healing of the lame man by the Beautiful Gate at the temple (3:12–26) and before the Sanhedrin (4:8–12), gives us a clue as to the focus of the apostles' proclamation: Jesus, of Nazareth, crucified on the cross, as the fulfilment of God's promise to Israel for the world as both Christ and Lord; and the command to repent and be forgiven in his name. It was all about Jesus, the way, the truth and the life; and this message demanded a response, the same response Jesus had demanded of the disciples and which they had made when they first heard him proclaim the kingdom of God.

The apostles' proclamation was accompanied by signs and wonders. There is a marked difference between the miracles performed by the apostles then and those of today's healing crusades. The apostles were not on a healing crusade; they were proclaiming the good news of Jesus crucified and risen, in whom and through whom God's kingdom had been revealed. Much of today's hype and publicity over miracles makes them simply an end in themselves. The miracles and wonders done by the apostles were signs of the finger of God at work. The apostles were always quick to put the miracles in the context of the revelation of God in Jesus Christ. They were simply signs of God's grace, mercy and favour revealed in Christ. The appropriate response was not "more of them", but rather repentance and believing the good news in Jesus.

Luke gives us the example of the healing of a lame man at one of the temple gates in Jerusalem, where "he was put every day to beg from those going into the temple courts" (3:2). After he was healed he went into the temple with Peter and John, "walking and jumping and praising God. When all the people saw him walking and praising God, they recognised him as the same man who used to sit begging at the temple gate ..." (3:8–10). It is noteworthy that this man entered the temple courts praising God: he acknowledged that it was God who had healed him. There was pandemonium in the temple grounds; people were amazed at Peter and John. Peter took time to explain that all this was the work of Jesus, for "By faith in the name of Jesus, this man whom you see and know was made strong" (3:16). Peter then proclaimed the message of the kingdom of God to them, calling them to repentance and faith in Jesus. In Acts 5:12 Luke simply says, "The apostles performed many signs and wonders among the people." "Crowds gathered also from the towns around Jerusalem, bringing those who were ill and those tormented by impure spirits, and all of them were healed" (5:16).

The apostles also taught the believers. As we saw in the previous chapter, this was at the centre of the shared life of the community. By their teaching the apostles were fulfilling their assignment. It was with the apostles that Jesus had spent the most time, teaching them and demonstrating to them the presence of the kingdom of God in him. It was this teaching that would build up the believers and by their obedience continue to set them apart as the Jesus community. This "ministry of the word" was also accompanied by prayer (6:4). These two aspects were so central to the life of the young community that when they were threatened by the growing demands of ensuring equity in the way material resources were being shared, the latter responsibility was passed on to a new cadre of leaders so that the apostles could "give [their] attention to prayer and the ministry of the word" (6:4).

Community life was expressed in three other ways: in gathering together in the temple courts and in their homes (2:46); in praying together; and in sharing together their material needs and resources (as we saw in the last chapter). In praying together they expressed their dependence on God as their Lord and King; in sharing their needs and resources they showed their dependence on one another. Glasser writes:

> The reality of their loving acceptance of one another and their pattern of selfless sharing (*koinonia*) was nothing less than the universalisation of the ministry of Jesus by the Spirit in and through each member. All sensed his call to participate in the new social reality that the Holy Spirit was sending forth into the world. Their sense of spiritual identity with one another enabled them to affirm their communal relationship "in Christ" by loving service "to anyone as he had need" (Acts 2:45). It was a magnetic fellowship, a corporate participation

in the gift of the Spirit that expressed itself in outward acts. These acts constituted the marks of the true church.[2]

The matter of sharing needs and resources was not only at the heart of their *koinonia*, but it also tested it. The first major internal challenges of the community were about sharing. First it was Ananias and Sapphira (Acts 5), and their dishonesty; later it was the ethnic tensions arising from inequitable distribution (Acts 6). The problem with Ananias and Sapphira was that they presented part of the proceeds of the sale of their property as though it were the whole. Perhaps it was a desire for recognition – to be acknowledged in the way Barnabas had been when he sold a property and brought everything to the feet of the apostles (4:36–37) – that was the snare that lured them to dishonesty. They lied about their possessions; lied to the fellowship; and, as Peter said, more importantly they "lied to the Holy Spirit" (5:3). Peter asked them, "Didn't it [the property] belong to you before it was sold? And after it was sold, wasn't the money at your disposal? What made you think of doing such a thing? You have not lied just to human beings but to God" (5:4). The folly was dishonesty before God, which manifested itself in dishonesty before the community.

The complaint by the Grecian Jews was the marginalization of their widows in favour of their Jewish counterparts in the daily distribution of food. The Grecian Jews were not being treated as equals in the fellowship. The apostles recognized this as striking at the heart of the fellowship, negating the work of the Holy Spirit among them, and dealt with it resolutely by choosing seven men "who are known to be full of the Spirit and wisdom" (6:3) to attend to it. Many commentators have rightly observed that all the seven were Grecian Jews. What is not equally appreciated is that this was not a case of appointing ethnic leaders for their separate *ethne* (ethnic people groups); the entire distribution was to be managed by them, in order to maintain mutuality and harmony, irrespective of ethnic identity.

Luke describes the phenomenal growth of that nascent Jesus community in simple terms: "the Lord added to their number daily" (2:47). The work of growing the community in numbers was the Lord's, for after all it is the Lord who knows who are his; it is he who brings in the other sheep as well (John 10:16). But the growth was a consequence of the visible witness of the community as well. Clearly their life together was not a private and secret

---

2. Arthur Glasser, *Announcing the Kingdom: The Story of God's Mission in the Bible* (Grand Rapids, Mich.: Baker Academic, 2003), 265.

affair, just among them. It was visible to the outsiders, and this visibility was not accidental; it was intentional. Their transparency was not just with one another but also with those outside. So powerful was their life together that those around them were in awe of them. In Acts 5:13–14 Luke observes that "No one else dared join them, even though they were highly regarded by the people. Nevertheless, more and more men and women believed in the Lord and were *added to their number*" (italics mine). It was the Lord himself, by the Holy Spirit, who was drawing them in. They were not a club you could join but a family into which you were born, and only the Holy Spirit gives new birth. The Holy Spirit created the *koinonia*; the apostles were obedient to him, working miracles, teaching and proclaiming Jesus as Lord and Christ. And the Lord added to their number daily.

This process of growth contrasts with much of today's church-growth theories and practices today, which lay a great emphasis on strategies and methods rather than the faithful life and witness of believers. If we are honest, as Gregory A. Boyd admits in his book *Repenting of Religion,*

> If anything the church today is largely known for its petty divisiveness along denominational, doctrinal, social, and even racial lines. On the whole it is perceived as being less loving and less accepting than most other communities. It is often known for its self-proclaimed and often hypocritical alliance with good against evil and for its judgmentalism towards those it concludes are evil. But tragically, as a corporate body it rarely is known as being distinctive because of its radical love.[3]

Sometimes I wonder whether these propaganda strategies arise from the impetus to make up for the churches' poor witness.

The Jewish religious leaders, the high priest, the priests, the Sadducees, the temple authorities, the rulers, the elders and the teachers of the law, were not at all happy about the growing influence of the Jesus community. Firstly, the message of the apostles was uncomfortable and unsettling: not only were they holding them accountable for crucifying Jesus, who was widely acclaimed by the people, but also they were proclaiming that he had risen from the dead. To make matters worse, the apostles were claiming that the one they had killed had been made Lord and Christ by God (Acts 2:36). Secondly,

---

3. Gregory A. Boyd, *Repenting of Religion: Turning from Judgment to the Love of God* (Grand Rapids, Mich.: Baker, 2004), 46.

they were jealous because of the crowds that were being drawn through the signs and wonders to hear them preach about Jesus. Therefore the Jewish authorities determined to stop it. They used all the power at their disposal: the highest Jewish council, the temple guards and the jails. But the more they persecuted them, the bolder the apostles grew in proclaiming the message of Jesus. So when Peter and John were asked "By what power or what name" the lame man had been healed, they were clear and bold in their report: "it is by the name of Jesus Christ of Nazareth, whom you crucified but whom God raised from the dead, that this man stands before you healed" (4:10). Peter went further and challenged them to respond: for "Salvation is found in no one else, for there is no other name under heaven given to mankind by which we must be saved" (4:12). When challenged to stop proclaiming the name of Jesus "Peter and the other apostles replied: 'We must obey God rather than human beings!'" (5:29). Seeing the boldness of the apostles, one of their own, Gamaliel, cautioned his fellow leaders to hold back lest they find themselves "fighting against God" (5:39). The apostles were not deterred but continued proclaiming Jesus as Lord and God's Messiah with boldness: "Day after day, in the temple courts and from house to house [where the believers were meeting], they never stopped teaching and proclaiming the good news that Jesus is the Messiah" (5:42).

The Holy Spirit was at work in them and through them. The proclamation, the signs and wonders, their *koinonia* and the courage and boldness with which they faced their persecutors deepened the faith and commitment of all the disciples. The Lord continually added to their number. Consequently, the "number of disciples in Jerusalem increased rapidly, and a large number of priests became obedient to the faith" (6:7).

In All Judea and Samaria

The way the disciples came to Judea and Samaria and preached the gospel there (Acts 8:1–8, 26–40) is one of the most amazing stories in the book of Acts. It was the opposition and persecution that arose from unlikely circles – the Synagogue of Freedmen (6:9) – that scattered the disciples. The problem for these Greek-speaking (Hellenistic) Jews who originated from North Africa (Cyrene and Alexandria) was with their fellow Grecian Jew, Stephen, whom God was using with great effect among the Grecian Jews in Jerusalem. They wanted to counteract his continuing influence. Luke describes Stephen as a "man full of God's grace and power, [who] performed great wonders and signs among the people" (6:8). They accused Stephen of speaking "blasphemous words against Moses and against God" (6:11) in order to mobilize support for their cause from the wider Jewish leadership.

They succeeded. Stephen was brought before the Jewish supreme council to defend himself against the charges. Just like the apostles, instead of making a personal defence he proclaimed Jesus as Lord and God's Messiah, whom the Jewish leadership had killed but whom God had raised from the dead, challenging them to repentance and faith in him. Then the Jewish mob, with the support of all the Jewish leadership (Saul being chief among them) dragged him away and stoned him to death. A great persecution then broke out against the church at Jerusalem. The Jewish leadership took advantage of this commotion to renew their hounding of the disciples. Saul, tasked by them, intensified the hunt: "going from house to house, he dragged off both men and women and put them in prison", and "all except the apostles were scattered throughout Judea and Samaria" (8:2–3). This was how God brought the message of the good news to all Judea and Samaria. The disciples preached "the word wherever they went" (8:4). The dispersion through persecution created a band of missionaries, not refugees.

There is no evidence to indicate that the apostles in Jerusalem were strategizing, in obedience to their master, about going beyond Jerusalem, to all Judea, then to Samaria and to the uttermost parts of the earth. After the first season of growth followed by persecution they seemed to settle down and even began to have squabbles among themselves. One wonders whether the growing numbers of believers and their growing acceptance in Jerusalem were making them complacent. As Luke noted, the number of disciples had grown rapidly, to the extent of including some from the temple establishment. Indeed, "a large number of priests became obedient to the faith" (Acts 6:7). Thus they had become a very influential community in Jerusalem, no longer one on the fringes as it had been at the beginning. The Jewish leaders were not tormenting them any more – but only for a season. There is another factor that may have hindered the disciples from "strategizing" for Samaria, the first cross-cultural mission encounter: the historic barrier that existed between Jerusalem and Samaria.

There was a long history – over a thousand years – of prejudice between Jerusalem and Samaria. It began around the tenth century BC with the defection of the ten tribes of Israel and the formation of the northern kingdom, with Samaria as its capital. When Samaria fell to the Assyrians in 722 BC its leaders were deported and the city repopulated with Assyrians, leading to intermarriages. The Samaritan schism was hardened with the erection of a temple at Mount Gerizim and the repudiation of all the Jewish Scriptures except the five books of Moses. For this reason the Jews despised the Samaritans. According to the Jews, the Samaritans had relegated themselves to a position of inferiority, hybrids in race and religion, heretics and schismatics. It needed persecution and scattering to get the Jewish followers of Jesus in Jerusalem to come to Samaria. The Samaritan mission was not the disciples' mission; it was God's mission, to which he brought the disciples. God used the death of Stephen and a violent and hostile Saul to make the apostles get Samaria on their radar. It was Philip who found himself in Samaria and, like all the other scattered disciples, he proclaimed Christ there (8:4–5).

Luke gives attention to the story of Philip to illustrate the way the Holy Spirit was working to bring the good news to the ends of the world. He tells us that Philip "proclaimed the good news of the kingdom of God and the name of Jesus Christ" (8:12) in Samaria, with signs and wonders. "When the crowds heard Philip and saw the signs he performed, they all paid close attention to what he said. For with shrieks, impure spirits came out of many, and many who were paralysed or lame were healed. So there was great joy in that city" (8:6–8). The proclamation of Christ with words was accompanied by a demonstration of his power. Philip preached the good news with words and works, pointing the Samaritans to the power and presence of the kingdom. Many people believed and the impact was evident on the whole city. Then Samaria caught the attention of the apostles because of the reports reaching them and they sent Peter and John (8:14). Philip's ministry was authenticated by their arrival. When Peter and John laid their hands on the Samaritan believers, they received the Holy Spirit (8:17).

The response of Simon the sorcerer to the remarkable work of the Holy Spirit when the apostles prayed for the disciples adds an interesting twist to the account. Simon's way of life had always been about striking deals. His philosophy was "money works all things". So he offered money to the apostles so that he too could access the power of the Holy Spirit (8:18–19). Peter's rebuke was stern: "May your money perish with you, because you thought you could buy the gift of God with money! … Repent of this wickedness and pray to the Lord" (8:20, 22). How relevant this rebuke is to us all! Consider the situation in the worldwide church and in many local churches. There are those who have more and those who have less. The former are tempted to use their money as a tool to dominate, and the latter are tempted to fold their arms and do nothing, because "there is no money". The rebuke comes to both: the gift of God is not for sale! The Holy Spirit is God's gift for God's people.

Philip's encounter with the Ethiopian[4] chamberlain was from beginning to end the work of the Holy Spirit in an obedient person. Firstly, it was an "angel of the Lord" who told Philip to take the road that he was travelling; secondly, when Philip saw the chariot, it was the Spirit who told him to approach it. Each time, Philip discerned the prompting of the Holy Spirit and obeyed, not knowing what these actions would lead to. What a joyful surprise for Philip when, on getting near the chariot, he heard the official reading from the scroll of the prophet Isaiah concerning the Messiah! We are not given the flow of the conversation, but Philip must have asked the man who he was and where he was coming from. That is how we have so much biographical data about him: he was a eunuch, a finance official in the palace of the queen of Ethiopia and a proselyte, returning from a pilgrimage to Jerusalem. When the eunuch asked what the prophetic writings were about, "Philip began with that very passage of Scripture and told him the good news about Jesus" (8:35). The good news about Jesus must have included "repentance for the forgiveness of sins … in his name" (Luke 24:47), the acceptance of which was symbolized in the act of baptism, because when the eunuch saw that they were passing some water, he made the connection and asked to be baptized. As was the case for the city of Samaria, the impact on the life of the eunuch was one of great joy.

Throughout the story of his encounter with the Ethiopian eunuch Philip was listening, discerning where the Holy Spirit was leading, and listening to the eunuch as well. Philip asked him questions in order to know him better and understand what God was doing. He did not offer to translate for the eunuch the meaning of the passage; he first asked whether he understood what he was reading (8:30). It was then that Philip, beginning with "that very passage of Scripture … told him the good news about Jesus". Philip was aware that since it was the Holy Spirit who had led him down that route, he must know what he was about. Philip was constantly eager to know and see what the Holy Spirit had in mind on this path. When it was time to move, the Holy Spirit whisked him away! The eunuch continued on his way rejoicing (8:39). He would bring the good news to his people of Nubia, "the ends of the earth". From the beginning to the end of the story, it was the Holy Spirit at work; Philip discerned and obeyed.

---

4. The kingdom of Ethiopia here is not to be confused with today's region and country of Ethiopia. At that time, the kingdom of Ethiopia lay on the river Nile, south of Egypt, between Aswan and Khartoum – an area called Nubia.

To the Ends of the Earth: Among the Gentiles

The "ends of the earth" meant, from the perspective of the Jewish people, the Gentile world. The story of the first proclamation among the Gentiles is also surprising. Again, because it was a major barrier for the Jewish apostles, the Holy Spirit dragged their leader, Peter, to them. We have to remember that the Jews despised the Gentiles, considering them aliens to the purposes of God, "excluded from citizenship in Israel and foreigners to the covenants of the promise, without hope and without God in the world" (Eph 22:12). All familiar association with Gentiles was forbidden because they were declared unclean. They were to be treated like dogs; not pet dogs, like those I saw when I first visited Europe and North America, which eat food from the supermarket, have blankets and are members of the family! No; these were "dogs" like the African guard dogs that eat leftovers, bones and other scraps. The story of that encounter, in Acts 10:1–23, is captivating.

Luke begins this narrative in a very surprising manner: with the story of the Gentile, Cornelius, a Roman soldier with the rank of a centurion (equivalent to a captain or company commander). What is even more tantalizing is that God had been at work in the life of Cornelius. His and his family's devotion to God was not a secret, reflected in the way he gave to the poor and kept the public prayer calendar. Cornelius was possibly associated with the local synagogue and was respected by the Jewish community. But his was not devotion for show; he desired God and was seeking him, to know him and his glory. One afternoon at three o'clock, he took a break from his work and retreated to his prayer chamber, as was his custom. Jesus had told his disciples that "everyone who asks receives; the one who seeks finds; and to the one who knocks, the door will be opened" (Matt 7:8), and that is what happened. Luke tells us that Cornelius "distinctly saw an angel of God" who told him that God had taken notice of his devotion and desire for him. The angel then told Cornelius about Peter – with amazing detail concerning the name and address where he was staying – and said that Peter was God's messenger for him.

Consider how incredible this story is. Cornelius was not a proselyte, but just a God-fearing Gentile. That there were God-fearing Gentiles could be understood by a Jew, but that God should listen to them and answer their prayers was unheard of. How can it be, then, that we read that Cornelius' prayers reached God and that God was answering his prayers? That is the point: there is no one and no place beyond God's reach. He is the sovereign God who rewards all who seek him diligently.

As I reflect on this truth I think of the many people whom our traditions and theologies have disqualified as beyond God's reach. The Jewish perspectives on Gentiles as outsiders could be compared to some evangelical Christian perspectives on people of other faiths (Islam, Hinduism, etc.). Is it possible that God may be working in them, even though we consider them outsiders? No one is beyond the reach of the sovereign God! God may be at work in them in ways we are not able to see because we have excluded them in our minds. What is also amazing is that when God spoke through the angel, Cornelius recognized this as coming from God and obeyed immediately. He sent for Peter.

As all this was happening, unknown to Peter, he was getting on with the work of visiting the saints in Jerusalem and Judea. At the time, he was in Joppa at the home of Simon, a businessman dealing in hides and skins. Peter, like all the Jewish disciples of Jesus, kept the prayer hours. So at the noon hour of prayer Peter went up on the roof to pray. Meanwhile, lunch was being prepared. He was feeling hungry and dozed off for a time. Then he had a dream – or should we call it a nightmare? A sheet containing all kinds of creatures that the law of Moses declared unclean – four-footed animals, reptiles of all kinds and birds – came down. And to his shock and disbelief, a voice instructed him to "Get up ... Kill and eat". What was even more unbelievable for Peter was that this was the voice of the Lord. In his dream he protested vehemently. He could not and would not eat these creatures that were prohibited, for they were unclean. I wonder whether at this point Peter reminded himself and God of all those animals and creatures prohibited in Leviticus 11: "some that only chew the cud or only have a divided hoof ... The camel ... The hyrax ... The rabbit ... the pig ... the animals that move about the ground ...: the rat, any kind of great lizard, the gecko, the monitor lizard, the wall lizard, the skink and the chameleon" (11:4–7, 29–30). They were the very ones on the sheet. How on earth could Peter, a Jew, eat pork? Then the voice came two more times, telling Peter not to "call anything impure that God has made clean" (10:15). The command was irresistible because he recognized that this was not just a dream: God was speaking to him. It was a vision from God.

As Peter was making sense of this vision, perplexed and bewildered as to what God was saying to him, the men from Cornelius came to the door asking for him. Even before the message got to Peter, who was still puzzled, the Holy Spirit told him about them and instructed him: "Do not hesitate to go with them, for I have sent them" (10:20). Having descended from the roof and seeing the men he announced himself as the one, Peter, whom they were looking for. He learnt that they were Gentiles sent by another Gentile – a God-fearing man, Cornelius. Then it all became frighteningly clear. He had to let them in, for he was not to call anything unclean that God had made clean. God had shown him in no uncertain terms that he who gave the regulations in Leviticus now declared clean that which then had been declared unclean. For the first time in Peter's life he had to welcome Gentiles and sit with them in a home. They even stayed there overnight. We are not told what Simon the tanner had to say about all this. The apostle must have explained that God had broken the rules.

Compare and contrast the two visions of the two men. Of the two of them, who needed more persuading and converting to the purposes of God for the Gentiles? For Cornelius, all happened when he was wide awake, while Peter was in a half-asleep, half-awake state (in a trance) when he saw the vision. The angel spoke just once to Cornelius and he obeyed, while for Peter the Lord spoke three times, and even after that Peter was still wondering (Luke makes reference to his "wondering" (10:17) and "thinking" (10:19)).

All of us are like Peter in one way or another. We have long-held views and traditions, theological or otherwise, that hinder us from engaging with God in unfamiliar places. We must open ourselves up to God's mission. What was common to both Peter and Cornelius was their willingness to hear God. God prepared both for the encounter; the Holy Spirit was at work in Cornelius just as he was in Peter. It was significant that Peter went to Cornelius' house on invitation by Cornelius, in obedience to God's revelation through the angel. Peter also went with the men from Cornelius' house in obedience to the Holy Spirit. It was God at work, God's mission.

Peter travelled with some other believers from Joppa to Cornelius' home, which was a day's journey (10:23–24). When they arrived they found a large gathering of Cornelius' relatives and close friends. Peter did the unthinkable for a Jew: he entered Cornelius' house, the house of a Gentile. Cornelius had never experienced this before in his life. The Jews he had associated with thus far had treated him as an outcast. He had come to believe that as a non-Jew he was inferior to them. Now a Jew, a man of God, had entered his house. He fell down at Peter's feet as though in worship (10:25). The barrier and prejudice was not just on Peter's side; Cornelius had it too, albeit from the opposite angle. He too was captive to a history and tradition that created a dividing wall of hostility. The tragedy with barriers built between races, cultures, nations and ethnic groups is such that narratives of superiority and inferiority are told for so long that they become not merely traditions but the truth people live by. I was amazed in 1983, when I visited racially segregated South Africa, to find that it was not just that the white community believed they were superior to the blacks, but also that the blacks believed they were inferior. Both Peter and Cornelius needed to be freed from their prejudices and the captivity of their history and traditions by the gospel. Peter discovered this on entering Cornelius' house.

Peter's response was also amazing. He "made him get up. 'Stand up,' he said, 'I am only a man myself'" (10:26). Peter no longer defined his identity in Jewish versus Gentile terms. In Christ these identities were no longer significant. He was just a human being like Cornelius. What a transformation! What a conversion in Peter towards God's purposes and indeed his kingdom, a realization that there was no intrinsic distinction between Jew and Gentile! Peter gave up believing and acting out of the narrative of superiority. He then addressed the gathering, explaining how God had brought him there and testifying to the change that God had brought about on the journey to Cornelius' house. He began explaining that he should not really be there: "You are well aware that it is against our law for a Jew to associate with or visit a Gentile. But God has shown me that I should not call anyone impure or unclean" (10:28). He wanted them to know that it was God who had brought him there. He then asked why they had invited him to come. He did not want to presume upon them. Cornelius then narrated the story of how God had told him to invite him, and explained that they were all eager to hear the message from God.

It was clear to Peter that the same message was to be proclaimed among the Gentiles as among the Jews, for "God does not show favouritism, but accepts from every nation the one who fears him and does what is right" (10:34–35). He then declared to them the story of God's revelation and mission in Jesus Christ, the Lord of all, the one appointed judge of the living and the dead, and how that message was entrusted to his disciples, and he concluded with the offer of forgiveness for all who turned to him (10:36–43). Cornelius needed someone to explain to him who it was that was calling him! "While Peter was still speaking these words, the Holy Spirit came on all who heard the message" (10:44) and they spoke in tongues, praising God. God did among the Gentile believers what he had done on the day of Pentecost with the Jewish believers. It was understandable that the Jewish disciples who had come with Peter were astonished. It was only fitting that these Gentile believers should be baptized, just like those who were baptized at Pentecost. The Holy Spirit came upon them, sealing their membership of the kingdom

A Missional Community: Keeping in Step with the Holy Spirit

It was the coming of the Holy Spirit at Pentecost that propelled the disciples into mission: God's mission and theirs. It was (and remains) God's mission first and foremost. It was the Holy Spirit who gave Peter the clarity and boldness to proclaim the gospel to the thousands gathered in Jerusalem at Pentecost; it was the Holy Spirit who formed the disciples into a *koinonia* of witness; it was the Holy Spirit who gave the apostles the power to perform signs and wonders and face opposition and persecution boldly and joyfully, because they had been "counted worthy of suffering disgrace for the Name" (5:41). It was the providence of God that used the persecution that broke out in Jerusalem to thrust the disciples out into all Judea. Mortimer Arias writes, "The experience of the Holy Spirit brings the touch of God's presence, the power of God's healing, the liberating experience of forgiveness, the reality of fraternal community, the joy of celebration, the boldness in witness, the blossoming of hope, and the fruitfulness in mission."[5]

Thus the initiative to break through the first cross-cultural boundary, that between Jews and Samaritans, was taken by God. It was the death of Stephen and the hostile-violent Saul that forced the Jewish believers to proclaim the gospel beyond Jerusalem, even among the Samaritans. Although Jesus had clearly instructed his apostles that they were to be his witnesses beyond Jerusalem, "in all Judea and Samaria, and to the ends of the earth" (Acts 1:8), it was only persecution that brought them there. The Holy Spirit used persecution as the agency of spreading the good news of the presence of God's reign in Christ in Judea and Samaria. The Jewish-Samaritan barrier was not a barrier to the gospel; the barrier was cultural, in the minds of the Jewish disciples. It was their prejudice against the Samaritans that God had to deal with. The cultural barriers and prejudices with which the disciples accepted the gospel were broken down by the persecution and scattering and seeing God at work among the Samaritans just as he had been among the Jews. Once scattered, instead of being preoccupied with self-pity, mourning and

---

5. Mortimer Arias, *Announcing the Reign of God and the Subversive Memory of Jesus* (Philadelphia: Fortress), 61.

regretting the persecution and trying to regroup, the disciples spoke about Jesus wherever they went. The Holy Spirit was at work in them.

In most contexts today where there seem to be insurmountable barriers the gospel will progress only through persecution and suffering. We must always remember that the barriers are not against the gospel; they are against the culture of the disciples of Jesus, often in the minds of the disciples themselves. It is in relocating to the perceived hostile cultures, led by the Holy Spirit, that we will be amazed to see how God has been at work among those we thought hostile. Consider the remarkable breakthrough that Philip experienced in Samaria, to the extent that one of the sorcerers, Simon, who had practised sorcery in Samaria and had clearly become renowned among the Samaritans, was brought to his knees in submission before the power of the gospel. It seems that today, the disciples of Christ have not responded to God's prompting to relocate to the so-called hostile cultures. Thus God is bringing them in, forcing them upon us. Consider the way Islam is growing all over the world, including in countries that thought of themselves as Christian. May God open our eyes and ears to discern what he is doing by all these cultural movements!

Likewise, the apostle Peter's invitation by Cornelius was all the work of God. We learn from Peter's experience that entering a different culture presents us with an opportunity to experience Jesus in a new way, to know him better and deepen our appreciation of God's world and God's mission. Christian mission in this sense is not a task we engage in to convert others. Rather, it is being caught up in God's project of drawing us and all the nations to himself; it is Jesus taking us to different places to show us who he really is as well as introducing us to those who are his that he "must bring … also" (John 10:16). The process of breaking new ground where the gospel crosses from one culture to another (which is what is usually meant by Christian mission) cannot be posited as uni-directional, as has traditionally been the case. Similarly, conversion cannot be assigned simply to the receptor cultures. Since authentic Christian mission originates in God's mission, Jesus' invitation to follow him to another culture bids us to re-examine our own perspectives, repent and believe the good news of the kingdom; it is an invitation to a journey of conversion, being transformed by God's grace and being drawn into fellowship with others whom he is drawing to himself through us.

The challenge is in discerning the voice of the Holy Spirit when he sends, and in obeying! That is one great lesson from the story of the progress of the gospel from Jerusalem, in all Judea and Samaria and to the Gentile world. The entire path was determined by the Holy Spirit. The responsibility of the apostles and disciples was to discern and obey the Holy Spirit. That is why the apostles devoted themselves to "prayer and the ministry of the word" (Acts 6:4). Through teaching and prayer the apostles led the growing church in understanding the will and purpose of God. Understanding, discerning and obeying: that is what Christian mission is primarily about. One of the biggest problems today is the over-dependence on methods, strategies, institutions and technologies in Christian mission. The challenge before us is to discern the voice of the Holy Spirit amid the noises of our histories, cultures and lifestyles. Priority must be given to Bible teaching and prayer. The demons of our times are akin to that of which Jesus said, "This kind can come out only by prayer" (Mark 9:29). There is an urgent need to rediscover authentic Bible teaching and prayer in order to discern the voice of the Holy Spirit for us today.

Mission strategy must first and foremost be about listening to the Holy Spirit to discover what he is doing, and then in obedience following. After all, it is the Holy Spirit in whom we live and he in us. It is he who "will prove the world to be in the wrong about sin and righteousness and judgement" (John 16:8). It is he who, as Jesus said, brings glory to him by making known to us what he has received from Christ (John 14:16). And it is the Holy Spirit who knows where Jesus' flock is, the "other sheep that are not of this sheepfold" (John 10:16) that Jesus must bring in. But it is only in stepping out in obedience, relocating to those places and spaces to which he invites us, that we become amazed, like Philip, at what God has been doing in preparing the ground and what he will do with the feeble and simple proclamation of Christ.

Mission strategy should also be about listening to those among whom the Lord takes us. Philip did not only listen to the Holy Spirit; he also listened to the eunuch. In fact, by listening to the eunuch he was listening to the Holy Spirit, discovering what it was that he was doing in him. A disciple's disposition is always that of a listener and a learner. It is also a reflection of faith in the Lord of the mission. He is at work in his world. A lack of listening is not only a sign of arrogance and triumphalism; it also shows that we are not aware that God is already at work wherever he calls us. By listening, we learn not only the language of the Holy Spirit, but also the language of those among whom he calls us. Learning the language entails translation. This is the other responsibility of the disciple: telling the story and work of Christ in the language of those to whom he calls us. Mission history is full of stories of how the translation of the Scriptures into local languages sparked a massive turning to Jesus of entire communities. After all, the Spirit who sends us has spoken to them in their language! As Paul put it, "Since [as disciples of Jesus] we live by the Spirit, let us keep in step with the Spirit" (Gal 5:25). That is the ethos and logic of Christian mission.

This raises an important question. If it is Jesus who brings them in, what then is the purpose for the Christian activity we call missions and evangelism? It is first important to say what it is not. The purpose of missions and evangelism is not to convert. As Lesslie Newbigin has stated, "Evangelism is not some technique by the means of which people are persuaded to change their minds and think like us. Evangelism is the telling of good news, but what changes people's minds and converts their wills is always the mysterious work of the sovereign Holy Spirit, and we are not permitted to know more than a little of his secret working."[6]

When followers of Jesus declare the good news of Jesus, the people Jesus has already earmarked as his own will hear his voice and turn to him. Evangelism may be considered the work of a believer in the search of brothers and sisters who have not yet believed, knowing that they will believe because they already belong to Christ. They do not yet know his voice because they have not yet heard it. It is fundamental that we realize that, as simplistic as it may sound, what brings men and women to know Jesus as Lord and Saviour is always his work by his Spirit, which is always beyond our understanding or control and is always the result of the love and presence of Jesus himself.

That was certainly the experience of the apostles and the Jewish believers when it came to accepting that the Samaritans and, worse still, the Gentiles would be accepted into the fold of followers of Jesus. We have seen what it took for Peter to accept that the Gentiles were part of God's plan of salvation, by his vision and encounter with Cornelius and his household. It was equally hard for the rest of the apostles and Jewish believers. Luke tells us that when the "apostles and the believers throughout Judea heard that the Gentiles also had received the word of God", they protested to Peter when he returned to Jerusalem, rebuking him for having gone into the house of uncircumcised men and eaten with them (Acts 11:1–2). Peter was only let off the hook when he explained that it had nothing to do with him but God, who had given the Holy Spirit to the Gentile believers in the same way he had done for them, the Jewish believers. "Who was I to think that I could

---

6. Lesslie Newbigin, *Evangelism in the City* (1987), in Paul Weston, *Lesslie Newbigin: Missionary Theologian – A Reader* (London: SPCK, 2006), 144.

stand in God's way?" Peter protested (11:17). It was only then that the Jewish believers reluctantly concluded that God had "*even to Gentiles* ... granted repentance that leads to life" (11:18, italics mine). It took a special meeting of the leadership of the church in Jerusalem and Judea, the apostles and other leading Jewish believers – the council at Jerusalem (Acts 15) – for the Jewish believers to accept that Gentiles could be accepted as fellow believers in Christ, albeit with a few requirements. We will follow that story when we recount the birth of a community of believers in Antioch, another amazing work of the Holy Spirit.

7

Churches of God: Communities of the Holy Spirit

Therefore, remember that formerly you who are Gentiles by birth and called "uncircumcised" by those who call themselves "the circumcision" (which is done in the body by human hands) – remember that at that time you were separate from Christ, excluded from citizenship in Israel and foreigners to the covenants of the promise, without hope and without God in the world. But now in Christ Jesus you who once were far away have been brought near by the blood of Christ...

Consequently, you are no longer foreigners and strangers, but fellow citizens with God's people and also members of his household, built on the foundation of the apostles and prophets, with Christ Jesus himself as the chief cornerstone. In him the whole building is joined together and rises to become a holy temple in the Lord. And in him you too are being built together to become a dwelling in which God lives by his Spirit. (Eph 2:11–13, 19–22)

Therefore, since we are surrounded by such a great cloud of witnesses, let us throw off everything that hinders and the sin that so easily entangles. And let us run with perseverance the race marked out for us, fixing our eyes on Jesus, the pioneer and perfecter of faith. For the joy that was set before him he endured the cross, scorning its shame, and sat down at the right hand of the throne of God. (Heb 12:1–2)

One Sunday morning in the late 1980s I was in Nairobi, the capital of Kenya. While the date is vague in my memory, the experience is vivid. I decided I would attend the later church service at All Saints Cathedral, an Anglican church in the heart of the city. I was greeted by singing at every corner – congregations meeting indoors and outdoors. Next door to the YMCA hostel where I was staying, a crowd meeting in an auditorium of a student centre was blasting out its songs. At one street corner others were meeting in traditional church buildings conspicuous by their distinctly ecclesiastical architecture; there were no fewer than three such buildings and they all looked full. I checked later and I learnt that they were Lutheran, Catholic and Presbyterian. In the adjacent Uhuru Park were clusters of people evidently engaged in an act of worship. The group that struck me most were all dressed in white robes with white headgear. Towards the east end of Uhuru Park I saw a huge tent into which people were streaming, evidently for a church service. As I was trying to make sense of everything I noticed the sound of drums behind me. I turned. A group of men and women, and boys and girls of all ages, were marching, singing to the beat of a drum, led by a man dressed in a purple gown. I finally made it to the cathedral, where there was also a large congregation of the faithful. After the service I asked one of the locals about the groups I had seen in Uhuru Park. He confirmed my suspicions: they were church worship services.

Nairobi is also home to myriad para-church, missionary and Christian non-governmental organizations (NGOs), which on Monday mornings open their offices to "serve" Christ, so they all claim. Yet it is noteworthy that in spite of a history of Christian presence in Kenya of over 150 years and in a country reckoned to have over 70 per cent of its population claiming a church affiliation, Nairobi still boasts the highest density of European and North American Christian missionaries in Africa. I was told by one of the student leaders in the Christian Union at the University of Nairobi in the early 1990s – then a campus of about eight thousand students – that there were no fewer than fifteen Christian organizations and churches, indigenous and foreign, working among students, often holding meetings at the same time during the week.

All these groups – churches and organizations – claim to be communities of Christ. That they have different forms and structures, both physical and institutional, is not really the issue. The question is, What is it that legitimizes any group or community to claim a connection to the biblical narrative of the people of God in the Old Testament and the new community in the New Testament? In this chapter we turn our attention to the record in the Acts of the Apostles of the earliest of the churches to better understand the nature and character of the new community. It is the story of the church beyond Jerusalem and Judea: in Antioch, Philippi, Corinth and Ephesus, cities that the Jewish believers in Jerusalem would have characterized as being at the "ends of the earth" and whose churches emerged in the apostolic era. What is it that marked out those early disciples in the different cities as communities of Christ?

In Antioch (Acts 11:19–30; 13:1–4)

The scattering after the persecution that brought Philip to Samaria and subsequently brought Samaria to the attention of the apostles was the same movement that brought other disciples to Antioch. At the time, Antioch was the third-largest city of the Roman Empire, after Rome and Alexandria. It was a large metropolis, a melting pot of cultures and nationalities. Luke identifies two groups of disciples that came to Antioch: the first, constituted by Jewish believers of Palestinian origin, are referred to as Jews; and the second are called Grecian Jews – Greek-speaking Jews, men from Cyprus and Cyrene. The second group is of primary interest because unlike the first, who proclaimed Christ only to the Jews, the second group spoke to Gentiles (Greeks) as well. The story was the same wherever the gospel was preached in the power of the Holy Spirit: "The Lord's hand was with them, and a great number of people believed and turned to the Lord" (11:21). In every case we have seen, all that was required of the apostles and disciples was to proclaim the good news of Jesus faithfully and clearly, in the language of the people. The Holy Spirit did the rest, bringing conviction, repentance and turning to God.

The news reached the apostles in Jerusalem of the large number of people turning to the Lord in Antioch. The story that needed checking was not the work among the Jews in Antioch, but that among the Gentiles. Joseph, who had proved himself trustworthy among the apostles in Jerusalem and was nicknamed Barnabas, the "son of encouragement", was sent to Antioch. Luke simply describes him as "a good man, full of the Holy Spirit and faith". It needed a man full of the Holy Spirit to discern the work of the Holy Spirit. Barnabas' visit is summarized in Acts 11:23: "When he arrived and saw what the grace of God had done, he was glad and encouraged them all to remain true to the Lord with all their hearts." The work of the Holy Spirit was visible in what Luke calls "what the grace of God had done". Barnabas encouraged them to continue in that grace. He realized that, like the believers in Jerusalem, in order to grow in grace they needed teaching. He therefore sought out Saul, whose life God had turned around and was now an apostle, to come and teach. They continued with this for a year. Then came the interruption by the Holy Spirit, recorded in Acts 13, where the Holy Spirit told the gathered believers that he wanted Barnabas and Saul set apart for "the work to which I have called them". The community released them and sent them off.

The way Luke summarizes Barnabas' experience of the life of the believers in Antioch – that God's "grace" was evident among them (11:23) – is startling. God was at work among them and there was evidence of it. What was the evidence of God's grace that Barnabas saw? The word translated "grace" is the Greek *charis*, from which the English word "charismatic" is derived; this word is related to *charisma* ("gift"), and *charismata* ("gifts of the Holy Spirit", as in 1 Cor 12:1–11) . Gifts of the Holy Spirit are therefore gifts of grace. There is a direct connection between grace and the Holy Spirit. Wherever the Holy Spirit is at work, there the grace of God is at work. What was it, then, that happened in the church in Antioch that reflected the working of the Holy Spirit? In today's language we are really asking, What does an authentic charismatic (Spirit-filled) community look like? Let us look at Luke's account of the life of the church in Antioch closely.

First of all, the story began with the proclamation of the good news of Jesus Christ to the Antiochians, Jews and Gentiles alike. When Barnabas came he too proclaimed the good news about Jesus. The result in both cases was many people turning to the Lord. The first mark, then, of the presence of the Holy Spirit in a community is that the gospel will be continually proclaimed. This is evangelism. It should be noted that the gospel was proclaimed not just to the outsiders; the believers needed to continue to hear the good news expounded, constantly hearing the call to turn their entire being towards God and his purposes and continue to follow Jesus. Hence there was a link between the preaching of the gospel and the teaching of the apostles: the teaching of the apostles, which was the expounding of the good news of the gospel to the believers, gave them confidence to proclaim it to the outsiders.

The second mark of the presence of the Holy Spirit is seen in the fact that the proclamation was not just made in words, but the very nature of their community life spoke volumes to the onlookers about the subject and centre of their devotion. They proclaimed Christ and lived Christ in the full view of the outsiders, so that the people around them, in scorn, called them "Christ-ians" (11:26)! For a primarily Gentile audience, Christ was like the second name for Jesus; hence Christians were the people of the Christ party. This was especially so because they defied the usual characterizations of Jew or Gentile. The leaders of the community (13:1) reflected this multi-cultural and multi-national character. Barnabas and Saul were Jewish; Lucius is a Greek name, and Cyrene was in present-day North Africa, so he may have been of dark complexion, but in any case he was most certainly Gentile and Greek culturally; Manaen had links with Herod's family and therefore was politically favourable towards the Romans (the Herodians were a Jewish political party that supported Roman occupation); and Simeon called Niger – meaning black – has been associated with Simon of Cyrene (Luke 23:26). They could not be called a professional guild, as was the case in Roman society where people worked and traded in guilds. There was no common trade or profession that they shared on the basis of which they could have been called a guild. But they were still a visible community, clearly of a different kind. While the ethnic and cultural composition of the community reflected the ethnic and cultural composition of Antioch, what bound them together was not their ethnicity, culture or trade, but Jesus the Christ.

A word here is necessary about the other collective titles that Luke uses in referring to the disciples. One study, "Names for Christians and Christianity in Acts" by H. J. Cadbury,[1] has pointed to as many as nineteen of these. There are six that recur most frequently. The first one is "disciples", a term certainly originating with Jesus while he was still with them in the body as a reference to his personal followers. The second is "believers", coming from the expression that the ones whom the Lord added to their number were those "who accepted" (e.g. Acts 2:41) and how the apostles in their preaching declared that "everyone who believes in him receives forgiveness of sins" (10:43). The third is "brothers" (14:2), a term that the Jews used of themselves as the people of God and now appropriate for the new people of God, the new family that was made up of believing Jews and Gentiles. The fourth is "saints" or "the Lord's people" (9:13, 32), a title used in the Old Testament of the people of Israel and so applied to the disciples of Jesus as the community that had taken the place of Israel in the purposes of God. The fifth

---

1. In F. J. Foakes-Jackson and K. Lake, eds., *The Beginnings of Christianity*, vol. 5 (London: Macmillan, 1933), 375–92.

is "church", which we discussed in Chapter 1. Lastly, is the title "the people of God" (15:14; 18:10), which, like "brothers" and "saints", originates in the Old Testament. In this book the collective title "new community" is used as well, to capture the idea of the continuity of God's purposes through a people, as well as the discontinuity, reflecting something new and radical in Jesus.

The third mark of the presence of the Holy Spirit was that the believers gathered together regularly. It was not just their gathering together that marked them out, but also what they did when they gathered. Just as it was with the nascent Jesus community in Jerusalem, so it was with the one in Antioch: when they gathered they received apostolic teaching, initially from the apostolic delegate, Barnabas, and then later from Saul, the persecutor-turned-apostle. What an irony that Saul was the teacher to ground the disciples in Antioch in their faith in Jesus! The scattering that had brought the disciples to Antioch resulted from the persecution of the believers in Jerusalem led by Saul, and it was the same Saul whom the Holy Spirit had called to teach the believers in Antioch! One of the things that qualified Saul was that he understood well the patriarchal origins of the Messiah, having been schooled in Jewish law and customs and having been a Pharisee. After Jesus revealed himself to him on the road to Damascus he called Saul to be his "chosen instrument to proclaim my [Jesus'] name to the Gentiles and their kings and to the people of Israel" (Acts 9:15). After that, he was received as part of the apostolic team in Jerusalem.

What exactly was the role of the apostles' teaching? We have already seen how Jesus' appointment of the Twelve signalled the beginning of a new people of God in the place of Israel. As the foundation of the new Israel it was to them that Jesus committed the responsibility of teaching the good news of the kingdom. Apostolic teaching centred on God's initiative, purpose and mission, beginning with creation, his revelation through Abraham, Moses and Israel, to the final fulfilment in Christ, as well as the appropriate response to God's initiative and action. Thus in each of the situations where the gospel crossed a new cultural barrier, it was the responsibility of the apostles to authenticate the believers as disciples of Christ, as we have seen in the case of Samaria. That is why it was necessary for Barnabas to come to Antioch, as the apostolic ambassador, to authenticate the work in Antioch. By the time the apostolic era ended, the foundations had been set, and the Scriptures penned by the apostles were circulating. It should be understood that the only way a book got into the canon of the New Testament was either because it was written by one of the apostles or because it contained evidence that it was authorized by one of them. The apostolic authority we possess today is the Holy Scriptures, and not any office or personality in the church. In that sense, there are no apostles today who are equivalent to the first apostles. The centre of the life of Jesus communities today, as then, must be the apostolic teaching, which for us is the Holy Scriptures.

As with the Jerusalem believers, so it was with those in Antioch: when they gathered together, they shared their needs and resources. It is in the context of this sharing that the Holy Spirit moved Agabus to predict the famine that was to come and which would have a serious impact on the believers in Jerusalem. This is a case of the Holy Spirit giving his gifts for the edification of the body. In response, the believers in Antioch took a collection for the more affected believers in Jerusalem. Grace at work among them resulted in generosity, for "the disciples, as each one was able, decided to provide help for the brothers and sisters living in Judea" (11:29). Their care for believers went beyond their locality. We should not confuse this with partnership in mission: it was simply an expression of *koinonia* – belonging to Christ together. They recognized that although they and the believers in Jerusalem were in different cities and circumstances, they belonged together and therefore were mutually dependent on one another. As with the Jesus community in Jerusalem, *koinonia* in Antioch meant meeting one another's material needs.

The incident recorded in Acts 13:1–3, during which the elders released two from among them, was a very significant turning point, not only for the disciples in Antioch, but also for the entire account of the book of Acts. It was not only the evidence of God's grace among them; it is also the moment the narrative shifts to the story of the work of the Holy Spirit in the Gentile world. The believers in Antioch were a seeking and listening community, desiring to continue in the purposes of God. The kind of prayer and fasting portrayed (13:2) was not for show or ritual or for a project they sought to achieve; it seems to have been part of their routine, communing with the Lord and one another as they listened to apostolic teaching. They were together seeking God's will and purpose. I am sure they were surprised when the Holy Spirit asked them to let Barnabas and Saul move on. I call it a disruption, because everything was going on very well under their leadership. But discerning that this might be God's will, they then more intentionally sought to confirm that it was the Holy Spirit speaking. The Holy Spirit confirmed that it was his will to let Saul and Barnabas go and do the work he had prepared for them, and had prepared them for. When God's will is revealed, obedience is the appropriate response of all the believers. Then "they placed their hands on them and sent them off" (13:3). Luke continues, "The two of them, sent on their way by the Holy Spirit, went down to Seleucia and sailed from there to Cyprus" (13:4). The evidence of grace was their seeking God's will and their obedience. The outworking of this was missionary outreach. The elders therefore sent Saul and Barnabas in obedience to the Holy Spirit. The sending of the elders in Antioch was subordinate to the sending of the Holy Spirit.

Where did we get the idea of a "sending church"? It is not the church that sends; the church is sent. It is not the church that sends; Jesus sends by his Spirit. We, the disciples of Christ, the new community, are the sent people of God.[2] Now as then, it is God who sends, and he sends those he has called first as his disciples. He then brings those he sends to the places where he is already at work in his world. He is the one who said to the early disciples, "As the Father has sent me, I am sending you" (John 20:21). The church sends no one anywhere! If the church dares send, it had better be in obedience to the one who sends it; in which case we should find a more appropriate word to describe that action. Is it not the case that because most of those we call missionaries are indeed sent by "their home churches" as part of "their missions programme", seeking to convert the "unreached peoples" of the world, that they plant churches like their home churches, multiplying members (we call them denominations)? It all feels like club work, club expansion! When it finally all crumbles we should not complain!

The church in Antioch thus gives us a portrait of a community in the Holy Spirit showing the evidence of the grace of God: an evangelistic community, proclaiming within and without the good news of Jesus Christ; a teaching community, where the apostolic truth of the gospel was the centre of its life; a caring community, locally and beyond, wherever there were brethren, an expression of *koinonia* in Christ; a charismatic community, in which the gifts of the Spirit were at work for mutual edification; a multi-ethnic, multi-cultural community, reflecting in its composition the composite society of which it was a part but defined by the unity they shared in Christ; a praying and seeking community, deriving its life and direction from God; and a missionary community, in obedience to God who called it into his mission. This gives us a useful checklist for examining the nature of our

---

2. This is well articulated in Darrell L. Guder, ed., *Missional Church: A Vision for the Sending of the Church in North America* (Grand Rapids, Mich.: Eerdmans, 1998).

church communities: whether they are the evidence of the grace of God in the cities or villages where they are.

Antioch is significant in the entire story of the new community as it was because of the remarkable turning to Jesus there that the apostles faced squarely, as never before, the matter of accepting the Gentiles as fellow believers. The spark was the response of some Jewish believers from Judea who, hearing the news of many Gentiles turning to faith in Jesus, were anxious to preserve Jewish distinctiveness as the DNA for the new community. They went to Antioch and "were teaching the brothers: 'Unless you are circumcised, according to the custom taught by Moses, you cannot be saved'" (15:1). Barnabas and Saul (now known as Paul) were back in Antioch at the time, having returned from the mission that the Holy Spirit through the church had commissioned them for, with the story of how "the Gentiles had been converted" (15:3). A debate ensued between the Jewish zealots and the apostles. It could not be resolved in Antioch. Appeal was made for the apostles and elders in Jerusalem to come to the aid of the church in Antioch. Paul and Barnabas were sent as the delegates of the church in Antioch. On their arrival in Jerusalem a meeting was convened of the apostles and elders to hear Paul and Barnabas. In the meeting were believers from the party of the Pharisees, who protested that the "Gentiles must be circumcised and required to keep the law of Moses" (15:6).

The gathering was an opportunity for the apostle Peter to tell his story, of how God "had accepted them [the Gentiles] by giving the Holy Spirit to them, just as he did to us" (15:8). Peter was emphatic that by this God had levelled the ground: "He did not discriminate between us [Jews] and them [Gentiles]." He was unequivocal: "We believe it is through the grace of our Lord Jesus that we are saved, just as they are" (15:11). Paul and Barnabas' submission was equally compelling. Then James concluded, affirming that what they were experiencing in their time was the fulfilment of the promise of God through the prophets: that from among the Gentiles would be those who bore the Lord's name. It was therefore not necessary to demand that the Gentiles be circumcised; there was no need for Gentiles to become Jews in order for them to be considered fellow believers. The compromise reached to keep the Jewish zealots in the fold was to require of the Gentile believers the adherence to basic but important food regulations, in order to keep both at the same table: the Gentiles should "abstain from food polluted by idols, from sexual immorality, from the meat of strangled animals and from blood"

(15:20). This was the message carried to all the young churches where Paul and Barnabas had seen the remarkable turning to Jesus among the Gentiles.

This was a landmark resolution. Gentiles did not have to become Jews in order to be accepted by the new community, because God had shown that he had already accepted those who believed by giving them the Holy Spirit. The gift of the Holy Spirit authenticated "belonging to God". There was no need for any other requirement; no religious ritual or mark. The new people of God, anywhere, were community by and of the Holy Spirit.

In Philippi (Acts 16:6–15)

The Acts of the Apostles (or, as we noted earlier we could call it, the Acts of the Holy Spirit) is full of drama, with many unscripted and unpredictable scenes. The story of how the gospel reached the people in Philippi is one such drama. It began with Paul and his companions in Troas, a place they did not plan to come to. We have a fairly detailed description of this journey because Luke, the author, joined Paul, Timothy and Silas. Their intention when they left Syrian Antioch seems to have been to break new ground in the regions of the province of Asia, but for some reason the Holy Spirit did not allow them to, so they passed through without preaching at all. Plan B was to get to the border of Mysia and enter the region of Bithynia to the north-east, but on reaching the border "the Spirit of Jesus would not allow them to" (16:7). That is how they found their way to Troas, a Roman colony, where Luke joined them. For them, getting to Troas was simply accidental; at least, it was not according to their plans. But clearly it was according to the Holy Spirit's plan.

I have often wondered how Paul and his companions in both situations discerned that the Holy Spirit was the one stopping them. Luke reports that in the first instance it was the Holy Spirit who "kept … [them] from preaching the word in the province of Asia"; then, when it came to entering Bithynia at the border, "the Spirit of Jesus would not allow them" to enter. I suggest that in the first instance they had a deep sense within themselves that it was not the right thing to do; in the second, there was a physical barrier that Paul and his team recognized as Jesus stopping them. Whatever it was, they realized that neither Asia nor Bithynia was the leading of the Holy Spirit. Note that they did not even attempt to preach in Troas. It was important that in preaching anywhere they were certain it was with the direction of the Holy Spirit. The question in their minds then was "What next?" It was during the night that Paul saw the vision of the man from Macedonia. Paul brought it to the attention of his colleagues, and together they determined that it was not a dream to ignore but a vision from the Lord telling them to go to Macedonia. The key word in the text is "concluding" (16:10); it was something that they discerned together. Just as it was at Antioch, when the Holy Spirit spoke to the elders of the church together, so it was for Paul and his companions now: the Holy Spirit led them together. The opening of the European frontier was the plan and work of the Holy Spirit. Philippi was their first stop in Europe, near the eastern end of the great Roman highway, the *Via Egnatia*, nestled on the edge of the plain at the initial descent up to a considerable acropolis.

Philippi was a Roman colony in the province of Macedonia. A Roman colony was an important political and commercial centre within the empire. It was more like a piece of Rome abroad: the Latin language was used; Roman law controlled the local administration and taxes; and the popular culture was Roman. The population of Philippi at the time of Paul's visit was both Roman and Greek. Although Latin was the official language, Greek was the predominant language of commerce and everyday life. Our interest in the story of the church in Philippi concerns who constituted the first community of believers there, how they became believers and what characterized their life together. First there was Lydia, a businesswoman, and her household; secondly, the slave girl who was delivered from demonic possession; and thirdly, the jailer of the prison in Philippi.

Paul and his companions met Lydia at a Jewish prayer meeting. Paul's custom in any city was to begin with a community of devoted Jews and proselytes. Traditionally this would have been a synagogue, but where there were no synagogues there usually was a place where they would congregate for prayer. So they joined a place of prayer where devout women gathered, among them Lydia – a businesswoman and possibly a proselyte, given her Greek name, who traded in purple dye for which her native town, Thyatira, was famous. Paul and his companions spoke to the women about Jesus and "the Lord opened" Lydia's heart to receive the message. She believed and was baptised, along with her entire household. What is intriguing is that the evidence that they acknowledged her faith in Jesus to be authentic was their accepting an invitation to stay at her house (16:15); sharing in earthly goods was evidence of sharing in the Spirit. Paul and his companions were persuaded of her faith so they moved into her house and made it a base for their continuing mission in Philippi.

Paul and his team continued to join the others at the place of prayer. It was as they were going there one day that they were accosted by a slave girl who persisted in shouting out who Paul and his companions were, "servants of the Most High God, who are telling you the way to be saved" (16:17). The surprising thing is that the demon got it right, but it was not a positive testimony given the source; the girl was possessed by a demon that predicted the future, by which she brought income to her owners. She was a celebrity in the city for the wrong reasons. This went on for a few days until Paul could not take it any longer. He commanded the demon to leave, "in the name of Jesus Christ" (16:18), and the girl was freed.

A word concerning demon possession in our times is appropriate here. There are some in the church worldwide, particularly in the West, who deny its reality and dismiss it simply as superstition. There are others who see a demon in every sickness or malaise and are quick to prescribe exorcism and deliverance as the means of healing and restoring wholeness. Neither position has biblical ground; both betray and deny biblical and contemporary witness. Demon possession is real. There are sicknesses and maladies that result from demon possession, and nothing short of exorcism and deliverance will restore health, both of individuals and societies; and there are others which result simply from biological malfunction and for which treatment with other biological–chemical products (which is what medicine is) is adequate.

How sad that the deliverance of the slave girl, rather than result in rejoicing for all, caused anger and outrage among some. Certainly her freedom meant financial loss to her owners. Indeed, when Paul exorcised the spirit that possessed her, he exorcised the source of her owners' income as well. In anger her owners framed charges against Paul and his companions, alleging that they were subverting the cultural norms and customs of the Romans. It is amazing how easy it is to get a mob mobilized for any cause whatsoever and how gullible political leaders can be! The text talks of magistrates (16:20), but they were not the equivalent of magistrates today; they were more like today's elected political leaders. There was uproar, and the authorities in Philippi ordered Paul and Silas' arrest; they were flogged, bound and thrown into a maximum-security prison.

Sadly, even today there are those who are beneficiaries of the darkness and oppression that continue to dehumanize many in our societies and cultures. Such will never rejoice at the signs of the kingdom of God restoring dignity to the oppressed. The reason why the oppressors fear the day of freedom of the oppressed is because that freedom is their loss; therefore they work to maintain systems and structures of oppression and resist any initiatives towards liberation. That is why the gospel of the redemptive reign of God will always provoke opposition; it is good news of justice for the marginalized and the oppressed. The gain in the kingdom of God is loss in the kingdom of darkness, hence the resistance and persecution faced by those who carry the good news. I experienced this first-hand in Uganda at the beginning of 2012. I was involved, together with other civil society leaders, in a campaign against the continuing plundering of public resources by politicians and other public officials in government. One of the strategies we employed was publishing a regular newsletter that exposed corruption. One would have expected support and cooperation from the government of the day, but our efforts to fight this were met with brute force from the government. Government security trailed, harassed and maligned the leaders of this initiative. One day, as I was distributing the newsletter on the campus of Makerere University, I was arrested by police, detained in a police cell for a day and charged in court for inciting violence. Charges were dropped three months later, but the corrupt regime did not relent from continuing to undermine our efforts to fight the vice of corruption, because curtailing corruption was tantamount to undermining the wealth and power of the regime.

In prison, instead of mourning and crying, Paul and Silas were praying and singing in the full view and hearing of their fellow prisoners – singing the good news of the kingdom of God, and telling the good news of salvation in Jesus. They were prisoners of a different kind! Then a miracle: an earthquake that was local to the prison building flung open all the prison doors. Understandably the jailer was frightened that the prisoners had escaped and was preparing to commit suicide when Paul, who together with Silas ensured that all the prisoners stayed put, shouted out to assure the jailer that all was well and he had no reason to fear for his life. The message on the lips of Paul and Silas of the good news of salvation, the transformed life of the messengers and the miracle at the prison all caused the jailer to ask, "Sirs, what must I do to be saved?" The jailer must have been highly ranked, given the freedom he had in handling the prisoners. He took them to his house so that his entire house could hear the message. They all believed and were baptized, "he and his whole household" (16:34).

It was these three groups – Lydia and her household; the slave girl; and the jailer and his household – that constituted the "brothers and sisters" that Paul and his companions found meeting in Lydia's house after they were released (16:40). Consider the socio-economic diversity: Lydia, a wealthy woman with her wealthy family; a prison warder, a Roman civil servant, and his family, possibly of the artisan class; and a slave girl, part of the dregs of society. Note too their religious diversity: one a proselyte; another a Gentile; and as for the slave girl, simply a property, for that is what a slave was. But in Christ they were brothers and sisters, members of the same family. No socio-economic barriers; no regional–cultural barriers; and no gender barriers: a reconciled community – that is what an authentic church is.

We are able to piece together what else characterized their common life by looking at Paul's letter to this church, written from his first Roman imprisonment at least ten years later, as well as his testimony about them to other churches, notably to the church in Corinth (2 Cor 8:1–5). Four things stand out: they were a community of joy; they contributed generously to the work of the gospel beyond them; they suffered for their faith; and there were tensions and conflicts.

The joy in the prison cell that the jailer saw, as Paul and Silas sang the good news of Jesus, and the joy with which he believed with his entire household (16:34) remained a characteristic of the young church. Paul's letter to the Philippians has been called the epistle of joy; sixteen times the noun "joy" or the verb "rejoice" is used in the letter. Giving testimony to the Corinthians about the Philippians' "sharing in the service of the Lord's people", Paul wrote how they gave generously "in the midst of a very severe trial, their overflowing joy and their extreme poverty" (2 Cor 8:2, 4). Out of this overflowing joy they had given "as much as they were able, and even beyond their ability" (8:3), because they considered it a "privilege" (8:4). They gave out of gratitude to God for the wonder of the good news of the gospel. The disciples in Philippi may therefore be called a *koinonia* of joy, the fruit of the work of the Holy Spirit.

The Philippians' generosity, about which Paul commended them as an example to the Corinthians, was the second characteristic of their life together. Lydia had showed it in the way she opened her home and put her resources at the disposal of the believers. It is no wonder that Paul, writing to them more than ten years later, commended them for their continued "partnership [*koinonia*] in the gospel" which they had shown "from the first day" (Phil 1:5). He acknowledged to them that they were the first church who "shared with me in the matter of giving and receiving" (Phil 4:15). This was in spite of their suffering; as we read the letter it is evident that the believers in Philippi were undergoing some form of opposition and suffering. Whether it was the same group that had caused Paul and Silas' imprisonment when they first came to Philippi who continued to oppose them is not clear; but the letter is explicit that they were undergoing suffering for the sake of the gospel

(Phil 1:27–30). While commending them to the Corinthians, Paul also made reference to their "severe trial" and "extreme poverty" (2 Cor 8:2). In fact, it is arguable that one of the reasons for the letter to the Philippians was to thank them for the expression of their care through the agency of Epaphroditus, the courier of their message to Paul and then of Paul's letter itself (Phil 2:25).

In addition to the external pressures, the Jesus community in Philippi had some internal tensions. Paul mentions explicitly a disagreement between Euodia and Syntyche that had become public in the fellowship. But that was possibly not the only challenge to the fellowship. Clearly, unity of the community was being strained, because Paul pleaded with them to live a life worthy of the cause of the gospel by standing firm together, "striving together as one" (Phil 1:27), as well as striving to consider the interests of the other above self. It was important that the internal life of the community reflect the nature of the gospel all the way: a reconciled and reconciling community; otherwise they would no longer be a credible witness to the kingdom of God.

The Christian community in Philippi has much to teach us: not because it demonstrates anything that Jesus did not say, but because by it we see in real life how a people that otherwise have nothing in common become one as a result of the gospel. But that unity is not to be taken for granted; for as we saw earlier, the enemy is always sowing weeds wherever the good seed of the kingdom is planted. We also see that everywhere the gospel finds fertile ground, its reception is accompanied by gratitude to God and his messengers. Gratitude is expressed in joy and generosity, the outward signs and spontaneous outflow of the deep work of the grace of God in the hearts of people. Joy and generosity are like Siamese twins; wherever the Holy Spirit is at work there is never one without the other, irrespective of the situation. For the Philippians, they were faced with opposition and all kinds of suffering and trial, but the situation did not take away their joy or generosity. In my work as a bishop in Kampala I was always amazed to find that the most joyful and generous congregations were not necessarily those constituted by the middle-classes who had the greatest wealth; often they were among the less able and less privileged. Joy and generosity have nothing to do with the amount of wealth, but with the work of grace in the hearts and lives of the people.

In Corinth (Acts 18:1–11)

Corinth in the first century was similar to any city today. A Roman colony and the seat of the Roman governor of the province of Achaia, it was a major commercial centre, with strategic communications and a network of roads and rivers – notably the Isthmus of Corinth, the land bridge that linked northern Greece with the Peloponnese, a large peninsula and region in southern Greece, and with the sea routes to the east and west. Corinth was noted for its wealth, culture and sexual immorality, the last a feature of the Corinthian lifestyle. Dominating the city was the Acrocorinth, a hill over 500 metres high on which stood the temple of Aphrodite (or Venus), the Greek goddess of love. The cult was dedicated to the glorification of sex. The temple is said to have employed the services of more than a thousand "priestesses" who were nothing more than common prostitutes. In addition, there was the temple of Apollo, the god of music, song and poetry and also the ideal of male beauty. The cult of Apollo therefore glorified homosexuality. Corinth's notorious reputation for sexual licence spawned the new Greek verb *korinthiazein*, which simply meant "to practise sexual immorality". It was to this city, the biggest Paul had encountered since his call and sending in Antioch, that he came "with great fear and trembling", as he later admitted in his letters (1 Cor 2:3), after his fruitful ministry in Macedonia. Paul's ministry there and the way a community of followers of Jesus emerged, as well as its witness and struggles in a pagan, idolatrous and morally decadent city, have a lot to teach us in the "Corinths" of our day – the highly populated, commercial-minded and sex-obsessed cities of the world.

As was his practice, Paul began his preaching in Corinth among the Jewish community. The most logical way to find them, as in any other city with a significant Jewish presence, was to locate a synagogue, find them on the Sabbath and join them. His immediate acquaintance was with a couple, Aquila and Priscilla; they shared not only Jewish roots, but also the occupation of leather-working (tentmaking). So Paul stayed with them, and was certainly instrumental in their turning to faith in Jesus. When Silas and Timothy later joined him after their extended stay in Macedonia the team grew to five. But it was the level of resistance and opposition that Paul faced with the synagogue establishment that caused him to wonder about the efficacy of his methodology of starting with the Jews in the synagogue. They not only resisted him; they became abusive. Paul turned to preaching to the Gentiles, and "many of the Corinthians who heard Paul believed and were baptised" (18:8). But the opposition from the leading Jews was relentless. They made a united attack on Paul and brought him before the Roman court. God used the most unlikely person to rebuff the Jews when they accused Paul: Junius Gallio, the Roman proconsul of the province of Achaia. Although some believed – notably the synagogue ruler Crispus with his household – Paul was so discouraged that he considered leaving Corinth. But the Lord told him, "Do not be afraid; keep on speaking, do not be silent. For I am with you, and no one is going to attack and harm you, because I have many people in this city" (18:9–10). For the next eighteen months Paul preached and taught in Corinth.

Paul was disappointed that the Jews had rejected the good news. He expected that given their Jewish background and his own, by explaining to them that Jesus was the Messiah they would have been the first to believe and turn to the Lord. But they opposed Paul because of the very reason he hoped they should have believed. His preaching was unsettling to their belief system, a system they felt it was for them to protect. Their Jewish background, instead of it serving as fertile ground for the seed of the gospel, caused the hardness of their hearts. Their religion was the enemy of faith in Jesus. The Lord's words to Paul, "I have many people in this city", both Jews and Gentiles, were what kept Paul there. This was a reminder to Paul that the Lord's people are not to be identified by religious background. In fact, it was the Corinthians who did not have the Jewish background who "believed and were baptised" in large numbers. The people's turning to the Lord did not depend on their background and Paul's persuasiveness, but on the Lord himself. Paul's responsibility was simply to proclaim Jesus faithfully.

What the Acts narrative does not tell us about in any detail is the life of the nascent community of believers, Jew and Gentile, in immoral Corinth. It is significant therefore that we have in the account the specific reference to the fact that during the year and a half that Paul spent in Corinth, not only was he preaching the gospel, but he also devoted himself to teaching the believers the word of God (18:11). Luke also tells us that after Paul and his companions left Corinth, Apollos, an Alexandrian Jew whom Priscilla and Aquila had met in Ephesus, came and continued where Paul left off (18:24–28). Apollos was a man well versed in the Jewish Scriptures and the story of Jesus, and had become convinced by himself that Jesus was the Christ, but Priscilla and Aquila, on hearing him in the synagogue in Ephesus, taught him the way of the Lord more correctly, because he "knew only the baptism of John" (18:25). So when Apollos went on his journey to Greece he was commended by Priscilla and Aquila to the disciples in Corinth. Thus, just as we have seen with all the other Jesus communities, teaching was central to their life together.

It is from Paul's letters to the church in Corinth, preserved for us as 1 and 2 Corinthians, that we are able to learn what else characterized the community life of the disciples in Corinth: their witness, strengths, struggles and challenges. Reading the letters we see clearly that they were occasioned by issues in the church that were a cause of great concern and in some instances heartache for the apostle. It is not feasible in this limited space to do justice to the complex nature of the life of that nascent community of Jesus followers as portrayed in these two letters. We can only highlight a few issues that feature prominently, among them misunderstanding and misuse of spiritual gifts; divisions and a party spirit; the presence of pseudo-apostles; and conflicts among believers leading to law suits and immorality.

Although there was no doubt about the presence and work of the Holy Spirit among the believers in Corinth and therefore no question as to their authenticity as "the church of God in Corinth", the misuse of spiritual gifts and resulting divisions was undermining their corporate witness. The presence and work of the Holy Spirit was manifest in the variety of spiritual gifts in the church. In fact, according to Paul, they did "not lack any spiritual gift" (1 Cor 1:7), but their use and misuse had brought confusion and bickering, requiring Paul to devote a significant portion of his first letter to teaching on spiritual gifts and their place in the ordering of the life of Corinthian believers, especially when they gathered together. The confusion over spiritual gifts must have been exacerbated by the party spirit that had cropped up in the church. Factions had emerged along lines of loyalty to the different apostles and teachers: some were saying "I follow Paul"; others "I follow Apollos"; others "I follow Cephas"; and still others "I follow Christ" (1:11–12; 3:3–9). The situation was further aggravated by the appearance of some from among the believers, it seems, as well as from outside, who claimed to be better teachers and apostles and who were deliberately undermining and discrediting the apostleship of Paul (4:15–17; 2 Cor 11:1–6). It was heartbreaking for Paul to hear how the very essence of community was being lost. They were all taking their eyes off the one who had died for their redemption.

The church was also beset by many ethical dilemmas. There were some in the church whose morality contradicted the ethics of their new-found faith, notably one member who was living in an immoral relationship: "a man is sleeping with his father's wife" (1 Cor 5:1). There were believers taking each other to court (ch. 6); questions were raised concerning sexual conduct and marriage in the context of the sexually decadent society (chs 6 –7); and there was confusion over "food sacrificed to idols" (ch. 8). These were big issues for the church. Many of the people in the church, before they became believers, had lived liked the rest of Corinthian society: they were sexually immoral, idolaters, adulterers, prostitutes, thieves, drunkards and the like. Now that they had entered the kingdom of God through repentance and faith, "were washed, … were sanctified, … were justified in the name of the Lord Jesus Christ and by the Spirit of our God" (6:9–11), how were they to live? The main thrust of Paul's ethical and moral teaching in the letters to the Corinthian believers is that that which was accepted as normal in the wider Corinthian society could not be acceptable in the community of believers, because "wrongdoers will not inherit the kingdom of God" (6:9). Paul's one and a half years with them and Apollo's subsequent teaching were not adequate in building a foundation.

One last feature of the community of believers in Corinth that is noteworthy is what Paul refers to in 1 Corinthians 16:1 as "the collection for the Lord's people". Paul dealt with this again in 2 Corinthians 8 – 9. The specific collection was in relation to supporting a relief campaign that Paul had undertaken for the believers in Jerusalem, who had suffered a severe and prolonged famine. In every church that was birthed through Paul's ministry he stressed the opportunity, privilege and responsibility of meeting the needs of the saints in Jerusalem. Clearly, there was an expectation from Paul and from the Corinthian believers that they too would participate in contributing to the needs of the believers in Jerusalem. What seems to have concerned Paul about the giving of the Corinthian church was that it was not as spontaneous and generous as it ought to have been. Their reluctance or slowness to complete what they had started was a reflection of a declining devotion to the Lord. He wanted them to understand that his urging them to excel in "this grace of giving" and the demand for an appropriate response was not intended to be burdensome but rather "to test the sincerity of [their] love" (2 Cor 8:7–8). Giving, he urged them, was not simply about "supplying the needs of the Lord's people but is also overflowing in many expressions of thanks to God" (2 Cor 9:12). Clearly, their divisions, squabbling and other internal struggles had undermined their zeal for the Lord.

From a superficial glance at the church in Corinth, given the divisions, confusion, bickering and immorality that beset its life, one might wonder how Paul could address them as "the church of God in Corinth, … those sanctified in Christ Jesus" (1 Cor 1:2). However, the basics of what we have seen so far that characterize a Spirit-born community were all there: an apostolic foundation, through the work of Paul; the presence and power of the Holy Spirit, evidenced in the variety of spiritual gifts in the community; and sharing in providing for needy believers. The problem for the Corinthian church was its stagnating at the infancy stage. Paul wrote to them that he could not address them as "people who live by the Spirit but as people who are still worldly – mere infants in Christ" (1 Cor 3:1) and he later rebuked them, "stop thinking like children" (14:20). I am persuaded that this is at the heart of much of the credibility crisis of the church today. The two letters of Paul to the Corinthians should be on the menu of teaching in the churches, especially in the urban centres, every three to four years, because they contain the corrective. There is so much in them that is needed in the contemporary church. Two themes deserve some brief attention: the community as a functioning body; and the continuing challenge for the church to be a distinctive gospel community in its context.

It was the dysfunctional nature of the church in Corinth that led Paul to expound the metaphor of a functional human body as descriptive of a well-functioning community of believers. We should note that while the metaphor of "body" was not original to Paul – for example, the Stoics described the cosmos as "the body of the divine world-soul" – "Paul was apparently the first to apply it to a community within the larger community of society and to the personal responsibilities of people for one another rather than their civic duties".[3] We should also note that although Paul used the term with other churches to elucidate the nature of Christian community – for example, in Romans 12 and Ephesians 1, 3 and 4 – he first used it for the church in Corinth. It was the local community at Corinth he described as the body of Christ. "Now you are the body of Christ, and each one of you is a part of it" (1 Cor 12:27). There is therefore a sense in which the entire Christian community, past and present, owes to this dysfunctional church in Corinth the understanding of a community of believers in any locality as the "the body of Christ", with each member granted a ministry to the other members of the community, thereby building the whole. As Robert Banks has put it, "This suggests that wherever Christians are in relationship there is the body of Christ in its entirety, for Christ is truly and wholly present there through his Spirit (1 Corinthians 12:13). This is a momentous truth."[4]

---

3. Robert Banks, *Paul's Idea of Community: The Early House Churches in Their Cultural Setting* (Peabody, Mass.: Hendrickson, 1994), 66.

4. Banks, *Paul's Idea of Community*, 59.

This leads to the other theme: the distinctiveness of the Christian community within the wider community of which it is a part. This was the real issue highlighted by the questions that Paul had to deal with in his correspondence with the church in Corinth. Not only did Paul give advice on the specific behaviour expected of the believers that was to be different from the behaviour of wider Corinthian society, but also for each recommended behaviour he gave an underlying principle. Thus in the matter of sexual conduct Paul made it clear to the believers that while the rest of Corinth revelled in all manner of sexual promiscuity, the believers were to "Flee from sexual immorality" (1 Cor 6:18); the reason was not so that they were different from society, or even because sexual immorality was evil, but because "your bodies are temples of the Holy Spirit, who is in you … You are not your own; you were bought at a price. Therefore honour God with your bodies" (6:19–20). The "ethical" grounds for appropriate sexual conduct are theological: we are the dwelling place of God, redeemed to honour him. To indulge in sexual immorality of any kind for the believers would be a denial of who they were in Christ, and more fundamentally, a denunciation of the efficacy of the sacrifice of Christ on the cross. Thus the distinctiveness of the believing community was not just behaviour, the "dos and don'ts", but rather a response to God's work of redemption in Christ. This is an important corrective to much of moralist Christianity today, which focuses primarily on immoral acts.

In Ephesus (Acts 19:1–41; 20:17–36)

The genesis of a community of believers in Ephesus, a major seaport, a prosperous business centre and the capital of the Roman province of Asia, is another intriguing story. That Paul did not visit Ephesus on his way to Europe does not make a lot of human sense. One would think that the more obvious route would have been the inland journey from Antioch through Galatia, then into the province of Asia, a route that Paul took during his second missionary journey. But as we noted earlier, he and his colleagues were not allowed by the Holy Spirit to preach in the province of Asia and were instead guided to Philippi. The progress of the gospel does not go according to human sense but according to the will of God and the obedience of his people.

When Paul first set foot in Ephesus it was with Priscilla and Aquila after their time in Corinth and a stopover at Cenchrea. He stayed briefly at the time, promising to return "if it is God's will" (Acts 18:21), before continuing to Antioch. During his short stay in Ephesus he "went into the synagogue and reasoned with the Jews" (18:19), clearly not enough to see new believers. It was Apollos' preaching in the synagogue that had an impact, producing disciples of John the Baptist rather than disciples of Jesus. Those who believed Apollos' message received a baptism of repentance and not a baptism of the Holy Spirit. Apollos left Ephesus and went to Corinth, as we saw earlier. And God's will it was: Paul returned to Ephesus within a few months. When he arrived there, he was startled that the "believers" he found did not even know "that there is a Holy Spirit" (19:2). So Paul took time to teach them about Jesus and they believed in him; they were then baptized by Paul into the name of the Lord Jesus and received the baptism in the Holy Spirit when he laid his hands on them. Thus a new community in Christ was born among the Jews in Ephesus.

Some have taken this story to be a justification of a two-stage process in conversion: the first, repentance, leading to faith in Christ; the second, a baptism in the Holy Spirit. The assumption on which this interpretation is built is that Apollos' believers were followers of Jesus, which as Paul quickly learned on asking them a few questions, it was clear they were not. They had not even heard that there was a Holy Spirit. This story is significant for this reason: it shows that becoming a disciple of Jesus post-Pentecost *begins* with a regenerating experience of the Holy Spirit. An immersion (which is what baptism means) in the Holy Spirit is the beginning of a journey in Christ. One cannot be a disciple of Jesus and not know experientially the Holy Spirit, because access to the Father is by the Spirit (Eph 2:18).

Luke tells us in his account that Paul devoted the next three months to proclaiming the kingdom of God among the Jews in the synagogue. The synagogue became divided, with some vigorously opposing Paul and maligning the message. At that point Paul left with the other followers of Jesus and took the gospel to the public square. He rented a lecture hall and for the next two years he proclaimed the gospel from there, to the extent that "all the Jews and Greeks who lived in the province of Asia heard the word of the Lord" (19:10). As we study the rest of the account of Paul's two-year stay in Ephesus, at least three things stand out that characterize his ministry and the new community that was growing there: a gospel power encounter; apostolic teaching and example; and the harmony in the community, in spite of its diversity.

Ephesus was the headquarters of the cult of Artemis (Diana), the goddess of fertility, with a temple that was reckoned to hold between 23,000 and 56,000 people; it was so magnificent that it was later counted as one of the seven wonders of the ancient world. An economy had been built around this cult consisting of related businesses, shrine makers, silversmiths and craftsmen, traders and pilgrims. Ephesus was also home to pagan high priests, some of them Jewish. Luke tells of one such priest and the sons of Sceva, who "went around driving out evil spirits" (19:13). This is the context in which Paul preached the message of the kingdom of God with a demonstration of power in signs and wonders. "God did extraordinary miracles through Paul, so that even handkerchiefs and aprons that had touched him were taken to those who were ill, and their illnesses were cured and the evil spirits left them" (19:11–12). It was an encounter with these spiritual powers that had cast a spell on Ephesus for generations. The sons of Sceva decided to mimic gospel power, casting out demons, after the style of Paul, saying, "In the name of the Jesus whom Paul preaches, I command you to come out" (19:13). One day, instead of the demons coming out of the man, the man attacked the sons of Sceva and "gave them such a beating that they ran out of the house naked and bleeding" (19:14).

When those who were under the spell of the cult of Artemis and the pagan priests heard about this they were terrified and sought out Paul and the disciples. The change in the city was phenomenal. "Many of those who believed now came and openly confessed what they had done. A number who had practised sorcery brought their scrolls together and burned them publicly" (19:18–19). This meant loss to the business enterprises around the cult. We have here a repeat of what happened in Philippi. The freedom of those who gave up all their fetishes meant financial loss to those who benefited from this business. The latter swung into action to reverse the influence of the gospel and save the demise of their business, led by Demetrius, who owned a franchise that made shrines and therefore patronized many craftsmen and traders. He mobilized them and organized a riot in the city against the believers and Paul, appealing to both business and spiritual sentiments by saying that there was "a danger not only that our trade will lose its good name, but also that the temple of the great goddess Artemis will be discredited; and the goddess herself, who is worshipped throughout the province of Asia and the world, will be robbed of her divine majesty" (19:27). The city clerk's intervention quelled the riot. He demanded to know whether there was a legitimate case against Paul; if so, Demetrius had the right to use the courts. What is amazing is the way Paul and the believers responded: they neither defended themselves nor showed bitterness, but simply demonstrated a continued reliance on the power of God to save and protect them.

When the people of God proclaim the gospel of God in the power of the Holy Spirit, God does wonderful things, delivering people from all manner of bondage. One of the consequences is opposition from those who benefit from the bondage of others. We should not, as Paul reminded the Ephesians, think of those who resist and oppose us as enemies, because our enemy is "not flesh and blood" but "the powers of this dark world ... the spiritual forces of evil in the heavenly realms" (Eph 6:12). Our enemy is also the enemy of those who oppose us. For they too are in bondage – a worse bondage than that of their victims, because not only do they not know that they are in bondage, but also they work to keep others in bondage.

We shall not dwell much on the apostle Paul's teaching ministry in Ephesus, although there would be a lot to say given the significance of Ephesians, the letter occasioned by the life of the community, in shaping the progress of the Christian faith through the ages. We simply observe here that it is in Paul's message to the elders who came to meet him at Miletus, as recorded in Acts 20:18–35, that we are able to appreciate how central teaching the believers was to building the faith and witness of the community. What is even more instructive, in a manner and depth we have not yet seen with previous churches, is to see the investment Paul made in building up the leadership of the community. Paul was intent in ensuring that they would follow his example. He could boldly declare to them that during his time with them he had not hesitated to preach anything that was important for them, and he had proclaimed the whole will of God (20:20, 27). We should not be surprised that it is out of that teaching ministry that we have the heritage of the letter of Ephesians, written to the church in Ephesus during Paul's first imprisonment in Rome, an epistle that John Stott described as a "marvellously concise, yet comprehensive, summary of the Christian good news and its implications".[5]

A final feature of the community, which at face value seems to be taken for granted in the Acts narrative of the church, is the harmony in the community in spite of its Jewish–Gentile composition. Paul devoted about a third of the letter to the Ephesians to it. The unity of the people of God should not be taken for granted because it does not just happen; it is an accomplishment of the cross of Christ. It was by the cross of Christ that Jesus'

---

5. John Stott, *The Message of Ephesians* (Downers Grove, Ill.: Inter-Varsity Press, 1979), 15.

purpose "to create in himself one new humanity out of the two, thus making peace, and in one body to reconcile both of them to God through the cross, by which he put to death their hostility" (Eph 2:15–16) was achieved. The only way it became a reality for the believers in Ephesus was because of the Holy Spirit. It was the unity achieved by the cross and given by the Spirit that Paul now enjoined them to "Make every effort to keep … through the bond of peace" (Eph 4:3). In other words, it is the responsibility of each believer to ensure that it is not broken, and that takes effort.

Churches Today

The churches in Antioch, Philippi, Corinth and Ephesus, in first-century southern Europe, serve as a mirror for us as communities of followers of Jesus in the twenty-first-century globalized world. As we look intently in this mirror and see "what the grace of God [has] done" (Acts 11:23), as Barnabas experienced in the church in Antioch, we must rejoice and praise the Lord for many who, as in the church in Philippi, reflect the generosity and joy of the gospel in spite of harsh environments. At the same time, we see that what matters most in exemplifying Spirit-filled communities is not what characterizes many that we call churches of Christ today. We cause grief to the Lord of the church, as Paul expressed concerning the church in Corinth that was not only dysfunctional as a community, but was stunted in its growth and carnal in its witness. Indeed, there are many today which, although they bear the label "church", demonstrate hardly anything in their life together that reflects the Spirit life in them. Many of the leaders in these churches, instead of teaching the "whole will of God" (Acts 20:27), as Paul did in Ephesus, are more like the sons of Sceva, mimicking gospel power and playing church. This mirror presents all of us who invoke God's name through Jesus with the challenge to examine ourselves as to whether we are genuine communities of the Holy Spirit.

8

The Church: God's New Pilgrim Community

Praise be to the God and Father of our Lord Jesus Christ, who has blessed us in the heavenly realms with every spiritual blessing in Christ. For he chose us in him before the creation of the world to be holy and blameless in his sight. In love he predestined us for adoption to sonship through Jesus Christ, in accordance with his pleasure and will – to the praise of his glorious grace, which he has freely given us in the One he loves. In him we have redemption through his love, the forgiveness of sins … [and] he made known to us the mystery of his will according to his good pleasure, which he purposed in Christ, to be put into effect when the times reach their fulfilment – to bring unity to all things in heaven and on earth under Christ. (Eph 1:3–10)

In putting everything under them, God left nothing that is not subject to them. Yet at present we do not see everything subject to them. But we do see Jesus, who was made lower than the angels for a little while, now crowned with glory and honour because he suffered death, so that by the grace of God he might taste death for everyone.

In bringing many sons and daughters to glory, it was fitting that God, for whom and through whom everything exists, should make the pioneer of their salvation perfect through what he suffered. Both the one who makes people holy and those who are made holy are of the same family. So Jesus is not ashamed to call them brothers and sisters. (Heb 2:8b–11)

In October 2006 my wife and I were invited by a Christian couple and their family to Sydney for two weeks' rest. This was their gift of love to two overworked, exhausted and nearly burnt-out people. Paula and Barry had previously visited Kampala and worked with Theodora, my wife, in her counselling ministry. We shall for ever cherish our time in Australia. One of our most memorable experiences was a Sunday evening at their home church. I was intrigued by the name they called themselves: The Journey. I was very curious as to who and what constituted The Journey. On the previous day, during an excursion to one of the beautiful sandy beaches of Sydney, we had met Steve and his family, all members of The Journey. I was surprised by how much Steve and I had in common as we compared notes on the nature and impact of the churches in Uganda and Australia. We clicked immediately, although this was the first time we had met. We talked at length about our faith journey – the desire to simply follow Jesus in the complex realities of life, and the challenges and frustrations of institutional church, dry orthodoxy and the growth of the prosperity gospel movement. "What is church all about?" we asked each other. Steve explained to me that The Journey had resulted from a shared frustration with church as he and fellow members had experienced it, and from a deep desire to find a place where as followers of Jesus they could meet and worship the Lord with authenticity, not just in ritual; a place to share their stories and find meaning for their corporate journey. Their desire was to be a community that was concerned not just for themselves but also with reaching out to a hurting world in the name of Jesus.

At The Journey, meeting in one of the classrooms in a local primary school, there were a group of about twenty-five people: men and women, young people in their teens and some people who looked to be in their sixties. That gathering was characterized by three things. Firstly, they connected all that they said and did to Jesus. Each person who spoke at the gathering invoked the name of Jesus. There was an expressed desire that Jesus should be at the heart of all they were and did. They were gathered in the name of Jesus, testifying to each other their experience of Jesus during the past week and seeking renewal from Jesus for the week ahead. They were, together, a community by faith in Jesus.

Secondly, they showed care for one another in the way they listened to each other's stories of joy and brokenness and as they read the Bible together.

It was not immediately evident that there was a preacher. Barry, our host, later informed us that each of the families at The Journey had gone through one form of crisis or another. For a while I was taken aback by Barry's description because listening to them share their stories, it was evident that their "crises" were experiences of brokenness such as are common to all of us. They had all found meaning in their separate journeys of brokenness in the love of Jesus that they shared. Clearly, they were glad to be together again on this Sunday evening. They loved to hear each other's stories. They were also eager to find ways of supporting one another. The Journey was clearly a community of love.

Thirdly, the people of The Journey cared about the "ends of the earth". They wanted to be connected to brothers and sisters in Christ around the world. They were happy to welcome us, not as visitors but as their own. They showed this in the way they listened intently to our story and to some of the stories of hope among the people we served in Uganda, particularly of a ministry of restoration that we were involved in, Wakisa Ministries (*Wakisa* is a Luganda word meaning "God is gracious"), for teenage girls with unwanted pregnancies. Some of the members of The Journey had previously visited Uganda and helped us in building a strong programme for the girls. As a result, they had got the entire community involved with the work through regular financial support. They also prayed regularly for Wakisa. They wanted to do more and to make a difference, with us, in Uganda, bringing hope. The Journey was not just a community of hope among its own membership; through it they sought to bring hope to others beyond their community.

"The journey" is an appropriate integrating metaphor for all the people of God. It is akin to the "pilgrim" metaphor that we discussed in Chapter 1. That is the point that Hebrews 11 – 12 makes: that God's people are those who journey with and in God. We have seen how the entire story of the people of God, from ancient times to the followers of Jesus in the New Testament, is that of a journey of a people being formed into a community and whose identity is defined by their faith relationship with God who "created the heavens and the earth" (Gen 1:1).

Israel, as a people of God, were formed in the exodus; when they lost track of their identity after they settled in the promised land they were taken into exile, from where the remnant rediscovered their identity and mission. The prophets had made clear to the people what God's will for them was: to be a distinct people of God, wherever they were – captured in the words of Micah 6:8: "To act justly and to love mercy and to walk humbly with your God." When those "called out" as his people abandoned their "walk with

God", they could no longer count on God's protection; hence the exile. It was the remnant – those who continued to walk humbly with God, seeking justice and mercy – that were custodians of God's promise, finally fulfilled in the coming of Jesus the Christ, who was the final revelation of God's purpose for humanity and indeed all creation. The story of the new community is one of following Jesus. Jesus formed the disciples into his own community as they followed him. Even after his ascension they would continue to be his as the "sent ones", announcing and demonstrating the kingdom of God by the grace and power of the Holy Spirit. And just like the ancient people, they too were to live in his mission, a kingdom of justice, peace and joy in the Holy Spirit.

The three aspects of faith, love and hope that I experienced at The Journey in Sydney seem to be the enduring features and character of the people of God throughout time. They capture in a nutshell what the authentic Christian community is all about: its life and witness, at any time and in any place. This is also how Paul summarized his understanding of Christian community in his words to the believers in Corinth: "And now these three remain: faith, hope and love" (1 Cor 13:13). Faith, love and hope: that is what authentic church is all about, yesterday, today and tomorrow. We have already seen the triad in Hebrews 11 – 12 of faith, community and pilgrimage; love and hope are the outworking of community and pilgrimage, respectively. There is no contradiction or conflict. It is a continuing story. Love is the hallmark of community's life, purpose and mission; hope is the fuel of pilgrimage. In this concluding chapter, therefore, we focus on these marks that are features of the new covenant community of the Spirit: faith, love and hope.

The Church: A Community Of Faith, By Faith, In Faith, For Faith

Faith is at the heart of the identity of Christian community; it is what defines and forms it. As we saw in Chapter 1, this is the perspective of Hebrews 11: that it was faith that formed all those listed into a people of God. But community formed their faith – belonging to God and to each other. They were all related to each other by a particular way of being in relation with God – a communion or sharing of faith. It was the common denominator of their lives: *they were all* commended for their faith; they were a "community by faith" and so can rightly be called a "community of faith". The basis of belonging together was their belonging to God and that was by faith. The reason for the community was faith. Thus, the entire roll of honour may be described as a "by faith" movement. The point of Hebrews 11 – 12 is also that the new people of God, believers in Christ, are part of that faith movement. Faith is therefore the first characteristic feature of the people of God, old and new.

I can hear my evangelical friends plead with me that we begin with the Bible as the source of authority, "without error in all that it affirms, and the only infallible rule of faith and practice", as affirmed in the Lausanne Covenant.[1] But we have to acknowledge that the Scriptures themselves were formed in faith, for faith. Moreover, the Lausanne Covenant itself states clearly in its preamble, as noted by John Stott in his commentary on the Lausanne Covenant, *Making Christ Known: Historic Mission Documents from the Lausanne Movement 1974–1989*, that the creators of the Covenant were "members of the Church of Jesus Christ, from more than 150 nations".[2] John Stott is right to point out that the value of the preamble is not simply as a formal statement but as "something important about who the participants were, what the mood of the congress was and how the Covenant came into being".[3] The Covenant is a document that is based on the assumption of faith in Jesus and is grounded in that faith.

Looking closely at what Hebrews 11 says about the nature of faith that forms a people of God, we note at least four things. Firstly, it is all about God. Hebrews 11 defines faith as "confidence in what we hope for and assurance about what we do not see" (11:1). The subject of hope is therefore the unseen; the indescribable; the mystery; and yet on this mystery depends all certainty of life. This mystery is God, who is both the subject and object, "because anyone who comes to him must believe that he exists and that he rewards those who earnestly seek him" (11:6). It is recognition that what is, what has been and what will be are God's prerogative, and our duty is to seek him. The latter implies a relationship with him. It is not any God, but only the God who created and therefore is in himself relational. This is how Moses was to name him: "I AM WHO I AM.... The LORD, the God of your fathers – the God of Abraham, the God of Isaac and the God of Jacob …' This is my name for ever, the name you shall call me from generation to generation" (Exod 3:14–15), distinct from the gods of the Egyptians. This truth of relationship is captured in expressions such as "Enoch walked with God" and "Abraham

---

1. The Lausanne Covenant, at http://www.lausanne.org/en/documents/lausanne-covenant.html. Accessed 29/10/13.

2. John Stott, ed., *Making Christ Known: Historic Mission Documents from the Lausanne Movement 1974–1989* (Carlisle: Paternoster, 1996), 13.

3. Stott, *Making Christ Known*, 13.

believed God". This is faith, a relationship through which God commits to reveal himself – "I AM" – and people seek him and obey him. The initiative is God's; human beings respond.

Secondly, authentic faith is a gift. As we saw in the account of Israel, the ancient people of God, it was God who called Abraham from among the people; Moses too was called by God. Moses was categorical in reminding the people of Israel that the Lord did not choose them because of their numbers or because of any achievement of theirs compared with those of other peoples and nations. Rather it was because the Lord wanted to fulfil his promise and purpose that he chose them (Deut 7:6–9); the prophets constantly reminded Israel of their squandering of the gift of God's favour upon them. Jesus told his disciples, "You did not choose me, but I chose you and appointed you so that you might go and bear fruit – fruit that will last" (John 15:16). Faith is a gift, because the initiative of choice comes from God.

As I have encountered many people and cultures that do not yet know of the love of Jesus I have come to appreciate this truth more and more. The fact that I know I belong to Jesus is a gift. I grew up in a home where Jesus was acknowledged as Lord. Consequently, the faith of my parents became my own, again through circumstances that were not of my choosing or creation. But I also know many who do not yet know of the love of God in Jesus even though they too were born of people of faith; also, there are many who have not been exposed to matters of faith in Jesus simply because of the circumstances of their birth and upbringing, and may die before they hear of the love of God revealed in Christ.

Since faith is a gift that begins in God's initiative, we should also acknowledge that becoming the community of faith is a gift. It is God who creates the community of faith. This is a common thread through the entire story: it was God who called a people his own; it was the Lord who added to "the number of those being saved"; it was the Holy Spirit that gave birth to a church; the churches of God were communities of and in the Holy Spirit. Thus, although "faith comes from hearing the message, and the message is heard through the word about Christ" (Rom 10:17), it is the Holy Spirit who proves "the world to be in the wrong about sin and righteousness and judgment" (John 16:8). Authentic church is not a result of any human strategy or engineering; it is Jesus, through his Spirit, building his church for God's kingdom and glory.

Thirdly, faith is active; it is visible. Faith, as a responsive disposition of trust, is demonstrated in actions. Not only does faith affirm that God acts, but the acts "of faith" are acts made in response to God, as well as resulting from and reflecting the people's faith in him. Although faith's subject is unseen, faith itself is visible and describable because it works in the lives of those who believe. Although God is unseen, he is, he acts and he communicates: to his people and through his people. The roll of honour of Hebrews 11 is indeed a list of those whose faith was vindicated by their actions. They heard his word *with faith*, demonstrated in their actions. Their actions were the faith-response of obedience to the gift of faith from God. Hence Abraham's willingness to sacrifice his only son in obedience to God's command was the prototype faith act. Thus for Israel, it was not enough that they were the biological heirs to Abraham; it was by the obedience of faith that they would inherit the promises of Yahweh's covenant with Abraham. Abraham is referred to as the father of all, including those who come to God through faith in Jesus, for "If you belong to Christ, then you are Abraham's seed, and heirs according to the promise" (Gal 3:29).

Thus, although all Israel was liberated by God from Egypt, not all of them entered the promised land because not all responded in obedience. Although they all heard his word, there were some for whom "the message they heard was of no value to them" because they did not combine it with faith (Heb 4:2). Lack of faith, reflected in the way they responded to God in their actions, disqualified them from inheriting God's promise. On the other hand, for each of those commended for their faith, there were visible, dateable and locatable acts within a particular historical moment that demonstrated their faith. They lived by faith in God; they died in faith, for they "were still living by faith when they died" (Heb 11:13). Living faith, in life and in death, is always visible in actions of obedience.

Fourthly, faith is relational. Relationship with God means relationship with others who share in the relationship with God. Faith is expressed in community. The essence of faith is about belonging: with God and with others. Hence God, in his revelation to Moses, referred to himself as "the God of Abraham, the God of Isaac and the God of Jacob" (Exod 3:6, 15, 16; 4:5); and to ancient Israel as "my people" (Isa 1:3). Israel referred to God as "the LORD our God" (this is the most common way Deuteronomy refers to God). John the evangelist says that to those who received and believed in Jesus, "he gave the right to become children of God – children born not of natural descent, nor of human decision or a husband's will, but born of God" (John 1:12–13). To embrace the gospel of the kingdom of God is to enter into community; a person cannot have one without the other. Jesus said, "For where two or three gather in my name, there am I with them" (Matt 18:20). Community is the place where seeking, knowing and growing in Christ take place. As Paul wrote to the believers in Ephesus, it is only "together with all the Lord's people" that we can "grasp how wide and long and high and deep is the love of Christ, and to know this love that surpasses knowledge …"; only together can we "be filled to the measure of all the fullness of God" (Eph 3:18–19). Dietrich Bonhoeffer put it thus:

> Christianity means community through Jesus Christ and in Jesus Christ. No Christian community is more or less than this. Whether it be a brief, single encounter or the daily fellowship of years, Christian community is only this. We belong to one another only through and in Jesus Christ.
>
> What does this mean? It means, first, that a Christian needs others because of Jesus Christ. It means, second, that a Christian comes to others only in Jesus Christ. It means, third, that in Jesus Christ we have been chosen from eternity, accepted in time, and united for eternity.[4]

A distinction must be made between faith and religion. Faith is relational and personal; religion is about dos and don'ts, rights and wrongs. Faith is grounded in God's initiative and is existential; religion is built on a set of traditions, norms, beliefs and behaviours passed on over generations. While faith affirms that only God knows who is in and who is out, in religion it is the traditions, codes and standards which determine membership. The Jewish believers and apostles initially found it difficult to understand that the Gentiles could also be accepted as believers without submitting themselves to the Jewish laws and customs; the apostles later realized that God had accorded to the Gentiles the status of "believers" by giving his Spirit to them. But union in the Holy Spirit involved union with one another, for the Spirit was primarily a shared, not an individual, experience.

In the late 1920s, through the itinerant preaching of some Ugandan young believers, a revival broke out in the Anglican Church in Uganda – a church that had become nominal and ineffective in its witness. One of the marks of that revival was "fellowship", which was understood by the adherents to mean "living in transparent sincerity, and a willingness to share

---

4. Dietrich Bonhoeffer, *Life Together* (trans. from the German *Gemeinsames Leben*; London: SCM Press, 1954), 21.

with one another the experiences of daily life".[5] That is still the case among the members of this movement. Everyone who turns to Jesus in repentance becomes a member of a local fellowship group, irrespective of race, ethnicity, denominational affiliation, age and sex. The members of "the fellowship" refer to each other as "members of the same clan-family", in Luganda *aboluganda*, rendered "brethren". Note that it is not the people of the same ethnic clan that constitute this "clan-family". The "fellowship" is an egalitarian community in which individual identity finds its basis in the community. Members pray together, share testimonies of what Jesus is doing in their daily lives and read the Bible together. Their common faith is expressed in everyday life concerns. For example, when a girl in the community is sought in marriage, the brethren may deny her the marriage if the suitor is not approved, particularly if he is not a *Mulokole* (saved one). "If they agree to the marriage, the brethren in the community undertake the arrangements, provide the feast, and the transport, and attend the ceremony in force".[6] The entire process of marriage, from courtship to marriage, is undertaken by the fellowship as a whole and not just by the two individuals getting married.

This is the belonging together, *koinonia*, which we have seen exemplified in the churches in Jerusalem, Antioch, Philippi, Corinth and Ephesus. This is what the gathered assembly, *ekklesia*, was to demonstrate; belonging together was concretized in the gathering or assembly, in a particular historical moment and a particular place. *Koinonia* was visible. One of the ways it was manifested was in the believers' ensuring that "there was no needy person among them" (Acts 4:34) within the local community, as well as in their contributing to the needs of those beyond the community through the agency of the apostles. The fellowship they shared together in God was expressed in giving and receiving.

Sadly, it is a fact that in the church today there is not much honest and genuine sharing of needs and resources, both locally – within a local congregation – and globally – between the materially richer churches and the poorer. We have a repeat of the Ananias–Sapphira phenomenon: dishonesty. Does this not reflect a weak or in some cases non-existent shared relationship with God? Do we belong to God together? Is the Holy Spirit at work among us? These are the fundamental questions we should be grappling with, rather

---

5. John E. Church, *Quest for the Highest: An Autobiographical Account of the East African Revival* (Exeter: Paternoster, 1981), 194.

6. John V. Taylor, *The Growth of the Church in Buganda* (London: SCM Press, 1958), 102.

than the issues of autonomy and dependence that characterize the debate in Christian mission circles today.

However, there is another aspect to *koinonia*: it is also invisible. The author of Hebrews makes the point that the succession of generations of the people of God over the passage of time, though invisible, belong together. Referring to the roll of honour of the faithful in past generations he observed that although they "were all commended for their faith, yet none of them received what had been promised, since God had planned something better for us so that only together with us would they be made perfect" (Heb 11:39–40). By "us" the writer means the miscellaneous group of believers in Christ, Jew and Gentile, to whom he was writing. In other words, the faith of heroes such as Abraham and Moses was incomplete in itself without the faith of those who followed them. By extension, the faith of Abraham, Moses, the faithful kings, the prophets, the early disciples, the apostles and the early church fathers has not yet been made perfect; they are waiting for us, as we too wait for those who will come after us. The whole company of faith is bound together as part of a single story, a single act of God's redemption. The "newness" of the Christian community is not a reference to a new story of redemption; what is new is the notion of "fulfilment" that we discussed at length in Chapter 4. Together, the old and the new wait for the consummation, "when the times reach their fulfilment" and when "all things in heaven and on earth" will be put under Christ (Eph 1:10).

The reason one generation waits for the next and all the generations are waiting together is because the experience of *koinonia* in a particular time and place is incomplete without the contribution of a different experience of *koinonia* in a different time and place. A community of believers in one cultural setting "waited for" and needed the experience of Christ in another culture, for it is only together that they would have a more complete, fuller *koinonia* in Christ. For example, the Jewish experience of *koinonia* was couched in Jewish culture and idiom: gathering in the temple courts and synagogues; rejoicing and celebrating Jesus as the Christ (Messiah). These Jewish believers saw and understood Jesus in terms of Jewish history, tradition and belief, which revolved around the expectation of a Messiah.

However, when the gospel came to the Greek-speaking Gentile peoples the word "Messiah" meant nothing to them; it was absent in their history and beliefs. As Andrew Walls put it, "they had to translate it, to find a new term that told something about Jesus and yet meant something to a Greek pagan. They chose the word *Kyrios*, 'Lord'; the title that Greek pagans used for their cult divinities (Acts 11:19–21)".[7] Thus among the Greek-speaking Gentile believers we find the transposition "Lord Jesus Christ" as a shared expression, an expanded understanding of who Jesus was. In fact, "Christ" became the second name of Jesus and the article "the" was dropped, his name becoming "Jesus Christ". Crossing a cultural frontier led to new discoveries about Christ that could not have been made only within the Jewish setting. Thus, all the generations, past, present and future, wait until "the times reach their fulfilment", when all will reach "unity in the faith and in the knowledge of the Son of God and become mature, attaining to the whole measure of the fullness of Christ" (Eph 4:13).

This gives us a different motivation for evangelism. We have already understood that it is not the work of the Christian community to "bring others" into the fold of Christ; Jesus will bring them. The longing to attain the "whole measure of the fullness of Christ" should compel us to go to the ends of the earth, to other cultures and nationalities, to search for those who belong to him, so that with them our understanding and appreciation of our redemption is enhanced and our experience of Christ deepened. The understanding of Christ – knowing the "whole measure of the fullness of Christ" – arises from the coming together of the fragmented understandings that occur within the culture-specific segments of humanity where he becomes known. None of us, in our locality and in our generation alone, can reach that fullness that God intends. We need all the cultures, all the nations and all the peoples in order to appreciate the multi-dimensional, multi-faceted fullness of fullness of Christ. It is the translation of the life of Jesus into the way of life of all the world's cultures and subcultures throughout history that will enable us all to correct, enlarge and focus our own understanding and experience in Christ.

A Community Of Love, By Love, In Love, For Love

It is with the subject of love that there is a division between the ancient people of God and the new community in Christ. This is because the latter was more distinctly a community of love and grace in a way that ancient Israel did not know. Although the Lord God had declared to Israel his love for them, saying, "I have loved you with an everlasting love; I have drawn you with unfailing

---

7. Andrew F. Walls, *The Cross-Cultural Process in Christian History* (Maryknoll, NY: Orbis, 2002), 79.

kindness" (Jer 31:3), they could not grasp the full extent of God's love; they could not appreciate the universal nature of that love. It was Jesus, in whom "God was pleased to have all his fullness dwell" (Col 1:19), who showed the very nature of God, for "God is love" – supremely in the act of dying on the cross for the world, which God so loved and loves. As we saw in Chapter 4 Jesus taught that his people were to let God's love reign in them as a sign of the presence of the kingdom of God.

Love – to love God and one's neighbour – was the essence of the Mosaic law. Love was the new commandment given to the followers of Jesus; it was by love that his disciples would distinguish themselves as belonging to him; and loving one another was the authentic testimony to the love of God among them. Jesus told them that their unity, resulting from love, would be their supreme witness to the world: then "the world will know that you [the Father] sent me and have loved them even as you have loved me" (John 17:23). It was clear to the apostle Paul that apostolic ministry was a ministry of love and in love: "For Christ's love compels us, because we are convinced that one died for all, and therefore all died. And he died for all, that those who live should no longer live for themselves but for him who died for them and was raised again" (2 Cor 5:14–15). Paul emphasized that reconciliation with God brought about reconciliation with others, because in Christ the dividing walls of hostility were demolished; in him "There is neither Jew nor Gentile, neither slave nor free, nor is there male and female", for "you are all one in Christ Jesus" (Gal 3:28). Love defines every aspect of Christian community, internally and externally; for love defines every aspect of God's life. God is love.

The new community is called by love, in love, for love and to love. Jesus made it clear to his disciples that they were to be a community marked out by love. The Holy Spirit would mediate the love of the Father and the Son to them and through them. As communities of the Holy Spirit the churches were to display the God of love. For the people of the kingdom, participants in the triune fellowship of love – Father, Son and Holy Spirit – love is the bottom line. Boyd puts it thus:

> This [love] is the only thing that gives value to anything we believe, say or do. This is the reason the world exists, and the reason the church exists. Whatever music we play, sermons we preach, churches we build, people we impress, powers we display, stances we take, doctrines we teach, things we

achieve – if believers are not growing in their motivation and ability to ascribe unsurpassable worth to people who have no apparent worth, *we are just wasting time.* We are not making true disciples.[8]

Living in Uganda in the 1970s, during the regime of Idi Amin, a dictator who unleashed the terror machine of his regime on any who were perceived to be an enemy, I saw and witnessed first-hand what it means for followers of Jesus to love our enemies. Among the "enemies" of the regime were some in the leadership of the Church of Uganda who challenged its brutality. Bishop Janani Luwum, then Archbishop of the Church of Uganda, was one of those who paid the ultimate price for his stand for justice in the country. Bishop Festo Kivengere, another of the fiery advocates for justice, was also one of those targeted. He was one of the last bishops in the company of Luwum hours before his death, and thereafter he fled for his life having received information that he too might suffer the same end. Festo Kivengere wrote a book that narrates some of the experiences of the church in Uganda during Idi Amin's regime and his flight into exile; its title is *I Love Idi Amin.* This echoes the paradoxical love that the church must live out. Kivengere says he wrote *I Love Idi Amin* to "share what God has done for ordinary Christians in an ordinary church in the middle of storms and stresses – because Christ does shine brighter when all around is darker".[9] While in exile he wrote, "We look back with great love to our country. We love President Idi Amin. We owe him a debt of love, for he is one of those for whom Christ shed His precious blood. As long as he is still alive, he is still redeemable. Pray for him, that in the end he may see a new way of life, rather than a way of death."[10]

Kivengere's point was that the church had only one option in its response to its enemies: love. This reaffirms the *raison d'être* of the church: to bear witness to the love of God as it was manifested in Christ. The church in Uganda, those who "walked humbly with God" beyond denominational boundaries, had to bear witness to the love of God for the people of Uganda by defending those traumatized by Idi Amin and his regime. But it also had to

---

8. Gregory A. Boyd, *Repenting of Religion: Turning from Judgment to the Love of God* (Grand Rapids, Mich.: Baker, 2004), 57.

9. Festo Kivengere, *I Love Idi Amin: The Story of Triumph under Fire in the Midst of Suffering and Persecution in Uganda* (Old Tappan, NJ: Revell, 1977), 7.

10. Kivengere, *I Love Idi Amin,* 63.

bear witness to the love of God *even* for Idi Amin himself and the perpetrators of carnage.

I cannot forget my encounter one afternoon with two girls at the international students' conference in Austria that I referred to in the Introduction. I had noticed that the two were hanging around together a lot. They came over to me. I wonder whether my face had betrayed my curiosity and they had noticed it. One of them introduced themselves to me. She said, "I am Aisha and she is Bilhah; she is a Jew and I am a Palestinian Arab; we both love Jesus!" It said it all. Now that I had grown to understand the historical enmity between Palestinian Arabs and Jews, what a joy to see the gospel there before my eyes!

And yet how true the opposite can be: the damage and harm done to the cause of Jesus when those who claim to be his reflect anything but the breaking down of the dividing walls of hostility. The examples of this are rife: separate communities – black churches, white churches, Asian churches, in white, black and brown neighbourhoods; separate social-class churches – upper-middle-class and working-class churches in mixed neighbourhoods; and so on. In 1984 I made my first visit to South Africa. I was eager to learn first-hand about the impact of apartheid on the evangelical Christian student movement. In 1970 the Bantu Homelands and Citizenship Act was passed to implement the apartheid doctrine of separate development according to race and colour. This act said that every black South African was a citizen of one of the homelands. Even if a person had never been to any homeland and had nothing to do with the homelands, they were still a citizen of a homeland – a *bantustan*. Their citizenship was determined by the language they spoke. A report published by the International Defence and Aid Fund of South Africa, *Apartheid: The Facts*, observed that the pass laws divided South Africa into two – *bantustans* and the rest. Every African outside the *bantustan* areas who was over the age of sixteen was to carry a pass book as an instrument of control. This pass book immediately identified the owner to any official and the limits set to their freedom of movement in the country.[11]. With the independence of each of these homelands between October 1976 and December 1981, all the black people lost their citizenship in South Africa and became foreigners!

The evangelical student ministry in South Africa founded in 1896 succumbed to the ideological pressures of apartheid and split into four

---

11. *Apartheid: The Facts* (London: International Defence and Aid Fund, 1983), 43–44.

racially based organizations in 1965: one for blacks; another for English-speaking whites; a third for Afrikaans-speaking whites; and a fourth for those of mixed race. From then on, Christian evangelical student work in the schools, colleges and universities in South Africa was carried out along racial lines. What a sad day it was for me when, in 1987, the International Fellowship of Evangelical Students (IFES) accepted into its membership two separate student organizations – one for whites (English-speaking), the Students' Christian Association (SCA); and the other for blacks, the Students' Christian Movement (SCM) – under the guise of effective student witness on the campuses. And what a joy it was when, in 1997, the two organizations disbanded and together formed the Students' Christian Organisation (SCO) of South Africa. Among the objectives of the new organization was "To urge students to commit themselves to the extension of God's kingdom throughout the world by evangelistic witness, by responding with compassion to the needs of society, by working for peace, righteousness and justice".[12]

The unity in diversity which love engenders in the Christian community is at the heart of Christian witness. Firstly, it provides a more complete, though always provisional, portrait of Jesus. It is only "together with all the Lord's holy people" that we can "grasp how wide and long and high and deep is the love of Christ ... that surpasses knowledge" and be "filled to the measure of all the fullness of God" (Eph 3:18–19). It is the diversity that adds value to the mutual experience of Christ. Secondly, unity in diversity creates space in which diversity thrives; unity does not mean the dissolution of diversity. The Jews did not become Gentiles and the Gentiles did not become Jews. And there were not two distinct Christian communities, one for the Jews, the other for the Gentiles. There was to be one Christian community in which both Jews and Gentiles fully belonged.

As we have seen, initially the apostles (all of them Jewish) and the other Jewish believers could not conceive how it could be possible to be Gentile and a believer. As we saw in Chapter 6 it took a crisis experience and encounter for Peter, the leading apostle at the time, to "realise how true it is that God does not show favouritism" (Acts 10:34). It was the great turning of Gentiles to Jesus at Antioch and during Paul and Barnabas' first journey that "forced" the leadership to address the question squarely. We saw in Chapter 7 how at the council at Jerusalem, although there was consensus that it would be an act of disobedience on their part to "make it difficult for the Gentiles who are

---

12. Students' Christian Organisation South Africa, at www.sco.org.za. Accessed 2013.

turning to God" (Acts 15:19) by requiring them to convert to Judaism, they nevertheless required some rudimentary Jewishness: they demanded that all the Gentile believers subscribe to some key Jewish food laws.

However, that requirement could only be provisional, for after all, there was no Gentile leader at the council. The council's resolutions regarding food laws were inadequate for the new situations in Philippi, Corinth and Ephesus. Thus, when Paul was asked about food offered to idols by the believers in Corinth, the answer he gave was not the Jerusalem council position but instead one based on the principles that "we know that 'An idol is nothing at all in the world' and that 'There is no God but one'" (1 Cor 8:4). He added that whether to eat or not to eat food offered to idols should be determined by the principles of love and freedom: love for the "weak brother or sister, for whom Christ died" (8:11) and freedom in Christ, since nothing can be added or taken away from Christ's sufficiency for our redemption.

Love turns out to be the primary motivation for mission and evangelism. The apostle Paul put it thus: "Christ's love compels us, because we are convinced that one died for all, and therefore all died. And he died for all that those who live should no longer live for themselves but for him who died for them and was raised again" (2 Cor 5:14–15). Authentic, liberating and life-giving mission and evangelism spring out of the experience of God's love in Christ and the Spirit-given desire for more of that love, and for others "to know this love that surpasses knowledge" (Eph 3:19). Grounded in any motivation other than God's love, mission and evangelism easily degenerate into an arduous duty and do not commend the gospel to the world.

Thus, by love and in love, the Christian community is to be a display of what community truly is, as God intended: unity and communion in diversity. In today's world, in spite of much talk of and hype about globalization we are faced with an unprecedented rate of breakdown of community in all its forms. In Africa the breaking down of community is simply on a spiral course. Hitherto cohesive clan communities were torn apart by divisions along religious and denominational lines with the introduction of Christianity and Islam in the late nineteenth and early twentieth centuries, and this community breakdown in African societies has been exacerbated by the rapid growth of urban centres, brought about by rural–urban migrations. As a reaction to this there is a growing revival in the urban centres of rural-based, regional-ethnic organizations as a way of recapturing the sense of community that rural life offered. The irony, however, is that rather than rebuild community, this phenomenon seems to cause further fracturing of our urban societies and the boomeranging of violence to the rural communities. The witness of the gospel is the presence of authentic Christian community in a world characterized by breakdown of community: a community in which unity thrives in diversity and diversity in unity.

A Community Of Hope, By Hope, In Hope, For Hope

We have seen how the writer of Hebrews locates the essence of faith in hope. All those the author listed were people of hope, looking toward to what they did not see and sustained in faith by the promise; a hope rooted in the trustworthiness of God. It is this hope that set the heroes and heroines of faith apart from the society of which they were part. Thus Noah, when "warned about things not yet seen", acted by building the ark, something that was incredible to his society at the time (Heb 11:7). Abraham, "when called to go to a place he would later receive as his inheritance, obeyed and went, even though he did not know where he was going" (11:8). Even Rahab the prostitute is numbered among the heroines of faith because her unpatriotic act of welcoming Israel's spies was due to her hope in the God of the Hebrews. The author tells of more extraordinary acts inspired by hope:

> Women received back their dead, raised to life again. There were others who were tortured, refusing to be released so that they might gain an even better resurrection. Some faced jeers and flogging, and even chains and imprisonment. They were put to death by stoning; they were sawn in two; they were killed by the sword. They went about in sheepskins and goatskins, destitute, persecuted and ill-treated – the world was not worthy of them. They wandered in deserts and mountains, living in caves and in holes in the ground. (Heb 11:35–38)

The phrase "the world was not worthy of them" sums it all up. They lived as strangers, so they "wandered in deserts and mountains, living in caves and in holes in the ground". Their "strangeness" was reflected not only in the wandering but also in the "extraordinary" happenings among them. "Women received back their dead"! God, in whom they hoped, did not let them down, working among them in extraordinary ways. They lived and acted in such a manner as to show clearly that they were "unlike" the rest of their society. "Wandering" is not simply a description of their lifestyle; it also describes their attitude to their entire life. It was because of this "unlikeness" of the faith community – the certainty of hope in that which was unseen – that they were able to endure suffering.

In Chapter 2 we saw how the identity of Israel as God's people was rooted in a promise that became their focus of hope and therefore shaped how they lived. In Chapter 3 we saw how it was the misplacing of their hope that led them astray, leading to God giving them up. The remnant of Israel were those who continue to live by the promise, looking forward to its fulfilment. In Jesus the hope of the world broke into human history. His resurrection from the dead was an attestation to the victory achieved on the cross and to the fact that the kingdom of God was indeed now present in human history. At Pentecost the new community in hope was born – born of the hope of the world, looking forward to the consummation and the summing up of all things under Christ. The new community were to be the hope of the world, proclaiming the good news of the reign of God, and demonstrating the transforming power of the kingdom of God as a sign of that which would finally be realized in the fullness of time.

The resurrection is central to the Christian hope. In his correspondence with the believers in Corinth the apostle Paul went to great lengths to explain that the historical fact of the resurrection of Jesus was the grounds of hope for the renewal of creation and eternal hope. For if Christ had not been raised from the dead there would be no reason for the certainty of faith and absolutely no grounds for Christian hope – or any hope at all for the world. But as Paul expounded:

> Christ has indeed been raised from the dead, the firstfruits of those who have fallen asleep. For since death came through a man, the resurrection of the dead comes also through a man. For as in Adam all die, so in Christ all will be made alive. But each in turn: Christ, the firstfruits; then, when he comes, those who belong to him. Then the end will come, when he hands over the kingdom to God the Father after he has destroyed all dominion, authority and power. For he must reign until he has put all his enemies under his feet. The last enemy to be destroyed is death. (1 Cor 15:20–26)

It is because Jesus was raised to life that those who by faith turn to him experience renewal and recreation in the here and now, and look forward to the total and complete restoration and renewal of all creation, the new heaven and the new earth. Jesus' resurrection attested to the adequacy and finality of the cross; it is the reason why Jesus is the only hope for the world.

This is the other motivation and the grounds for confidence in evangelism: the realization that only those who possess this resurrection hope have a true understanding of history and hence bear the responsibility to share it with those who do not. As Newbigin has explained, in reference to Jesus' words to his disciples recorded in John 14–16, in preparation for his departure from them and for their mission in the world, the evangelistic mandate is grounded in this understanding:

> … that a particular community in history, that community which bears the name of Jesus, will be given, through the active work of the Spirit of God, a true understanding of history – the ongoing history that continues through the centuries after Jesus, an understanding which is based on the particular events of whose memory they are the custodians. But this privileged position is not for their sake but for the sake of the world into which they are sent as the witnesses to Jesus in whom God's purpose for his entire creation has been disclosed.[13]

I have often wondered whether much of the lack of evangelistic zeal in many churches today is a manifestation of the disconnection with the resurrected Lord. What is needed therefore is not more training programmes on how to share the gospel, but rather to proclaim afresh in these churches the resurrected Saviour of the world on whom all hope depends.

It was this hope that motivated and inspired the early communities of believers to endure suffering in anticipation of the final victory over sin, the evil one and the world. We saw how every one of the churches of God endured all manner of suffering, and that without bitterness. On the contrary; many of the believers rejoiced in their sufferings, because they were counted worthy to suffer for Christ's sake. The same hope continues to inspire followers of Jesus today to face suffering, just as their Master did. This is especially so in the most difficult situations, particularly where Christianity is a minority faith. It is the dominant story of believers in Muslim lands – such as in North Africa, the Middle East and South Asia – where converts from Islam live in very hostile environments and are not even recognized as former Muslims

---

13. Lesslie Newbigin, *The Gospel in a Pluralist Society* (Grand Rapids, Mich.: Eerdmans, 1989), 78.

following the Lord Jesus. They constantly live under death threats and many have paid the ultimate price. Kamal Fahmi, my dear friend and a long-time missionary in North Africa and the Middle East with Operation Mobilisation, has told me many stories from these regions, stories of courage and love in the Lord Jesus inspired by hope.

Mehdi Dibaj's story is one, as shared with me by Kamal. Dibaj was the head of the Bible Society in Iran for many years. He was arrested and imprisoned without trial in Sari for ten years, where he was systematically tortured. Finally tried in an Islamic court on 3 December 1993, he was sentenced to death on charges of apostasy. Kamal tells how, at his trial, Dibaj said, "I am not only satisfied to be in prison for the honour of his holy name, but I am ready to give my life for the sake of my Lord." Following a worldwide outcry initiated by his friend and colleague Bishop Haik Hovsepian Mehr, Dibaj was finally freed in January 1994, although the death sentence was not lifted. Just three days later Bishop Haik Hovsepian Mehr himself was abducted and murdered. Dibaj was abducted on 24 June 1994. His body was found in a west Tehran park on 5 July 1994.

This persecution of believers is still going on today in Iran. Yousef Nadarkhani is a pastor within the Full Gospel Church of Iran denomination in the northern city of Rasht. He was arrested in October 2009 and was charged with apostasy – conversion from Islam – a crime punishable by death. Yousef received a death sentence in September 2010. Yousef and his wife, Fatemeh, had two young sons, aged nine and seven, at the time. Fatemeh was also detained for four months in 2010. Through his lawyers Yousef appealed to the Supreme Court of Iran, which then directed that his case be reviewed specifically to verify whether Yousef was previously a practising Muslim. Yousef claims that, although raised in a Muslim home, he was never a Muslim by choice, conviction, belief or consistent practice, and that he should therefore not be regarded as an apostate. In spite of the death sentence, separation from his family and the continuous pressure from the authorities for him to recant his faith in Jesus, Yousef is steadfast in his faith.

This is not only happening in Iran. Kamal has shared with me stories illustrating how Sudan continues to be a dangerous place to live for those who turn to faith in Jesus from Islam. In September 2011, 129 people were arrested for apostasy in Khartoum. In 2000 Al-Faki, who refused all offers of money and property to return to Islam, preferred to stay in prison rather than deny his Lord. When asked "What do you want?" he said "I want my Lord." In Egypt, many Muslim converts to faith in Christ have had to flee the country since the revolution that saw the fall of President Hosni Mubarak in 2011. One such is El-Gohari in 2011. He converted to Christianity from Islam as an adult. As other people were fleeing Egypt, El-Gohari, then aged fifty-six, also wanted to leave the country, but he was prevented because he wanted Christianity to be named as his religion on his ID card. Since then he has been attacked in the street, spat at and knocked down in his effort to win the right to officially convert. He and his fourteen-year old daughter continue to receive death threats by text messages and phone calls. El-Gohari told Kamal, "Our rights in Egypt as Christians or converts are less than the rights of animals. We are deprived of our social and civil rights. Deprived of our inheritance and left to the fundamentalists to be killed. Nobody bothers to investigate or care about us." In spite of all these threats, El-Gohari and his daughter have not given up or betrayed their Lord and Master.

But it is not just in the lands where Christians are in the minority that those who seek to be true followers of Jesus suffer persecution. In fact, one of the challenges to authentic Christian community in countries and contexts where Christianity is accepted is the fact that acceptability breeds conformity and compromise. What Paul said to Timothy, that "everyone who wants to live a godly life in Christ Jesus will be persecuted, while evildoers and impostors will go from bad to worse, deceiving and being deceived" (2 Tim 3:12–13), is still true today. There is a sense in which this persecution attests to the authenticity of Christian faith grounded in the hope and certainty of that which is not seen.

Authentic Christian community is the hope of the world. The turmoil of our world, torn apart by conflicts and wars – between nations, communities, families and individuals, is caused by selfishness, greed and injustice. Selfishness and greed – for wealth and power among others – fuel injustice. Injustice fuels conflict and wars. Selfishness, greed and injustice are the very antithesis of love. Generosity and justice are the outworking of authentic love, rooted in faith in God – the One who alone is love and justice. As Jesus said of his followers, they "hunger and thirst for righteousness (justice)" and are "peacemakers" (Matt 5: 6, 7) Thus, authentic Christian community not only reflects love and justice in its internal life but strives and acts for love and justice in the world. The stories of Dietrich Bonheoffer of Nazi Germany, bishops Janani Luwum and Festo Kevengere of Uganda who faced the greed and injustice of brutal and autocratic regimes were a testimony both to the love and justice of God and the hope of a future for their countries. Authentic churches engage the powers and structures of greed and injustice in love, challenging corruption and abuse of power, speaking and acting on the behalf of the marginalized and the oppressed.

Ordering the Community for Faith, Love and Hope

What structure of organization of community life and witness embodies and reflects faith, love and hope in the new community in Christ? This is a matter that has attracted much debate and acrimony in the story of the church down through the ages, since the nascent community of believers in Jerusalem. A close look at the ordering and organization of the various communities of followers of Jesus in the New Testament shows that they were shaped by at least two factors: the need to enable the life and witness of community to thrive, and the historical–cultural context of the particular community. The use of the image of the body to characterize the ordering of the life of believers together, such as in Paul's letter to the believers in Corinth, is especially instructive. "Just as a body, though one, has many parts, but all its many parts form one body, so it is with Christ.... Now you are the body of Christ, and each one of you is a part of it" (1 Cor 12:12, 27). The different parts of the body are ordered according to their functions for the thriving of the entire body in a particular environment.

As we noted in Chapter 5, Jesus organized community life to enable teaching and learning: Jesus was the teacher – the rabbi; the others were learners – disciples. Jesus did not start a new synagogue for himself and his disciples; he did not institute a "new Sabbath"; he did not create a hierarchy among his disciples; and his disciples came from all sects, backgrounds and classes. It is noteworthy that the basic organization of the Jesus movement in first-century Palestine was modelled on the Jewish rabbinic tradition.

The nascent Spirit-filled community in Jerusalem was ordered around "the apostles' teaching and ... fellowship, ... the breaking of bread and ... prayer" (Acts 2:42). The structure was simple: there were the apostles and the rest of the believers. As the communal life of sharing goods and possessions became more complicated, a new tier was introduced: deacons, to "wait on tables", to release the apostles to devote their "attention to prayer and the ministry of the word" (Acts 6:2, 4). The ministry of the word was both evangelistic (announcing the good news of the kingdom) and devotional (strengthening the faith of the believers). The ministry of the apostles enabled the believers to live more fully by the Spirit, in fellowship with one another, as well as to witness to the gospel of the kingdom. The service of the deacons enabled the believers to thrive as an egalitarian and harmonious community of faith, love and hope.

When the numbers of believers multiplied and persecution arose, resulting in the scattering of the believers beyond Jerusalem, the apostles' ministry became itinerant. In each place where there were followers of Jesus, the apostles made sure that the two functions – the ministry of the word (evangelistic preaching and teaching, as we call it today) and the "service to the saints" – were provided for. In Ephesians 4:11–13 Paul makes the point strongly that the ministries of gifts are to provide for the ordering of the community life of the believers, so that there may be a thriving of life towards maturity:

> It was he who gave some to be apostles, some to be prophets, some to be evangelists, and some to be pastors and teachers, to prepare God's people for works of service, so that the body of Christ may be built up until we all reach unity of the faith and knowledge of the Son of God and become mature, attaining to the whole measure of the fullness of Christ.

The "whole measure of the fullness of Christ" that Paul speaks about is surely to do with the fullness of God's love in Christ in all its dimensions. Note that of all the five categories of ministers – apostles, prophets, evangelists, pastors and teachers, four are ministries of the word, and one (pastors) connotes the service of the needs of believers. Pastors have the duty of shepherds – ensuring that all in Christ's fold in a particular place have access to spiritual and physical nourishment. In some translations, the two – pastors and teachers – are combined into one, "pastor-teacher", to show that the pastoral role is fulfilled through teaching. However, this misses out a critical function of the pastor – the ministry of administration. A better way to draw the distinction is to speak of pastor-teachers and pastor-deacons. The form that all these ministries take will differ from one context to another, depending on what forms of community organization exist in the wider society.

There are some who have created an institutional hierarchy out of this characterization by Paul in Ephesians, particularly among Christian communities within the Western tradition. Contemporary forms of church organization that originate in the West (e.g., the Roman Catholic Church, the Anglican tradition and other Protestant Reformation church traditions) were developed during the Middle Ages, when most Western societies were feudal and hierarchical. Although there is value in hierarchical forms of church governance, it is difficult to justify them from this text. On the contrary, rather than promoting an institutional hierarchy, Paul is clear that authority is resident in the message and spiritual gifting. There are others who have suggested that some of the offices were limited to particular historical epochs: that, for example, apostles were the specified twelve plus Paul, those who were eye-witnesses of the earthly life and ministry of Jesus, and were commissioned by him as such and had a unique role as the founders of the church; therefore there can be no apostles today. This view is often justified from 1 Corinthians 12:28: "God has placed in the church first of all apostles, second prophets, third teachers, then miracles …" While there is no doubt that the twelve and Paul were uniquely chosen and sent by Jesus and that therefore there are no apostles of the same standing today, we must affirm that apostolic ministry is present today: the pioneering, ground-breaking proclamation of the gospel across new frontiers, commonly called cross-cultural mission, is in this category.

In Paul's letters to Timothy and Titus we read of three forms of leaders: overseers (translated as "bishops" in some translations), deacons, and elders (translated as "presbyters" in some translations). Space does not permit an extended discussion on the varying interpretations of these passages and the debate among scholars, theologians and church leaders from different denominations. It suffices to note that from the plain reading of these texts and others cited above, there are no standard normative forms and no standard structure for the ordering of ministry of the new community in Christ for every time and in every place. As communities of faith, love and hope come into being in new cultures and contexts, resulting from the preaching of the gospel of Christ, fresh forms of ordering community life emerge that enable the flourishing of the Spirit life in those contexts. The compulsion of faith, love and hope means that the story itself is incomplete until these communities go beyond themselves.

The Church: God's New Pilgrim Community

The Journey, the community with whose story we began this chapter, is an apt conclusion of our journey through the story of the people of God in the Scriptures. How well its name captures the story of the people of God, old and new! How well it captures the nature of authentic Christian community: not just a people on *a* journey together, or considering the journey, as though it was apart from them, but actually on the journey itself – the entire narrative of the people, from the first coming of Jesus in first-century Palestine to the last coming at the end of time. They are the body of Christ, and "the journey" is an appropriate metaphor of the character and nature of the people of God. This is the story, as we have surveyed it, from ancient Israel to the young churches in Jerusalem, Antioch, Philippi, Corinth and Ephesus. This is the continuing story of the authentic church: a people of faith, love and hope; God's new pilgrim community, looking forward to the fullness of time when the "kingdom of the world has become the kingdom of our Lord and of his Messiah, and he will reign for ever and ever" (Rev 11:15) – indeed, in Paul's words, when God will finally "bring unity to all things in heaven and on earth under Christ" (Eph 1:10).

In the course of history and up to the present day there have been and there are many Christian communities known as "churches" that are not equally faithful to Christ and his Spirit; some even deny totally the very tenets of being church while continuing to pride themselves on being called churches. As Avery Dulles, in his classic work *Models of the Church*, argued, "It is necessary to distinguish between the church as a sociological and as a theological entity. From the point of view of sociology, the term 'church' would designate a group of men who consider themselves to be followers of Christ ..." We may add that the community's self-awareness and consciousness of being followers of Christ, though critical, is not enough to authenticate them. Dulles clarified that "sociologically, the church is a fact of observation, accessible to persons who do not have faith. Theologically, the church is a mystery of grace, not knowable independently of faith".[14] The mystery of grace manifests the evidence of grace; just as the presence of salt in food is evidenced in the savoury taste of the food.

> The Church is the pilgrim people of God. It is on the move – hastening to the ends of the earth to beseech all men to be reconciled to God, and hastening to the end of time to meet its Lord who will gather all into one. Therefore the nature of the Church is never to be defined in static terms, but only in terms of that to which it is going. It cannot be understood rightly except in a perspective which is at once missionary and eschatological, and only in that perspective can the deadlock of our present ecumenical debate be resolved.[15]

---

14. Avery Dulles, *Models of the Church* (Dublin: Gill and MacMillan, 1988), 123.
15. Lesslie Newbigin, "The Nature and Calling of the Church", in Paul Weston, *Lesslie*

The motif of pilgrim, presented in Hebrews 11, is at the heart of the identity and ethos of the church as the community of the kingdom of God, a community of faith in Jesus. The following words from the Epistle to Diognetus, reckoned to date from the second century, capture the pilgrim character of the authentic Christian community:

> For Christians are not distinguished from the rest of humanity by country, language or custom. For nowhere do they live in cities of their own, nor do they speak some unusual dialect, nor do they practise an eccentric life-style ... But while they live in both Greek and barbarian cities, as each one's lot was cast, and follow the local customs in dress and food and other aspects of life, at the same time they demonstrate a remarkable and admittedly unusual character of their own citizenship. They live in their own countries, but only as aliens; they participate in everything as citizens, and endure everything as foreigners. Every foreign country is their fatherland, and every fatherland is foreign.[16]

Thus the motif of pilgrim is a clue to "being authentic church". We can deduce that "becoming church" is authenticated by "being pilgrim people", like their pilgrim Saviour; that God is, "through them", displaying his works of grace and wisdom revealed in Jesus and fulfilling his promise to restore creation-community. Authentic church is a community of a people on pilgrimage over the passage of time, looking forward to its consummation, when "the journey" will be over – in the new heaven and new earth, with the multitude "from every nation, tribe, people and language" (Rev 7:9) and generation!

Newbigin: Missionary Theologian – A Reader (London: SPCK, 2006), 126.

16. "The Epistle to Diognetus" in J. B. Lightfoot and J. R. Harmer (trans), *The Apostolic Fathers* (Leicester: Apollos / Inter-Varsity Press, 1990), 299.

Bibliography

Apartheid: The Facts. London: International Defence and Aid Fund, 1983.

Arias, Mortimer. *Announcing the Reign of God and the Subversive Memory of Jesus.* Philadelphia: Fortress.

Atkinson, David. *The Message of Genesis 1–11.* Leicester: InterVarsity Press, 1990.

Banks, Robert. *Paul's Idea of Community.* Peabody, MA: Hendrickson, 1994.

Bonhoeffer, Dietrich. *Life Together.* London: SCM Press, 1954.

Boyd, Gregory A. *Repenting of Religion: Turning from Judgment to the Love of God.* Grand Rapids, MI: Baker, 2004.

Brother Andrew with John and Elizabeth Sherrill. *God's Smuggler.* London: Hodder and Stoughton, 1967.

Church, John E. *Quest for the Highest: An Autobiographical Account of the East African Revival.* Exeter: Paternoster, 1981.

Dulles, Avery. *Models of the Church.* Dublin: Gill and MacMillan, 1988.

Dumbrell, William J. *Covenant and Creation: An Old Testament Covenantal Theology.* Exeter: Paternoster, 1984.

Ferguson, Everett. *The Church of Christ: Biblical Ecclesiology for Today.* Grand Rapids, MI: Eerdmans, 1996.

Foakes-Jackson, F. J. and K. Lake, eds. *The Beginnings of Christianity, vol. 5.* London: Macmillan, 1933.

Giles, Kevin. *What on Earth Is the Church?* London: SPCK, 1995.

Glasser, Arthur F. *Announcing the Kingdom: The Story of God's Mission in the Bible.* Grand Rapids, MI: Baker Academic, 2003.

Goldingay, John. *Theological Diversity and the Authority of the Old Testament.* Grand Rapids, MI: Eerdmans, 1987.

Guder, Darrell L., ed. *Missional Church: A Vision for the Sending of the Church in North America.* Grand Rapids, MI: Eerdmans, 1998.

Hauerwas, Stanley. *The Peaceable Kingdom: A Primer in Christian Ethics.* Notre Dame, IN: Notre Dame University Press, 1981.

Hauerwas, Stanley and Gregory Jones, eds. *Why Narrative? Readings in Narrative Theology.* Grand Rapids, MI: Eerdmans, 1989.

Idowu, E. Bolaji. *African Traditional Religion: A Definition.* London: SCM Press, 1973.

Kaiser, Walter C., Jr. *Toward an Old Testament Theology.* Grand Rapids, MI: Zondervan, 1978.

Kasozi, Abdu B. K. *The Spread of Islam in Uganda.* Nairobi: Oxford University Press, 1986.

Kenyatta, Jomo. *Facing Mount Kenya.* Tel Aviv: Am Hassefer, 1963.

Kivengere, Festo. *I Love Idi Amin: The Story of Triumph under Fire in the Midst of Suffering and Persecution in Uganda.* Old Tappan, NJ: Revell, 1977.

Klaus, C. Norman. *The Community of the Spirit: How the Church Is in the World.* Scottdale, PA: Herald Press, 1993.

Labberton, Mark. *The Dangerous Act of Worship: Living God's Call to Justice.* Downers Grove, IL: InterVarsity Press, 2007.

Ladd, George E. *Jesus and the Kingdom of God: The Eschatology of Biblical Realism.* New York: Harper and Row, 1964.

Lightfoot, Neil R. *How We Got the Bible.* 2nd ed. Grand Rapids, MI: Baker, 1988.

Lightfoot, J. B. and J. R. Harmer. "The Epistle to Diognetus." In J. B. Lightfoot and J. R. Harmer (trans), *The Apostolic Fathers.* Leicester: InterVarsity Press, 1990.

Mbiti, John. *African Traditional Religions and Philosophy.* London: Heinemann, 1969.

Mutebi, Wilson. *Towards an Indigenous Understanding and Practice of Baptism Amongst the Baganda, Uganda.* Kampala: Wavah Books, 2002.

Newbigin, Lesslie. "On Being the Church in the World." In *The Parish Church? Exploration in the Relationship of the Church and the World,* edited by G. Ecclestone, 25–42. Oxford: Mowbray, 1988.

———. *The Gospel in a Pluralist Society.* London: SPCK, 1989.

———. "The Nature and Calling of the Church." In Paul Weston, *Lesslie Newbigin: Missionary Theologian – A Reader,* 114–157. London: SPCK, 2006.

Niles, D. T. *Upon the Earth: The Mission of God and the Missionary Enterprise of the Churches.* London: Lutterworth Press, 1962.

Padilla, René. *Mission Between the Times: Essays on the Kingdom.* Grand Rapids, MI: Eerdmans, 1985.

Saneh, Lamin. *Translating the Message: The Missionary Impact on Culture.* Maryknoll, NY: Orbis, 1993.

Skydsgaard, K. E. "Kingdom of God and the Church." *Scottish Journal of Theology* 4 (1951): 383–397.

Stott, John R. W. *Christian Counter-Culture: The Message of the Sermon on the Mount.* Bible Speaks Today. Leicester: InterVarsity Press, 1978.

———. *The Message of Ephesians.* Downers Grove, IL: InterVarsity Press, 1979.

———, ed. *Making Christ Known: Historic Mission Documents from the Lausanne Movement 1974–1989.* Carlisle: Paternoster, 1996.

Students' Christian Organisation South Africa, at www.sco.org.za. Accessed 2013.

Taylor, John V. *The Growth of the Church in Buganda.* London: SCM Press, 1958.

The Lausanne Covenant, at http://www.lausanne.org/en/documents/lausanne-covenant.html. Accessed 29/10/13.

Van Gelder, Craig. *The Essence of the Church: A Community Created by the Spirit.* Grand Rapids, MI: Baker, 2000.

Walls, Andrew F. *The Cross-Cultural Process in Christian History.* Maryknoll, NY: Orbis, 2002.

Weston, Paul. *Lesslie Newbigin: Missionary Theologian – A Reader.* London: SPCK, 2006.

Wright, Christopher J. H. *Knowing Jesus Through the Old Testament.* Downers Grove, IL: InterVarsity Press, 1992.

———. *Walking in the Ways of the Lord: The Ethical Authority of the Old Testament.* Downers Grove, IL: InterVarsity Press, 1995.

———. *The Mission of God: Unlocking the Bible's Grand Narrative.* Downers Grove, IL: IVP, 2006.

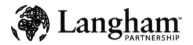

Langham Literature and its imprints are a ministry of Langham Partnership.

Langham Partnership is a global fellowship working in pursuit of the vision God entrusted to its founder John Stott –

to facilitate the growth of the church in maturity and Christ-likeness through raising the standards of biblical preaching and teaching.

Our vision is to see churches in the majority world equipped for mission and growing to maturity in Christ through the ministry of pastors and leaders who believe, teach and live by the Word of God.

Our mission is to strengthen the ministry of the Word of God through:
- nurturing national movements for biblical preaching
- fostering the creation and distribution of evangelical literature
- enhancing evangelical theological education especially in countries where churches are under resourced.

Our ministry

Langham Preaching partners with national leaders to nurture indigenous biblical preaching movements for pastors and lay preachers all around the world. With the support of a team of trainers from many countries, a multi-level programme of seminars provides practical training, and is followed by a programme for training local facilitators. Local preachers' groups and national and regional networks ensure continuity and ongoing development, seeking to build vigorous movements committed to Bible exposition.

Langham Literature provides majority world pastors, scholars and seminary libraries with evangelical books and electronic resources through grants, discounts and distribution. The programme also fosters the creation of indigenous evangelical books for pastors in many languages, through training workshops for writers and editors, sponsored writing, translation, strengthening local evangelical publishing houses, and investment in major regional literature projects, such as one volume Bible commentaries like *The Africa Bible Commentary*.

Langham Scholars provides financial support for evangelical doctoral students from the majority world so that, when they return home, they may train pastors and other Christian leaders with sound, biblical and theological teaching. This programme equips those who equip others. Langham Scholars also works in partnership with majority world seminaries in strengthening evangelical theological education. A growing number of Langham Scholars study in high quality doctoral programmes in the majority world itself. As well as teaching the next generation of pastors, graduated Langham Scholars exercise significant influence through their writing and leadership.

To learn more about Langham Partnership and the work we do visit **langham.org**

CPSIA information can be obtained
at www.ICGtesting.com
Printed in the USA
BVHW081119071119
563183BV00009B/216/P